4451836

HONEY, W.
Shakespeare
epitaph deciphered
35/-

822 SHAK

Please renew/return this item by the last date shown.

So that your telephone call is charged at local rate, please call the numbers as set out below:

	From Area codes 01923 or 0208:	From the rest of Herts:
Renewals:	01923 471373	01438 737373
Enquiries:	01923 471333	01438 737333
Minicom:	01923 471599	01438 737599

L32b

CENTRAL RESOURCES
LIBRARY
01707-281530

W.E
14 DEC
LOA

17 JUL 1997

28 JUL 1997

- 7 NOV 2005

Essex
17/11/06

D1321056

The Shakespeare Epitaph
Deciphered

In Memory of Tony Costello

On the 5th February, 1944, Sub-Lieutenant (A) A. F. H. Costello, R.N.V.R., piloting a Swordfish, returned from an operational flight and attempted to alight on the heaving, handkerchief-small deck of the escort carrier H.M.S. "Nairana", which was then attached to the Western Approaches Command. His aircraft, carrying primed depth charges, overshot and plunged into the sea. He was twenty-two years old.

Henry Wriothesley, Third Earl of Southampton
(Reproduced by courtesy of the National Portrait Gallery)

WILLIAM HONEY

The Shakespeare Epitaph Deciphered

LONDON:
THE MITRE PRESS
52 LINCOLN'S INN FIELDS, W.C.2

I wish to present my thanks to H. V. Hodson for advice regarding the positioning of the decipherment; G. Mathias Tucker for counsel concerning the handling of its assessment; and Leonard and Barbara Wooding for assistance with what I have called the Christ-cursed theme in *Doctor Faustus*. All the above were kind enough to read this book in manuscript.

HERTFORDSHIRE
COUNTY LIBRARY

822 SHA

4451836

07051 00472

© WILLIAM HONEY, 1969
SBN 7051 0047 2
*Printed in Great Britain for The Mitre Press
(Fudge & Co. Ltd.) London*

CONTENTS

1

It is a strange irony, in the light of what I am about to disclose, that in 1964 so much attention was lavished upon Shakespeare's quatercentenary, when Marlowe's was hardly noticed at all.

At the Marlowe Theatre in Canterbury, the dramatist's birth-city, there were performances of one of his plays in February, the birth-month, but that was all: at any rate on a professional scale.

They are not terribly proud, it seems, of Marlowe in Canterbury. When visiting the city a few years ago, I decided to look for the house held traditionally to be his birthplace; but nobody could tell me where it was. Policemen, assistants in postcard shops, the staffs of the official Information Bureau and the Public Library all looked at me vacantly when I put the question to them. Finally, wandering among the shelves of the Library, I got down a book on Marlowe I remembered having read some years earlier, and this had in it a map on which the site of the birthplace was marked. The house, it then became clear, had been in an area damaged during the war; and, instead of restoring it, the good citizens (I found when I got to the spot indicated) had demolished what remained and erected over the site and its surroundings (of all things!) a supermarket. Marlowe's birthplace had been swamped in modernity.

I went back to the Information Bureau and remarked that I thought it peculiar.

"The truth is," replied a matron on voluntary duty, bridling, "that we never cared much for Marlowe down here. Whenever he visited us he was drunk."

They were holding his drunkenness against him nearly four hundred years after his death. Yet Canterbury is the centre of the Church of England.

I have trifled for a long time, in fact ever since the

7

appearance of Calvin Hoffman's book on the subject, with the idea that it might have been Marlowe who wrote the Shakespeare plays. It has seemed to me odd that Marlowe's death should have exactly coincided with Shakespeare's birth as a writer. And there is the classical objection to Shakespeare's authorship: the unlikelihood that, in those days of limited education a bumpkin could have travelled to London to become the world's greatest poet and playwright. How could such a person, it is argued, have acquired the familiarity with Court circles and immense knowledge of History, the Law, Philosophy and the Science of the period that the plays show? But there is a point that with me outweighs all the others. There is no known incident in the life of the traditional Shakespeare that would appear to give rise to the urgency of creation that the author of the plays (and the Sonnets) must have felt: no intensity of experience that would account for the immense range of emotion he traverses. The figure of Shakespeare, beside that of the vital, tempestuous Marlowe, is as inanimate as a dummy. It might even be called a vacuum. Here you have a man destined to become the world's greatest literary creator who, for a period of eight years in the critical formative part of his life, was not able to attract the attention of his contemporaries; and for a period of twenty-eight, but for the records of his baptism, his marriage, and the baptisms of his three children (all required by the law in respect of even the lowest in the land), drew forth no historical reference at all. Those same twenty-eight years were, on the contrary, packed with references to Marlowe.

"His murder at Deptford," declare the scholars almost unanimously, "at the age of twenty-eight is an insuperable obstacle to his authorship." But is it? Graver blunders have been perpetrated than the misidentification of a corpse. And that is exactly what happened.

Having read Calvin Hoffman's book, I pondered over the implications of his theory for some years, never entirely convinced by it, because of its weaknesses, but always hoping, oddly enough, that it might in the end

THE SHAKESPEARE EPITAPH DECIPHERED

be proved. The strange story of Marlowe fascinated me. The tragedy of his early death, implying waste and unfulfilment, seemed so unreasonable; though the author of the Shakespeare plays would not have cavilled at it. Did he not write:

> To-morrow, and to-morrow, and to-morrow,
> Creeps in this petty pace from day to day,
> To the last syllable of recorded time;
> And all our yesterdays have lighted fools
> The way to dusty death. Out, out, brief candle!
> Life's but a walking shadow, a poor player
> That struts and frets his hour upon the stage,
> And then is heard no more; it is a tale
> Told by an idiot, full of sound and fury,
> Signifying nothing.

Or was this only one side of a dialectical argument put into the mouth of Macbeth? Whatever it was, the man who wrote it was not unacquainted with atheism.

It was not until the early part of the quatercentenary year that I suddenly came across fresh evidence which shed an abundance of light on the subject. This was to be my own contribution to the theory, and it seemed to me that it proved conclusively Marlowe's authorship of the plays. (A rash statement, perhaps, when the teasing problem of the authorship has provoked so much controversy over the years!) It had to do with the epitaph on the Shakespeare tomb. About a month before the birthdate (23rd April) one of the Sunday newspapers published an article on William Shakespeare in its colour supplement, and in a caption under a picture of the tomb suggested that the epitaph might contain "a cipher never satisfactorily explained".

One of the minor reasons for doubting Shakespeare's authorship of the works attributed to him is the poorness of the doggerel rhyme of this inscription, which the dramatist himself is said to have written only a few days before his death. How, it is contended, could the author of such marvellous lines as those quoted above or:

Our revels now are ended. These our actors,
As I foretold you, were all spirits and
Are melted into air, into thin air;
And, like the baseless fabric of this vision,
The cloud-capped towers, the gorgeous palaces,
The solemn temples, the great globe itself,
Yea, all which it inherit, shall dissolve,
And, like this insubstantial pageant faded,
Leave not a rack behind. We are such stuff
As dreams are made on, and our little life
Is rounded with a sleep.

have been guilty of perpetrating the jingling:

Good friend for Jesus' sake forbear
To dig the dust enclosed here.
Blest be the man that spares these stones,
And cursed be he that moves my bones.

So that by the presupposition of a cipher, the badness of the verse seemed to be accounted for and the difficulty smoothed away. But then I saw that a cipher indicated a secret message; and that this, in its turn, pointed to a revelation of the true authorship and the fact that it could not be Shakespeare's. I determined to try to decipher the rhyme and spent several weeks pondering over it at odd moments during the day. I had more success than I had ever dared hope for. The underlying message came out in what might be called a species of "Shakespearean" verse; it listed the contents of the tomb and implied that the occupant was not Shakespeare, but Marlowe.

In the light of this information I restudied the Calvin Hoffman book, and soon understood why he had failed to establish his case. The book, it has to be admitted, as a piece of scholarship, was not carefully enough written. Its main fault lies in the fact that its arguments are sometimes unsupported by any reference to historical sources. Its judgments, therefore, often appear arbitrary. And indeed I see now, having penetrated deeply into the jungle of critical and historical material that exists on the subject of Shakespeare, that some of them, those for which, after the most exhaustive search, I have been unable to find any support whatever, are in fact arbitrary. The all-important statement, for instance, that *Venus and Adonis* was published in the *September* of the year 1593. How does Mr. Hoffman know that? Nobody knows, I am convinced, in exactly which month the poem appeared on the bookstalls, and if Mr. Hoffman has exclusive knowledge deriving from some esoteric source, he would be more likely to be believed if he named it.

Next, the argument is clumsy. Based to a large extent upon parallels that he has found in the Marlowe and Shakespeare plays and poems, he tries to prove that, because of these, everything was the work of a single author: an argument which naturally misfires because, if Shakespeare were indeed a separate author, he would undoubtedly have had experience of the plays of Marlowe, who towered above his contemporaries, and would unconsciously have echoed certain passages in his own work. This is the accepted explanation. Had Mr. Hoffman, on the other hand, limited his range of application to the contemporaneously written poems *Hero and Leander* (the work of Marlowe) and *Venus and Adonis* (attributed to Shakespeare) which teem with parallels many of which he has missed, he would have been more successful; because, if there were indeed two authors, neither of these poems, as I shall show, could have been seen by the author of the other. Calvin Hoffman failed to spot that fact. The parallels would accordingly have had to be separately conceived, and the odds against the possibility of such a lengthy series of coincidences would be in the region of thousands to one.

Then again, Calvin Hoffman did not dig deeply enough into the subject matter. The printers and publishers of the period, vitally concerned though they were with the appearance of the hinge-poem *Venus and Adonis,* are hardly mentioned. The beautiful young Earl of Southampton, against all reason, yields pride of place to Mr. Walsing Ham. And what of the Burbages? What part did this powerful theatrical family

play in the whole affair? Calvin Hoffman does not
appear to have thought it necessary to read his way
into the complex history of the Elizabethan theatre to
supply an answer. The financial state of the "Theatre",
the rivalry between the Burbages and Philip Henslowe,
and the possible rôle of other great theatrical names of
the period are alike ignored by him; yet all these in-
fluences had considerable bearing upon the story.

More important, however, is the fact that he mis-
interprets the evidence. He believes that Marlowe, after
the supposed murder, went abroad, continued writing
his plays and sent them back to be published under the
name of Shakespeare: a peculiar theory! For if
Marlowe did indeed go abroad, he had the money to do
so; and if he was not short of money and did not want
to remain in the country, no murder was necessary.
There was no Interpol in those days. Walsingham, in
other words, would not have had to involve himself in
so unpleasant and dangerous a crime. Indeed one of
Calvin Hoffman's major mistakes, it seems to me, was
in allowing himself to become obsessed with the idea
of Walsingham and the part he played in the deception.
"Keeping Sir Thomas Walsingham as an ever-present
background figure", he says early in the book, and so
runs into error. In my belief Thomas Walsingham, when
Marlowe went to him for assistance, did exactly what
was necessary and no more. To have involved himself
further would have been much too risky.

Calvin Hoffman, therefore, on account of the blurred
presentation of his theory, was greeted, when the book
was published, with scornful incredulity and when he
succeeded in opening the Walsingham tomb, in which,
for some unaccountable reason, he expected to find
documents which would clinch his argument, he was
rewarded by the critics with a laugh of derision, and
pictures were published in the newspapers showing
him gazing into emptiness. It was a pity; because he was
the first to perceive the possibility of Marlowe's having
been the author, not only of the six plays known to
be his, but also of the entire Shakespeare canon; and

for his original flash of inspiration and the clarity of his insight, based on intuition rather than reasoning, he deserves all possible credit.

After deciphering the epitaph, I set to work to bolster up my discovery with historical fact and, paying scrupulous attention to dates and the order in which events occurred, began a meticulous examination of the literature and documents available. I was again successful: so successful, indeed, that in the end people seemed more likely to be convinced by the argument from fact, which, it was said, itself created an atmosphere of belief, than by the evidence of the deciphered epitaph.

I have decided on that account, in planning this book, to state the argument from historical fact first and then proceed to a description of the decipherment of the epitaph, which will thus gain plausibility. Let us therefore see how the finding of Christopher Marlowe's body in Stratford-upon-Avon can be brought into accord with the records. The story is packed with irony and dramatic interest.

2

It should be remembered that Marlowe, at the time of his supposed death, was facing charges of atheism, high treason and homosexuality; and that all these (let us call them) breaches of convention were, in those sanguinary days, if proven, punishable by death. Homosexuality, but for a short respite, oddly enough in the reign of Queen Mary, had been, if practised, a capital offence dealt with by the secular courts ever since the much married Henry VIII had, in 1535, made the "detestable and abominable vice" a felony. Hitherto the Church had dealt with it, though equally savagely, burying such offenders alive or burning them at the stake.

Born in Canterbury on, or shortly before, the 26th February, 1564 (two months almost to the day before William Shakespeare was born in Stratford-upon-Avon), Marlowe was educated at the King's School and Corpus Christi, Cambridge, to both of which, since his father was only a poor shoemaker, he was awarded scholarships. The scholarship to Corpus Christi was one of several created under the Will of Matthew Parker, Archbishop of Canterbury, who had died in 1575 and whose wish it had been that all those benefiting from his charity should eventually take holy orders. Marlowe, however, instead of abiding by the Archbishop's direction, allowed himself to be beguiled by the new Humanism. Besides studying Divinity, he spent a great deal of his time reading Ovid and Lucan, some of whose works he translated, Virgil and other classic poets, and Holinshed's *Chronicles,* which was to become the chief source of his *Edward II.* All these, and many other profane works, were to be freely had from the university library shelves.

It is interesting to note that Shakespeare was drawn by the very same authors. Dr. A. L. Rowse in *William*

Shakespeare, in an imagined reconstruction of his subject's schooling, tells us: "In the upper school he (Shakespeare) went on to Ovid, and this was the love of his life among Latin poets. Ovid made an overwhelming impression upon him, which he carried with him all his days. Four times he refers to him directly by name, five times to the swan's singing at death as described in the *Heroides*. The story of *Lucrece* comes from Ovid's *Fasti*. But it is the *Metamorphoses* above all that echo throughout his work . . . Along with the Bible and the Prayer Book, Ovid made the most constant and fertilising impression upon his mind . . . Francis Meres wrote, 'the sweet witty soul of Ovid lives in mellifluous and honey-tongued Shakespeare'." In addition, there was "a little Virgil and rather more Horace"; whereas of Holinshed's *Chronicles* he "made splendid use" throughout his working life. The strangest feature of this coincidence is that everything that has to be inferred for Shakespeare's classical education is explicit for Marlowe's. It is as if Stratfordians, in deducing the nature of Shakespeare's intellectual equipment from his works, were creating a perfect Identikit picture of the mind of Marlowe. Yet they do not seem to be aware of this fact.

Marlowe received his Bachelor of Arts degree in the spring of 1584 at the age of twenty and stayed up for a further three years to read for his Master's degree. It was during the latter part of this period, or just after it, that he is thought to have written both Parts of *Tamburlaine the Great*. Dr. F. S. Boas, in *Christopher Marlowe*, writes: "Marlowe's last period of residence in Corpus Christi College was for five weeks and a half between Christmas 1586 and Lady Day 1587. He may . . . have begun *Tamburlaine* towards the end of this Cambridge period. Otherwise both Parts must have been written in the summer and autumn of 1587."

Marlowe's Master's degree was conferred in the same year, but only after a series of delays on the part of the Cambridge authorities. It is generally accepted that he had aroused their displeasure by sometimes absenting

himself from the University to work as a spy in Sir
Francis Walsingham's foreign espionage service and so
neglecting his studies. The fact that the degree was
eventually conferred in response to a written request of
the Privy Council stating that "he had done her majestie
good service and deserved to be rewarded for his faithfull dealinge" certainly adds support to the belief; as does
his record of attendance at the University, which, during
these years shows frequent and prolonged absences.

Marlowe, then, though only the son of a poor shoemaker, already had access to the mighty, and his work
for Sir Francis Walsingham could have involved travel
to Rheims and even to Rome, in both of which cities
there were Catholic seminaries actively engaged in training English priests who were to be returned to England
to further the Catholic cause. I quote from A. K. Gray's
article, *Marlowe as a Government Agent* (P.M.L.A.,
September, 1928): "If Marlowe did leave Cambridge
for Rheims, he can only have gone there as a spy on the
seminarists. He ostentatiously announced his liking for
Catholic ritual, etc., and so fell in with a Jesuit agent in
Cambridge, by whom he was smuggled over to Rheims
as a sympathiser, perhaps even a possible convert. Once
in Rheims with his excellent introduction he could
spy with impunity."

But what of a journey to Rome, which, from the
standpoint of the Shakespeare plays, since several are
set in Verona, Padua and Venice, would be much more
arresting! For any such journey, in those days, would
in all probability have been made via the Brenner Pass.
The Great Brenner Road has, since the time of the
Romans, run through Verona; and a turning off, for a
curious young man, to Padua and Venice, would not
have been unthinkable. I do not believe, however, that
Marlowe ever went to Rome. Another point that he and
the author of the plays have in common is that both
appear to have been extraordinarily ignorant of the
geography of the Italian Peninsula. In *The Two Gentlemen of Verona*, when the scene is set in that very city,
which, as everybody knows is a good sixty miles, as the

crow flies, from the Port of Venice, one of the characters is made to say: "Launce, away, away, aboard! thy master is shipped, and thou art to post after with oars. What's the matter? why weepest thou, man? Away, ass! you'll lose the tide, if you tarry any longer . . . lose thy voyage." To which Launce is made to answer: "Lose the tide, and the voyage . . . Why, man, if the river were dry, I am able to fill it with my tears; if the wind were down, I could drive the boat with my sighs."

Now Launce and his master were travelling to Milan, a city still further inland. And Milan is not linked with Verona by river, only by road, along which any sensible traveller, wishing to get from the one to the other would ride. So that this, despite the arguments of the pundits to the contrary, is not the language of a man who has a specialised knowledge of canals, but of one who, at the time of writing, had no idea of the position of Verona in relation to Milan or the sea, and had not even bothered to look at a map. The author, indeed, would appear to be thinking of the Port of London.

Marlowe, too, in *Doctor Faustus,* written at approximately the same time as *The Two Gentlemen,* displays similar ignorance.

Having now, my good Mephistophilis,
Pass'd with delight the stately town of Trier . . .
From Paris next, coasting the realm of France,
We saw the river Maine fall into Rhine,
Whose banks are set with groves of fruitful vines;
Then up to Naples, rich Campania,
Whose buildings fair and gorgeous to the eye,
The streets straight forth, and pav'd with finest brick,
Quarter the town in four equivalents:
There saw we learned Maro's golden tomb . . .
From thence to Venice, Padua and the rest,
In one of which a sumptuous temple stands,
That threats the stars with her aspiring top . . .
But tell me now what resting place is this?
Hast thou, as erst I did command,
Conducted me within the walls of Rome?

To which Mephistophilis replies: "Faustus, I have". One cannot help asking what Mephistophilis was about (when Faustus had erst commanded him to conduct him within the walls of Rome) in conveying his protégé from Mainz to Naples (via Rome) to see Maro's golden tomb (which is not golden), then (again via Rome) hundreds of miles north to Venice, Padua and the rest (only one of which had a sumptuous temple, though most of the great churches were by that time in existence) and not until all that mileage had been accomplished to their final destination (retracing their steps some two hundred and fifty miles due south). A most roundabout route! Surely Mephistophilis, using his magic arts, would have travelled more directly!

While still at the University, or while travelling in France, Marlowe had met Thomas Walsingham, second cousin of Sir Francis, and Calvin Hoffman believes that the two men had become linked by a homosexual attachment. He bases his argument on the assumption that Marlowe, in dedicating the Sonnets to Mr. W. H., had had in mind Mr. Walsing Ham. Walsingham, at any rate, was, from the time of their meeting, to play an important rôle in Marlowe's life, "bestowing upon him," according to Edward Blunt the publisher of *Hero and Leander,* "many kind favours and entertaining the parts of reckoning and worth which he found in him with good countenance and liberal affection".

On his arrival in London Marlowe immediately became famous as a dramatist. The first Part of *Tamburlaine the Great* was successfully produced, and the Lord High Admiral's company, who had bought the rights of it, was soon clamouring for its sequel. Both Parts had been produced by the 10th November, 1587. (Boas). But in certain quarters he was already paying the price of fame. His spontaneous success at the age of only twenty-three had aroused the jealousy of the established writers some of whom were regarding him with hatred. For, in writing *Tamburlaine,* he had evolved a new form of artistic expression. In the words of the Edwardian writer Edward Thomas, *"Tamburlaine* was the first notable English poem in blank verse that was also essentially a play". And this "new-found means of expressing his burning thought" was to the poet "as direct and worshipful as the smile of love, the dance, the nakedness of beauty, the running of athletes".

At this point there is a curious hiatus in Marlowe's history. Two years pass from which there emerge no records. And when he is next heard of his character has undergone a peculiar transformation. Dr. Boas sums the matter up in more scholarly fashion: "There is a remarkable contrast between the large amount of evidence extant concerning Marlowe's career at Cambridge and the almost complete dearth of it for his first two years in the capital after his triumph on the stage with the *Tamburlaine* plays. And when the earliest record of him for this period leaps to light it is startlingly at variance with the certificate of the Privy Council in 1587 that in all his actions he had behaved himself orderly and discreetly."

What happened to bring about his bitterness and disillusionment? I shall suggest an answer later. Meanwhile to continue with the story.

On the 18th September, 1589, in a small street called Hog Lane in the Liberty of Norton Folgate where he lived, and not far from Shoreditch in which the playhouses "The Theatre" and "The Curtain" stood, in which his plays were performed, he became involved in a duel with a man called William Bradley, twenty-six-year-old son of an innkeeper, who had quarrelled with the poet Thomas Watson, Marlowe's and Walsingham's friend. Watson arrived on the scene shortly after the duel had begun, intervened and killed Bradley. For this suspected murder both Watson and Marlowe were committed to Newgate prison, where Watson was to remain for five months, before finally being freed by Royal Pardon. Marlowe was more fortunate. Having been able to prove that he had withdrawn from the affray before the death blow was struck, he was released on bail after spending only twelve days in the prison and on the 3rd December was "quit by proclamation." Charles Norman in *The Muses Darling* makes an interesting comment on this duel. "It was," he says, "like the clash between Tybalt and Mercutio in *Romeo and Juliet*—save that Marlowe was unscratched." He recognises the similarity, but not the coincidence.

It must have been about this time (though it could have been earlier) that the now rebellious Marlowe associated himself with the avant-garde of the period, becoming a member of Sir Walter Raleigh's highly secret school of atheism. Consisting of the "wizard" Earl of Northumberland, the Earl of Derby (though his membership is not sure), Sir George Carey, the poets Marlowe, George Chapman, Matthew Roydon and William Warner, and the mathematician Thomas Harriott, this met once weekly at one of Raleigh's London residences and discussed matters of a speculative metaphysical nature. Miss M. C. Bradbrook in *The School of Night* claims that its teachings were Hermetic, and it is certainly likely that, under the mastership of the crazily brilliant Harriott, who is thought to have trafficked with the Devil, experiments of an advanced alchemistic nature were carried out. The exact character of the school's activities is not known. The joint editors of The New Cambridge Shakespeare (Sir Arthur Quiller-Couch and John Dover Wilson), while asserting that there was indeed such a school, state only that its members affected astronomy and mathematical calculations; though they go on to declare, rather curiously, that Shakespeare, in writing *Love's Labour's Lost* "was having his fling at it as an offence *contra naturam*". By this, however, though the comment has been otherwise interpreted, they probably meant no more than abstinence, in which Raleigh and Marlowe were both singularly to fail. It is easy to see why Raleigh was attracted to Marlowe. Apart from the fact that both were poets, both were passionate and hot-blooded, and both had in their make-up a streak of cruelty. In November 1580 Raleigh, in helping to put down the Desmond rebellion, had been involved, as one of Elizabeth's captains, in a military exploit which had "excited general horror through Europe". This was the massacre at Smerwick in Southern Ireland, where six hundred Spaniards and Italians, after surrendering, had been butchered in cold-blood. "Six hundred stripped bodies, 'as gallant and goodly personages as ever were beheld', were laid out on the sands." (Henderson). Raleigh, comments his biographer Stebbing, was capable of unspeakable cold-blooded cruelty. The creator of the horrific *Tamburlaine* must therefore have been a man to whom Raleigh felt himself strongly attuned.

Under the influence of this school, and also on account of his acquired embitterment, Marlowe, then, seems to have become a sort of Elizabethan rebel, and before long was disseminating unorthodox beliefs wherever he went. His imprudence could not have failed, in the end, to get him into serious trouble.

Several more years passed, during which he produced a series of magnificent verse dramas—*The Jew of Malta, The Massacre at Paris, Edward II* and *Doctor Faustus,* to place them in their probable date order—and continued to live riotously and recklessly. He never hesitated to indulge freely in intellectual argument, or give expression to opinions which in those days were dangerous and even in these would (in polite circles) be considered shocking. Talking and acting without restraint, he antagonised heedlessly. Small wonder that informers began to gather round him, taking note of his actions and utterances and reporting them to the relevant authorities! By 1593 his improprieties had become so flagrant that he could no longer avoid the impending crisis. On the 12th May the playwright Thomas Kyd was arrested by the Privy Council on charges of atheism and, on being interrogated under torture, implicated Marlowe with whom, he said, he "had written in the same chamber" some two years previously, when their papers had got mixed. Marlowe's arrest followed a week later; though, for lack of immediate evidence, he was less harshly treated. After being examined, he was released with the injunction that he was to appear daily before the Council until a decision had been reached as to the best means of dealing with him. That is how matters stood shortly before his supposed death.

Now, several years earlier—the date given tentatively is 1586, but it could have been even a year earlier than that, for there is a gap of eight years in the traditional chronology—William Shakespeare, coming from Stratford-upon-Avon, had arrived in London and attached himself to one of the troupes of players performing at the "Theatre". It is said by some that he simply held the horses of the rich people who came to see the play and by others that he was merely a call-boy. But by 1592 he seems to have prospered in the lowly profession he had chosen and become a reasonably successful actor. He was a loud-mouthed swaggering fellow, one fancies, inclined "to tear a passion to tatters" and it is certain that, in imitation of the mighty, he was attempting to write verse plays. For Robert Greene, in his last bitter diatribe against "players", when, repentant and deserted by his former friends, he was dying of the pox in a shoemaker's house near Dowgate, first extravagantly praises Marlowe, beseeching him to give up atheism and render due thanks to Him who endowed him with his talent ("Why should thy excellent wit, His gift, be so blinded, that thou shouldst give no glory to the Giver?"); then turns to attack Shakespeare. "The first public notice of Shakespeare," says G. B. Harrison in *Introducing Shakespeare*, "was hostile and unkind". Here it is:

> There is an upstart Crow, beautified with our feathers, that with his Tiger's heart wrapped in a Player's hide, supposes he is as well able to bombast out a blank verse as the best of you: and being an absolute Johannes factotum, is in his own conceit the only Shake-scene in a country.

A Groates-Worth of Witte, from which this extract is taken, was written only a few days before Greene's death on the 2nd September, 1592.

Dr. Boas comments: "Greene . . . in his *Groatesworth of Wit* was attacking the actor, Shakespeare, for daring to compete with his superiors, the dramatists, in their own field."

Now, that Shakespeare must have been a fairly successful actor by this time is clear, or he would not have attracted the attention of Greene, who had been the most popular writer of his time. Greene, it is true, was closely associated during the latter years of his life with the companies at the "Theatre" (with one of which Shakespeare is thought to have acted), and there are no records whatever of Shakespeare's appearances. Shakespeare must still have distinguished himself in some way, good or bad, or he would hardly have aroused such venom. Equally clear is the fact that Greene had not a very high opinion of the quality of Shakespeare's blank verse, or he would not have called him a Johannes factotum, or declared that in his own conceit he was the only Shake-scene in a country. It would moreover be strange if one so skilled in writing had been wrong. Perhaps his judgment was impaired, it may be argued, since he was dying. But he himself comments: "The Swan sings melodiously before death, that in all his life useth a jarring sound. Greene though able enough to write, yet deeplier searched with sickness than ever heretofore, sends you his Swan-like song, for that he fears he shall never again carol to you wonted love lays, never again discover to you youth's pleasures." Perhaps, then, there is truth after all in the traditional story that the Stratford actor, when a young man, had found himself in trouble with Sir Thomas Lucy over a poaching escapade on his estate; that to avoid arrest he had abandoned his wife and three young children and fled to London to seek his fortune; and that, before departing, he had nailed, in dudgeon, a satirical poem to Sir Thomas's gate, one verse of which has survived:

A Parliament member, a Justice of Peace
At home a poore scare-crow, at London an asse
If lowsie is Lucy, as some volke miscall it
Then Lucy is lowsie, whatever befall it:
He thinks himself great,
Yet an asse in his state
We allow by his ears but with asses to mate
If Lucy is lowsie; as some volke miscall it
Sing lowsie Lucy, whatever befall it.

No wonder that Shakespeare scholars refuse to include this vulgar little composition in the canon, for it shows no promise of the glory to come. Yet it may well have been an example of the actor Shakespeare's early capabilities.

Now, an all-important factor in my argument is the coincidence that the critical year 1593 was a plague year. Stalking about the stinking streets of the period, the pestilence was carrying off thousands. Everyone who could move out into the untainted air of the country was doing so; the theatres and other places of entertainment were closed, and, since no plays were being performed, few were being written. Marlowe, at this time, turned his attention to the writing of verse and produced the first two sestiads of *Hero and Leander,* a long poem which he was to leave unfinished and which was eventually to be completed by George Chapman; whereas Shakespeare it is believed, wrote *Venus and Adonis,* which, to the perplexity of Stratfordians, he called the "first heire" of his invention. More important, however, to the development of the unfolding drama is the fact that, owing to the Privy Council's decree, Marlowe had to remain in, or near, London—where his affairs rapidly deteriorated.

Somewhere about the time of Marlowe's supposed death, the Privy Council received a report from a government informer, Richard Baines, listing the playwright's opinions in detail: his contempt for orthodox religion and preference for the hated Catholicism ("If there be any God or good religion, then it is the Papists', because the service of God is performed with more ceremonies."); his scorn of Jesus and doubt of his godhead ("Christ deserved better to die than Barrabas: the Jews made a good choice."); his equal scorn of the apostles ("They were fishermen and base fellows: only Paul had wit, but he was a timorous fellow in bidding men to be subject to magistrates against his conscience."); his blasphemous beliefs concerning Jesus ("St. John the Evangelist was bedfellow to Christ and leaned always in his bosom: he used him as the sinners of Sodoma: and the woman of Samaria and her sister were whores

whom Christ knew dishonestly."); and his disparage-
ment of the Queen ("That he had as good a right to
coin as the Queen of England, and that he was acquainted with one Poole a prisoner in Newgate who had great
skill in the mixture of metals and having learnt some
things of him he meant through help of a cunning stamp
maker to coin French crowns, pistolets and English
shillings").

Equally bad, there was an accusation of homosexuality ("They that love not tobacco and boys are fools");
while the suggestion that Marlowe might be on the point
of fleeing north to embrace the cause of the Scottish
King James, which added high treason to the charges,
was to be made by Kyd in a letter to Sir John Puckering, the Lord Keeper.

Marlowe's situation was becoming desperate. His
tormented state of mind at that time can easily be
imagined, for he must have known that he was facing
trial and execution. Francis Kett, by an odd coincidence
also of Corpus Christi, had been sent to the stake for
atheism alone and had died screaming from the flames:
"Blessed be none but God!" On the 30th May, in a
tavern in Deptford, Marlowe was murdered.

3

Now the Baines Note was undated, so that it is not certain when the Privy Council received it. All that is known as regards the date of its receipt is that, because of its importance, a copy of it was made and sent to the Queen; and at the head of this copy were written the words: "A Note delivered on Whitsun eve last of the most horrible blasphemes vtteryd by Christofer Marly who within iii days after came to a soden and fearful end of his life."

This mention of Whitsun Eve is puzzling; for Whitsun Eve, in the year 1593, fell on the 2nd June, and, since the date of the Deptford murder was the 30th May, it would appear that the murder preceded the receipt of the note by three days. The writer of the comment, however, declares that it took place "within three days after", so that obviously an error was made.

Calvin Hoffman, considering that it lies in the use of Whitsun Eve, states unequivocally that the date of the note's receipt was the 29th May; and since, had it actually been received before Marlowe's reported death, it would seem to make the need for an arranged murder all the stronger, Dr. H. N. Gibson, in attempting (in *The Shakespeare Claimants*) to disprove Hoffman's theory, reaps considerable harvest from what he believes to be a mistake. "I would first call in question what I consider to be Hoffman's exaggeration of Marlowe's danger . . . Of course, if the Baines report had been in the hands of the Privy Council from the first the situation would have been different; but we have seen that there is good reason to suppose that it did not arrive until after Marlowe was officially dead. In any case its arrival must have been very late in the proceedings or the Lords would certainly have ordered Marlowe's close arrest, and not merely invited him to drop in daily until further orders."

I am in full agreement. Had the Privy Council received the note before they had heard of the Deptford murder, they would have undoubtedly ordered Marlowe's arrest. One is forced to the conclusion, therefore, that the scrivener's error lies not in one of the dates in question, as Dr. Gibson and others have presumed it to do, but in his use of the word 'after'. What he meant to write was 'before'. The comment should read, "who within iii dayes *before* came to a soden and fearful end of his life". The dates are then brought into harmony, and the strange circumstance that, though indicted by Baines of such heinous offences, Marlowe was not arrested is explained.

Now, does this question of the late delivery of the note weaken our case? Of course it does not. Marlowe had been aware of what was going on for very nearly a year: ever since, I am prepared to wager, the June of 1592 when Raleigh's fall from favour had removed his comfortable protection. For nearly a year the menace had been building up. Evidence of this is to be seen in Greene's diatribe against players (September 1592) and criticism of Marlowe. Moreover, had this criticism done the dramatist no harm? He was a known and acknowledged atheist and a known and acknowledged homosexual. In the words of Dr. Boas: "Homosexual affection, without emphasis on its more depraved aspects, had a special attraction for Marlowe. Jove and Ganymede in *Dido,* Henry III and his 'minions' in *The Massacre,* Neptune and Leander in *Hero and Leander,* are all akin, though drawn to a slighter scale, to Edward and Gaveston" in *Edward II.* "The parallel to Jupiter and his cup-bearer is a fact brought home to the audience by the deserted queen (l. iv. 178-81):

Like frantic Juno will I fill the earth
With ghastly murmur of my sighs and cries;
For never doted Jove on Ganymede
As much as he on cursed Gaveston.

Even more significant is the roll-call of illustrious precedents in 1. iv. 390-6 :

The mightiest kings have had their minions:
Great Alexander loved Hephaestion;
The conquering Hercules for Hylas wept;
And for Patroclus stern Achilles droop'd.
And not kings only, but the wisest men:
The Roman Tully loved Octavius;
Grave Socrates, wild Alcibiades."

So that, if he flaunted his atheism in his daily life and his homosexuality in his plays, is it not likely that he flaunted his homosexuality in his daily life also? Marlowe's vulnerability, it is clear, dated from the day of Raleigh's eclipse. Thereafter he was like a lobster that has shed its carapace.

Two pieces of documentary evidence support this view: first, Marlowe's apparent reaction to Greene's criticism. This is enlarged upon by Henry Chettle, publisher of *A Groates-Worth of Witte* in the introduction to his *Kind-Harts Dreame*. (Neither Marlowe nor Shakespeare, incidentally, are mentioned by name in either of these works. Scholars, however, are unanimously agreed as to the identities of the persons concerned, and there would have been no doubt in the minds of contemporaries). Chettle says: "About three months since died M. Robert Greene, leaving many papers in sundry Booke sellers hands, among other his Groatsworth of wit, in which a letter written to divers playmakers, is offensively by one or two of them taken . . . For the first (Marlowe), whose learning I reverence, and at the perusing of Greene's Booke, stroke out what then in conscience I thought he in some displeasure writ: or had it been true, yet to publish it, was intollerable."

Since Marlowe's atheism had been frankly discussed by Greene, this matter which could not be published, and which so offended Chettle, can have referred only to his homosexuality, which will have been well known to Greene, who had confessed earlier to having seen and committed, during his travels in Italy, "such villainy as is abominable to declare". Chettle now seeks to defend himself against the charge of having added to the pamphlet, asserting that it could not have been licensed, had the offending passages not been deleted. "I had only in the copy this share . . . licensed it must be, ere it could be printed which could never be if it might not be read. To be briefe I writ it over and as neare as I could, followed the copy, onely in that letter I put something out, but in the whole booke not a worde in, for I protest it was all greenes, not mine nor Master Nashes, as some uniustly have affirmed."

The second piece of evidence comes from Kyd. In the already mentioned letter to Sir John Puckering written a few days after the murder at Deptford, he tries further to denigrate Marlowe: "He wold perswade with men of quallitie to goe vnto the k(ing) of Scotts whither I heare Roydon is gon and where if he had livd he told me when I sawe him last he meant to be." The operative words are "when I sawe him last" which point to a period antecedent to the 12th May, the date of Kyd's arrest, and well antecedent to the date of the murder. But why, even before the 12th May, had the great dramatist been on the verge of leaving the seat of his profession, abandoning his gains and fleeing to the barbarian north where a means of livelihood would have been so much less secure? Obviously because the writing was already on the wall. He had to make a break with his present type of life and start all over again. Because he felt himself to be in extreme personal danger. There could also have been the fact that the abnormal proclivities of the young James were already being talked about over the grapevine, and Marlowe was looking for a sympathetic protector.

There is another important consideration. How long did it take Baines to compile his note? Dr. Gibson cannot be so naive as to hold that all this information was accumulated in the course of one period of eavesdropping. The note is too complex: the wording too pat. Baines may have been compiling his list of charges for months. And can it be believed that Marlowe, during that period, was never aware of the fact that he was being watched: that his actions were being observed and his conversations written down: that all this evidence was being accumulated against him? Can it moreover be thought that his highly sensitive and perhaps paranoid mind remained calm after his first summons to the Privy Council? Or did he feel himself rather to be in the position of a modern criminal on the run, who, while the police are getting together a watertight case, lies quaking in a hideout, waiting for the official rap on the door which will betoken the end of his liberty and perhaps even worse. It is just this state of suspense that is so wearing to criminal nerves; for under the influence of an active imagination and a sense of guilt, it builds up, until the mind reels and the nerves snap.

Having lost the protection of Raleigh, Marlowe, we know, had gone after his arrest, to seek that of his other friend Thomas Walsingham at Scadbury where he was waiting for the next development in the drama.

It is indeed fortunate that the murder was organised three days before the note was handed in. Otherwise, as Dr. Gibson says, Marlowe would surely have been detained—and then it would have been too late.

4

The story of the murder is well known and would appear to be easily verifiable, for every moment of the dramatist's supposed last day was recorded in an official document, which was discovered by Dr. Leslie Hotson in 1925 in the Public Record Office. It tells how, on the 30th May, 1593, Marlowe met Ingram Frizer, Nicholas Skeres and Robert Poley in Deptford; how he retired with them at about ten o'clock in the morning to a small upper room in the house of a widow named Eleanor Bull (which stood facing the Green beside the royal shipyard on a small part of the site occupied to-day by the crushing horror of the huge Deptford Power Station); how they "dined, walked in the garden of the house until about six in the afternoon, then returned to the room and supped"; how, after supper, Marlowe lay down on a bed in the room, while Frizer, Skeres and Poley remained seated on a bench facing the table; how after a time a quarrel arose concerning the payment of "le recknynge", and Marlowe drew Frizer's dagger which was slung behind him and, from his position on the bed, struck at Frizer, inflicting two superficial wounds on his forehead; how Frizer, jammed in between Skeres and Poley, could not move away, but instead turned and, having received the wounds, wrestled with Marlowe, twisting the blade so that he eventually succeeded in giving him "a mortal wound over his right eye of the depth of two inches, of which mortal wound the aforesaid Christopher Marlowe then and there instantly died". The report, dated the 1st June, 1593, was drawn up by one William Danby, Gent., Coroner to the Household of Queen Elizabeth, and was signed by him and sixteen named witnesses all of whom, the day following the murder, had viewed the body "lying dead and slain". Its official reliability cannot

31

therefore be doubted: the accuracy of its detail can.

In order to account for the presence of Marlowe's body in Stratford-upon-Avon, it now becomes necessary to hypothesize one extraordinary characteristic about the actor Shakespeare. He was remarkably like Marlowe to look at: so like him, indeed, that he might have been taken for his twin. And this coincidence is not nearly so improbable as it may at first seem; for it derives from an inverted syllogism based on the assumption that the presence of the body in Stratford indicates an imposture, and that all impostures presuppose a likeness.

Because is it not reasonable to assume that the influential Thomas Walsingham, too, had known for some time of his protégé's plight and been worried by it? That for some months past, as suspicion of Marlowe had been building up, he had even been taking steps to prevent an execution that would rob his country (and the wide world, though he did not know it) of an incomparable talent? And that, in looking about for a scapegoat, in the purest sense of the word, who could be slaughtered in Marlowe's stead, and whose place in society Marlowe could take, his eye had fallen upon Shakespeare, the loud-mouthed air-sawing player from Stratford, who, by a freak of nature, happened to be Marlowe's double? Moreover, if he selected Shakespeare, there was the additional advantage, indicated so unmistakably in Greene's *Groates-Worth of Witte,* that the actor had been trying to write; for how could the coarse clay of Shakespeare suddenly become animated with Marlowe's genius, as it would seem to do if Marlowe took his place and went on producing his splendid verse dramas.

For corroboration let us revert to Chettle's introduction to his *Kind-Harts Dreame.* Chettle, it would seem, though "not caring if he were never acquainted with the first of the two play-makers" who had taken offence at Greene's *Groates-Worth of Witte,* was nevertheless disturbed by the reaction of the second. He apparently sought Shakespeare out, for he says: "The other, whome at that time I did not so much spare, as since I wish I had, for that as I have moderated the heate of living writers, and might have used my owne discretion (especially in such a case) the Author beeing dead, that I did not, I am as sory, as if the original fault had beene my fault, because myselfe have seene his demeanour no lesse civill than he exelent in the qualitie he professes (i.e. his acting): Besides, divers of worship have reported, his uprightnes of dealing, which argues his honesty, and his facetious grace in writting, that aprooves his Art."

This piece of literature is akin to the handsome apology made by a modern newspaper after being threatened with a libel action, with the difference that Chettle, in much of what he says, seems to be sincere, whereas the average modern editor, in penning such a fulsome piece of praise, would only be looking after his company's financial interests. It should therefore be noted that, whereas Chettle claims immediate knowledge of Shakespeare's civil demeanour and excellence in the quality he was professing, he had only *heard* of his uprightness of dealing, which argued his honesty, and his facetious grace in writing, that approved his art. These had been reported by divers of worship. So that it is pertinent to ask: Why had Chettle, an educated man, an author and a publisher, not *seen* any of Shakespeare's writing, if Shakespeare was already emerging, as the Stratfordians assert he was, and had outstanding talent, as the Stratfordians say he had, and Chettle had actually met him?

The answer lies, of course, in the poor quality of Shakespeare's writing and in the strange fact, always minimised by Stratfordians, that not one of the works that are to-day attributed to William Shakespeare can be linked with that name before the 30th May, 1593, the date of the Deptford murder. Any such linking is based upon the purest assumption. Parts II and III of *Henry VI,* called in their early form *The First Part of the Contention betwixt the two famous Houses of Yorke and Lancaster* and *The True Tragedy of Richard Duke*

of Yorke and the death of good King Henry the Sixth,
are thought to belong to the years 1591 and 1592,
because of the quotation from Part III (already contained in *The True Tragedy*) that is parodied in Greene's
A Groates-Worth of Witte (September 1592): ". . . with
his Tiger's heart wrapped in a Player's hide."

The line "O tiger's heart wrapped in a woman's hide"
is included in the curse the dying York flings at Queen
Margaret.

Whereas on the 3rd March, 1592, a play listed by
Henslowe simply as *Harey the VI*, with no reference to
an author, was acted at his theatre the "Rose", and this
is thought to have been *Henry VI*, Part I. The entire
trilogy was therefore in existence, *in some form*, at the
time of the Deptford murder; but all three parts of
Henry VI, as we know them to-day, were not to be
published *at all*, let alone under the name of Shakespeare, until 1623 when the collected works appeared
in the First Folio. They are not even mentioned by
Francis Meres, in 1598, as being among "Shakespeare's"
completed plays. Only *The Contention* and *The True
Tragedy* and the mysterious *Harey the VI* are known to
have been actually in existence at the time of the Deptford murder, and the first two of these are attributed
by the more enlightened scholars to Christopher Marlowe. (*Harey the VI* I believe to have been written by
Greene and shall substantiate the theory in a later
volume.)

As for the first two plays, Dr. Boas, whom I quote
rather too freely, deals with their authorship exhaust-
ively: "Tucker Brooke has championed Marlowe as
the author of *The Contention* and *The True Tragedy*
on grouds which may be summarised broadly as
follows. Thomas Millington, who entered *The Contention* on the Stationers' Register on the 12 March
1593/4, on the following 17 May entered, with Nicholas
Ling, *The Jew of Malta*. In neither case was the author's
name given, nor did it appear on the title-page of *The
Contention* (1594) or *The True Tragedy* (1595). But the
latter play and presumably the former was acted by

Pembroke's company, for which Marlowe wrote
Edward II, and with which Shakespeare is not known
to have been associated. . . .

"The literary quality of *The Contention* and *The True
Tragedy,* in Brooke's view, points to Marlowe as being
their author. They exhibit 'a brilliant synthesis of plot
and emotion', and 'the whole tangled story is resolutely
pitched in a single key'. Moreover, the respective relations of Henry VI, Queen Margaret, Suffolk, and Prince
Edward in these two plays are closely akin to those of
Edward II, Queen Isobel, Mortimer, and Prince Edward
in *Edward II.* The versification, with its predominant
number of end-stopped lines, and its absence of double
endings, is characteristic of Marlowe. But the most con-
crete support for Marlowe's claim is found by Brooke
in the remarkable number of passages in *The Contention*
and *The True Tragedy* which have parallels in Marlowe's
accepted plays or which are repeated in the quartos
themselves. Such parallelism and repetition are both
characteristic of Marlowe's technique."

It is nevertheless certain, if Greene's reference to the
only Shake-scene in a country is to be taken literally,
that some sort of dramatic work is ascribable to the
actor and Johannes factotum, who was trying his hand
at writing, and who was not, and was not to be, the only
actor to write, or collaborate in the writing of, plays.
Richard Tarleton had written; Robert Wilson had col-
laborated, and there were to be a number of others. But
still there was no mention of Shakespeare by name.

Even when, six weeks before the murder—on the
18th April, to be exact—*Venus and Adonis* was entered
in the Stationers' Register, it was done so anonymously.
Only later in the year, when the poem was published,
did the name William Shakespeare appear in print; and
for the first time. But the author himself states that
the poem was "the first heire" of his invention, and why
should we disbelieve him! *Venus and Adonis* was the
first composition written by Marlowe under the new
pseudonym.

5

It now becomes necessary to consider the major point put forward by Dr. H. N. Gibson in his attempted refutation of Calvin Hoffman's theory. After the business has been arranged, says Dr. Gibson, "Walsingham sets the ball rolling by causing the poem, *Venus and Adonis* . . . to be published under the name of William Shakespeare, the first work to be printed with this name attached". And he appends a footnote: "This part of Hoffman's case can be disposed of at once. *Venus and Adonis* was entered in the Stationers' Register, with Shakespeare's name as author, on April 18th, 1593— that is, nearly five weeks before Marlowe was arrested, and therefore before there could be any plot against him. Moreover Field, the publisher who was responsible for the registration and eventually published the poem, was a Stratford man and a friend, or at least an acquaintance, of Shakespeare's. This would entail his being let into the 'secret', and thus more danger and expenditure in bribery"—he has already postulated some—"for the poor Sir Thomas Walsingham. In the light of such facts this purely supposititious plot becomes absolutely incredible."

Now this question of the anonymity of the registration of *Venus and Adonis* is of great importance; not for the reason given by Dr. Gibson, but because, if the poem had been entered on the 18th April under the name of William Shakespeare, one would then have to explain how it was possible to use the pseudonym fully six weeks before the murder: that is to say, in the actual lifetime of the Stratford player. I should very much like to know, therefore, why Dr. Gibson, who writes the letters M.A. and Ph.D. after his name and unmercifully castigates Calvin Hoffman for slovenly and slipshod scholarship, states categorically that *Venus and Adonis* was entered in the Stationers' Register on April 18th, 1593, with *Shakespeare's name as author*. Surely he cannot have checked the entry in the Stationers' Register, as I have. He cannot even have referred to E. K. Chambers' quotation of it from Edward Arber's transcript, or to the transcript itself, which is freely accessible on the open shelves of the British Museum Reading Room. Had he done any of these things, he would have seen that the entry in the Stationers' Register for "xviij Aprilis" reads in the margin: "Richard Feild (sic) Assigned over to master Harrison senior 25 Junij 1594"; and in the body of the page: "Entred for his copie under thandes of the Archbisshop of Canterbury and master warden Stirrop, a booke intituled Venus and Adonis", which is followed by a note of the registration fee, 6d., and the initial 'S' of Master Warden Stirrop. There is no mention of Shakespeare's name at all. But this is not unusual. The majority of the entries in the Register are anonymous so far as the author of the work is concerned. It was the publisher or printer who took out the copy, and more often than not the book was described by its title alone. I refer Dr. Gibson (whom, incidentally, I am not accusing of intellectual chicanery, but simply of ignorance of an elementary fact) to H. G. Aldis's chapter on the book trade of the period in *The Cambridge History of English Literature*.

"The only form of copyright recognized at this time was the entry of a 'copy' in the Stationers' Register by a member of the company, and the right to print the work so entered became vested in the stationer in whose name it stood. So far as the author was concerned, no right existed . . . The author was thus at the mercy of the stationer. He could, no doubt, take his manuscript in his hand, and, making the round of the shops, conclude a bargain with some bookseller whom he found willing to undertake the publication of his work; but, except by agreement, he could retain no control over his book: it would be entered in the register in the stationer's name and become his property. As for the author who allowed his writings to be circulated in manuscript, as was often done in the case of poems and other forms of polite literature, he was in a still more defenceless state, for his manuscript was liable to be snapped up by any literary scout who might scent a paying venture and the first stationer who could acquire it might forthwith proceed to Stationers' Hall and secure the copyright of the work, leaving the hapless author without recompense or redress, and without even the consolation to his literary pride of correcting the errors of copyist and printer."

There is then Dr. Gibson's over-glib statement that Field was a Stratford man and a friend, or at least an acquaintance, of Shakespeare; that he would have spotted any deception and therefore have had to be let into the secret. And thus more danger and expenditure in bribery for the poor Sir Thomas Walsingham! (Walsingham, incidentally, was not knighted until 1597). The facts are these.

Richard Field, son of Henry Field, tanner of Stratford-upon-Avon, arrived in London in 1579 at the approximate age of fifteen. He would therefore appear to have been Shakespeare's exact contemporary. He apprenticed himself, on his arrival, to George Bishop for a period of seven years, but was immediately transferred for the first six to Thomas Vautrollier, master-printer, bookseller and bookbinder; and publisher, with John Wright, in the very same year, of Sir Thomas North's translation of Plutarch's *Lives,* which was to become one of the most popular books of the period. Vautrollier and his wife Jacqueline were Huguenots, who in 1562 had fled from the Continent and settled in England. In 1584 Vautrollier, who had recently printed the writings of the Italian philosopher Giordano Bruno, fled to Scotland to avoid the consequences of so reckless an action and there attempted to set up a bookselling business in Edinburgh, but was prevented from doing so by the Scottish booksellers on the grounds of his being a foreigner. In 1586 he returned to London, bringing with him in manuscript form John Knox's *History of the Reformation,* but when he got the book into print the edition was suppressed. Where was Field all this time? One fancies with Vautrollier. For the following year, when Vautrollier died (perhaps from frustration), we find young Richard, now aged about twenty-four, marrying his master's elderly widow, inheriting the printing business and putting up his own sign. The Will that Vautrollier left, says R. B. McKerrow, "settles once and for all that he had no daughter and that Richard Field the apprentice married his widow and thus secured a good business". So that clearly Field was a man of ambition; and by the time William Shakespeare arrived in London to hold horses, or act as call-boy, or walk on the stage in supernumerary parts, or do whatever else it was he did before graduating to the rank of fully fledged player, Field was already well advanced on the road to success. What then would have been the reaction of the ambitious Master Field towards the newly arrived and probably hopelessly provincial William Shakespeare whom he had known in Stratford? We all know the Englishman's traditional love of a compatriot when he meets him abroad; and a Shakespeare holding horses, or even practising his humble profession of player, would probably have aroused more antipathy than love in the breast of the rising Richard Field. One of the most distressing features of Shakespearean scholarship is the tendency everywhere to whitewash Shakespeare and all those who can be considered sympathetic to him, and to build up cosy little romances about him. M. M. Reese uses up pages of his *Life* in trying to establish the fact that John Shakespeare could not possibly have gone bankrupt—because he was Shakespeare's father. Sir Sidney Lee, in dealing with the social status of players (who were thought in Elizabethan times to be a lowly breed of men), says that, once they had passed under the patronage of a person of high degree, "the licence gave them the unquestioned rank of respectable citizens"—as though anything but respectability would be unthinkable for Shakespeare. And others argue at length, vitriolically, that the dramatist could not possibly have been homosexual (though the Sonnets reek of homosexuality) or homocidal (though the plays abound in parricide, matricide, fratricide, sororicide, nepoticide, regicide, suicide, straightforward murder, assassination, butchery, war, civil war and blood-letting of every variety)—simply because he was Shakespeare. Now, this sort of prejudiced thinking, to which also belongs the cosy little friendship that is thought to have existed between Shakespeare and Field (because they both came from Stratford and Field appears to have been the first to recognize Shakespeare's genius) is downright dangerous so far as scholarship is concerned, because it prevents the establishment of truth. Stratfordians, however, are fortunately not unanimous. "Nothing is known of Field's connection with Shakespeare," R. B. McKerrow assures us, "and after the two early poems, he printed no more of his work. But as Field's output consisted mainly of large and serious volumes, and as he hardly touched popular literature at all, this fact has no significance."

It has, however, considerable significance; for Field may have been the publisher of *Venus and Adonis* only by accident, and may never have come into contact with the author of the poem at all. I am indebted to J. Denham Parsons for leading me to the following interesting line of argument.

Before the year 1593, John Harrison Senior of the White Greyhound in St. Paul's Churchyard (Master of the Stationers' Company in 1583 and 1588) had employed Richard Field to print three Latin and three English works for him.

The trade notices on the English works read as follows:

Imprinted at London by Richard Field for Iohn Harrison and are to be sold at his shop in Paules Churchyard at the signe of the Greyhound 1590.
Imprinted at London by Richard Field for Iohn Harrison and are to be sold at his shop in Paules Churchyard at the signe of the Greyhound 1591.
Imprinted at London by Richard Field for Iohn Harrison 1592.

The trade notice on the first edition of *Venus and Adonis* read:

London. Imprinted by Richard Field, and are to be sold at the sign of the white Greyhound in Paules Church-yard, 1593.

And of the second:

London. Imprinted by Richard Field, and are to be sold at the sign of the white Greyhound in Paules Church-yard, 1594.

But according to H. E. Rollins, Editor of the Variorum Shakespeare, this edition was published by John Harrison Senior, to whom Field, as has been noted, assigned it on the 25th June of the same year.

Whereas the trade notice on the first edition of *Lucrece* read:

Printed by Richard Field, for Iohn Harrison, and are to be sold at the sign of the white Greyhound in Paules Church yard 1594.

Now, why do the notices of the first two editions of *Venus and Adonis* fall out of step? Mr. Parsons believes that the scrivener of the Stationers' Company made a mistake, and so do I; though here Mr. Parsons and I part company.

The next thing to observe is that, coupled with this strange inconsistency, there is the assignment of the copy from Field to Harrison on the 25th June, 1594. Under the name of Master Harrison Senior, the Stationers' Register shows:

Assigned over vnto him from Richard ffield in open Court holden this Day a booke called Venus and Adonis.

And a postscript follows:

The which was before entred to Richard ffield 18 aprilis 1593.

This, apart from the fact that it is an assignment, has, oddly enough, caused no comment (so far as I can see) among scholars. W. W. Greg, one of the leading Shakespeare authorities, in his introduction to *The Records of the Court of the Stationers' Company,* though referring to a number of what he calls interesting cases, does not mention this one. One must assume, therefore, that he was not struck by the words *in open Court.*

Because "in open Court" means before a judge and in public; so that it would seem that there had been some sort of dispute over the copy—and of a serious nature. It was the custom for disputes between members to be ironed out by the Company's own Court of Assistants, and only referred to a higher Court if both parties did not agree to abide by the Assistants' decision. According to the Register, however, this case was heard 'in open Court'. And there is a strange corroboratory circumstance. In the Company's Court Records (quoted above), there is no corresponding minute to cover the assignment of the copy of *Venus and Adonis* from Field to Harrison. Indeed, though the entry in the Register expressly states "assigned this day", no court appears to have been held on the 25th June, 1594. And though, in my opinion, there could be doubt as to the completeness of the records, W. W. Greg quite confidently asserts in his introduction, "We certainly have here the Court Book for the years in question (1576-1603)". It seems, therefore, that one would have to look for the relevant minute in the records of some other Court of the period; perhaps the Court of Requests. I have not yet done so. The magnitude of the task of tracing such a needle in a haystack has overawed me, and I have regretfully had to set it aside until I have time for so much labour.

Further corroboration of the fact that there had been a dispute comes from Harrison's own assignment of the copy of *Venus and Adonis* to William Leake, by a strange coincidence also on the 25th June, but in 1596. The terms of this are in marked contrast to those of the earlier one of Field.

William leeke. Assigned ouer vnto him for his copie from master harrison thelder, in full Court holden this day by the said master harrisons consent.

The words 'by the said master harrisons consent' seem to hark back to the earlier assignment and imply that here there was no dispute.

Now what happened? One explanation could be that Field "pulled a fast one".

"Oh, dear!" say the scholars. "He couldn't have done that. He was a friend of Shakespeare's."

Very well, then. Equally conceivable is the fact that an error was made and that, when it came to light, Field was not prepared to have it rectified.

The poem was submitted to Harrison and bought by him. Harrison then entrusted the manuscript to Field, whom he was employing as his printer, asking him to register the work for copy. Field walked into the Stationers' Hall with the manuscript, and the clerk, who had frequently dealt with him on his own account before, erroneously made out copy to him. When the error came to light, Field, sensing a valuable property, was unwilling to relinquish the copy which stood in his name. The Stationers' Company, since their prestige was involved, refused to admit their mistake, and Harrison took Field to court to recover what was his by right. After the hearing on the 25th June, 1594, the matter was corrected by the Stationers, and Field reprinted *Venus and Adonis* for Harrison, though the words "for John Harrison" were still omitted from the trade notice.

If this is so, Field had still not met the author of the poem.

There is then the question of the quality of Field's printing, about the merits of which scholars violently disagree.

H. E. Rollins, in the Variorum Shakespeare, declares that "the correctness of the text has led authors to believe that Shakespeare not only furnished the printer with a carefully prepared holograph copy but also read the proofs".

Sir Sidney Lee, however, states: "On the whole, Field's text of 1593 may be held to have adhered to Shakespeare's manuscript with reasonable closeness, but it presents defects of the sort which confutes the theory

that Shakespeare himself corrected the proofs . . . Very
little time must have been spent on the revision of proof-
sheets of a book in which some of the commonest words
were spelt indifferently two or three ways in contiguous
stanzas. Elizabethan spelling was impatient of strict
law, but well-printed books observed within their limits
a definite system in the treatment of ordinary words.
In the first issue of *Venus and Adonis* chaos reigns
supreme."

So that the author may have stayed away—and for
a very good reason. He was just then falling foul of the
Privy Council over the question of his suspected
atheism. And for the reading of proofs Field may have
employed his literary adviser.

One more point is of interest in this consideration
of Field's friendship for Shakespeare. In 1596 we find
Field, still resident in Blackfriars (for that is where
Vautrollier's business had been) adding his name to a
petition to the Privy Council, signed by a total of thirty-
one residents, requesting that the new theatre that
James Burbage was erecting in their district should be
suppressed. This shows Field's opinion of theatres and
doubtless of players; and perhaps demonstrates that
his friendship for "Shakespeare", who, as we know,
was closely associated with Burbage at the time, had
lapsed.

I come now to a very difficult problem: one in regard to which I am on much less secure ground: and
that is the actual date of publication of *Venus and
Adonis*: the date on which the poem actually appeared
on Harrison's bookstall. For I have still to prove that
the pseudonym was not used in the actual lifetime of
the Stratford player, and there is an interval of six
weeks between the registration of the poem and the
Deptford murder. Calvin Hoffman categorically states
that it did not appear until September, but I have been
able to find no support for this claim. At the other
extreme is Sir Sidney Lee's fantastically improbable
assertion that it was perhaps on the bookstalls some
two or three weeks after registration. All we have to

go on is Edmond Malone's mention (in 1796) of an entry "in an ancient MS Diary, which some time since was in the hands of an acquaintance of Mr. Steevens, by whom it was communicated to me: '12th of June, 1593. For the Survay of Fraunce, with the Venus and Athonay pr Shakespeare, xii.d'."

This sets us two weeks on the right side of the critical 30th May; but, since the diary no longer exists, Malone's report of the entry must be treated as distinctly suspect, passing, as it does, through so many hands: from George Steevens' acquaintance (the only one to see the diary) to George Steevens, and from George Steevens to Malone. There is a possibility of error in three places. Though the reference to the *Survay of Fraunce* falls into line. Written by John Eliot, it was entered to John Wolf on the 29th April, 1592, and published later that year.

But in my opinion it was not possible for the impression of *Venus and Adonis* to have been ready so soon. To begin with the book must have been in manuscript when it was entered for copy on the 18th April. The main purpose of such entry was the obtaining of licence to publish, and to have set up such a book before entering it would have been extremely risky. Moreover, that was the normal order of things. Having obtained the manuscript, the publisher, before sending it to press, would have to see that the work was properly licensed and, if he thought fit, would enter it at Stationers' Hall. (McKerrow). Then we all know (and Arber states) that printing in those days was a slow and painful process. Each page had to be set up, and the impression taken, by hand. Each page had to be proofread, if not by the author, then by the printer's literary adviser. Finally there was a factor of no small importance in that particular year: the plague. Since many of the leisured, book-reading class were out of London, there was no need to rush into print; Field's staff of apprentices may have been depleted, and he himself may even for a time have escaped from London. The poem would probably have been on Harrison's bookstall when, after the heat of summer, the incidence of the plague was beginning to wane, and people were beginning to filter back to the city. That would have been in September. So that Calvin Hoffman's date is likely to have been the correct one.

There is a further, more technical, consideration, which I have drawn from the New Variorum Edition of Shakespeare (1938). Having studied Shakespeare's orthography along the lines suggested by Sir Sidney Lee (quoted above), Wilhelm Marschall, writing in *Anglia* 1927, makes the astute observation that he sees in it a sudden change at line 1027 of *Venus and Adonis* and that the new system is carried over into *Lucrece*. Marschall decides that it is more reasonable to explain the change of spelling on the ground of the weariness of the poet as he approached the conclusion of *Venus*. Shakespeare put the poem aside after line 1026 and completed it later, while he was also writing *Lucrece* and *Richard III,* at which time his orthography (to some extent under the influence of Marlowe's *Hero and Leander!*) had undergone a change. For this view he finds support in the repetition after line 1026 of words, phrases, and motives from the earlier part of *Venus and Adonis* and in the metrical and literary inferiority of the concluding portion.

It is possible then that Harrison had bought a manuscript only four-fifths complete; though this would not be unusual for a publisher.

Admittedly the Editor of the New Variorum Shakespeare derides Marschall's theory; but it is no more far-fetched than the "nervous breakdown" diagnosed from the text by E. K. Chambers and seconded by A. L. Rowse, which took place during the writing of *Timon of Athens.* Moreover, it finds support in the fact that the author's name does not appear on the title page of the earlier editions of either *Venus and Adonis* or *Lucrece,* but simply under the dedications, as though both name and dedication had (in both cases) been supplied after the manuscripts: which is exactly what would have happened, in the case of the earlier poem, if the pseudonym had not been decided upon at the date of registration. And this is borne out by the Editor of the Variorum (at least in part) who expressly states that "the text of *Lucrece* beginning on (page) B.1. was set up before the preliminary matter on (pages) A.1. and A.2." which are respectively those of title and dedication. He is silent as regards the order of printing of *Venus and Adonis*. (It is one of those scholarly gaps.) Yet it seems clear that the title and dedication pages of *Venus and Adonis* were also set up after the text,* and that Field, in printing *Lucrece,* simply followed the same pattern, even to the ornament of the two title pages, the block for which, one author tells us, was not used again until 1612, when it appeared on the title page of the Genealogies in the first quarto of the Authorized Version of the Bible; it seems clear too that, if the last 168 lines of *Venus and Adonis* were completed while the author was also writing *Lucrece* (and *Richard III*), there would inevitably have been a delay in the publication of the poem.

There is one point upon which I am not in agreement with Wilhelm Marschall and that is his contention that the poem was set aside as a result of the "weariness of the poet" as he approached its conclusion. Any such shelving is more likely to have been due to the circumstances which led up to the Deptford murder.

---

*E. K. Chambers states uniquivocally: "The title-page and other preliminaries, such as epistles by an author or publisher, were generally printed, at any rate in first editions, after the body of the book." (*William Shakespeare* Vol. 1. p.174).

6

But to return to the story.

We come now to the important fact that Frizer, Skeres and Poley, the three men concerned in the murder, were all closely associated with Thomas Walsingham; and all appear to have been unscrupulous rogues. Calvin Hoffman summarizes their various misdeeds and offences, some of which, he says, had been committed actually for Walsingham's benefit. I quote at random. "Ingram Frizer was the Elizabethan version of to-day's 'con' man. He was commonly used as a foil by Walsingham in a series of fraudulent litigations. Up to almost the very day of the Deptford murder records show him associated with the Walsinghams (Thomas and his wife Audrey). Nicholas Skeres was a robber and cutpurse habitually in and out of jail. He was involved, as Frizer's accomplice, in a swindle undertaken for the benefit of Thomas Walsingham. And Robert Poley, perhaps the least scrupulous of the three, had been sentenced to terms of imprisonment at various intervals, often for the purpose of getting him to inform on prisoners. One of the more able government spies, he had been engaged in espionage and counter-espionage in both England and on the Continent. In May, 1593, he left England for the Hague on Government business, returning on the day of Marlowe's murder with secret information for Thomas Walsingham, and from that meeting with his employer went to Eleanor Bull's house in Deptford, there to meet Marlowe, Frizer and Skeres."

Much of this is confirmed by Dr. Boas. Frizer was indeed in Thomas Walsingham's employ and, with Nicholas Skeres, is known to have been involved in a shady deal with some people called Woodleff in which Walsingham also played a dubious part. But it is almost

48

impossible, says Dr. Boas, to identify him with the Nicholas Skeres mentioned by William Fleetwood in a letter dated the 7th July, 1585, as being amongst a number of "maisterles men and cut-purses, whose practice is to robe Gentlemen's chambers and Artificers' shoppes in and about London". He still seems to have been involved with Poley in the Babington Plot and, after the year 1593, to have been lodged in one London gaol after another. Of his early history we learn from Miss Eugenie de Kalb that "he was in Government Service with Poley and Walsingham between 1580 and 1593".

Robert Poley was the most "eminent" of the trio, and, not unnaturally, his history is the most completely documented. Dr. Boas describes his "tortuous career" in detail, dwelling upon "his equivocal activities as a Government agent and his double-faced attitude to recusants and plotters".

In 1585 Christopher Blount, who was the youngest brother of Lord Mountjoy and who had embraced the Catholic faith, threw himself ardently into the plotting that was being conducted on behalf of Mary Queen of Scots. He chose for his agent Robert Poley; and from the outset it is not clear whose side Poley was on. He may even, at one and the same time, have been working for both parties.

On the 18th January, 1586, Thomas Morgan, one of Mary's agents, who was then imprisoned in the Bastille but was able to communicate with her in cipher, mentioned in a letter "one Robert Poley who hath geven me assurance to serve and honor your majestie to his power being but a poore gentleman . . . If you know not how to be better served for conveyance to Scotland you may cause the Embassador to address the sayd Poley with your letters into Scotland . . . And if your majestie will have him to remayne in some place nerer for your purpose & service he will accommodate himself accordinglye to your pleasure. He is a Catholike and Blount has placed him to be Sir Phillipp

Sydneys man that he may more quietlye live a Christian life under the sayd Sydney."

They had secured him a place in Sidney's service, comments Dr. Boas, because in 1583 Sir Philip had married Sir Francis Walsingham's daughter and taken up his abode in his father-in-law's house. Poley would thus be in a favourable position for learning Mr. Secretary's movements and plans.

His relationship with Sir Francis Walsingham at the time was certainly ambiguous; for, according to one William Yoemans (a London cutler who was suing Poley for alienating the affections of his wife), Poley had, early in 1586, been examined before Sir Francis "by the space of two hours touching a book which was made against the Earl of Leicester. And although Mr. Secretary did use him very cruelly yet woulde he never confes ytt. And he saied that he putt Mr. Secretary into that heate that he looked out of his wyndowe and grynned like a dogge." To Yoemans' question as to how Poley "durst to denye the having of the said booke because he verie well knewe that he had the same," Poley replied: "Marye, it is noe matter for I will sweare and forsweare my selffe rather than I will accuse my selffe to doe me any harm".

"What an avowal," comments Dr. Boas, "from one of the trio on whose evidence the Coroner's jury were to be dependent later for their verdict on how Marlowe met his death!"

"During the summer of 1586 Poley was becoming more and more deeply involved in plots and counterplots." On the 17th October Sir Philip Sidney had died in the Netherlands, but by July Poley "had already wormed his way into the secrets of the hot-headed youth rich and well born, who staked everything for Mary's sake and in losing brought doom upon her as well as himself . . . His relation to the conspiracy is curiously equivocal. He appears to have been an agent of Walsingham, but he won Babington's complete confidence, and after the arrest of the conspirators was committed to the Tower, where he was examined on various charges and made a lengthy confession."

He remained in the Tower until the autumn of 1588 and was then released on the intervention of none other than Sir Francis, who appears to have thought that he had suffered long enough. "Had I not good lucke to gett owt of the Tower?" asked Poley of the long-suffering Yoemans with whose wife he was again on terms of intimacy; and he declared that Mr. Secretary did deliver him out.

"You are greatlie beholding unto Mr. Secretarie," was Yoemans' reply.

"Naye," went on Poley, "he is more beholding unto me then I am unto him for there are further matters between hym & me then all the world shall knowe of." And as though to demonstrate his complete familiarity with the private affairs of Mr. Secretary, he added the surprising detail that Walsingham had contracted the pox when in France.

Oddly enough, he was re-engaged by the Government later in the year and from then on throve in its service until the close of the century when he disappears from view. Dr. Boas sums up: "Whatever his crimes and follies, the adventurer was born under no ordinary star who crossed the paths of Christopher Blount and Anthony Babington, of Francis and Thomas Walsingham, of Philip and Frances Sidney, of Mary Stuart and Christopher Marlowe. He is the very genius of the Elizabethan underworld."

Before leaving this account of the double-dealings of Robert Poley, it is particularly important to note that, among the payments entered to him in the Declared Accounts of the Treasurer of the Chamber, there is one that especially concerns us:

"To Robert Poolye upon a warrant signed by Mr. vice-chamberlayne at the Courte xijmo die Junij 1593 for carrying lettres in poste for her Majesties speciall and secrete afaires of great ymportaunce from the Courte at Croyden the viijth of Maye 1593 into the Lowe Countryes to the towne of the Hage

in Hollande, and for returninge backe againe with lettres of
aunswere to the Courte at Nonesuche the viijth of June 1593
being in her majesties service all the aforesaid tyme—xxx[li]."

So that Poley was believed by the Government to
be abroad throughout the month bounded by the dates,
the 8th May and the 8th June, 1593. Though from the
evidence of the Coroner's report of the Deptford
murder, we know differently. He had slipped back to
England for a couple of days during the second half
of this period.

Calvin Hoffman, as has already been stated, claims
that Poley returned on the day of Marlowe's murder
with secret information for Thomas Walsingham, and
from that meeting with his employer went straight to
Eleanor Bull's house in Deptford. But there is nothing
to show that the day of the return coincided with the
day of the murder; and nothing to support the assertion
that secret information was brought to Walsingham.
Only one official journey is mentioned in the note of
payment: for carrying letters in post from the Court at
Croydon to the Hague and for returning back again
with letters of answer to the Court at Nonesuch. Poley
obviously returned on a flying visit to England to undertake business of a private nature. He arrived before the
30th May, and then (when the inquest was over) went
back to the Hague to pick up his despatches. He would
have just had time to do it. And that he did go back is
sure. The Government believed Poley to have been away
right up to the 8th June, or they would not have said
in the note of payment "being in her Majesty's service
all the aforesaid time", and here we can believe them
to have been right; for, whereas they may have had no
check on their messenger's activities while he was waiting for his letters of answer, they will have certainly
had proof as to the moment of his homecoming, because
the despatches he carried will have been dated. Now
the question the traditionalists have to answer is this:
Can it truly be believed that Poley came all the way
back to England merely to dine and sup and walk in

the garden with three friends at a tavern in Deptford? Or was the murder premeditated?

Equally important to the argument is the fact that much in the Coroner's report does not stand up to close investigation. There are, to begin with, the peculiar circumstances of the meeting. Miss Eugenie de Kalb writes in *The Times Literary Supplement* of the 21st May, 1925 : "It is legitimate to ask why Marlowe (under citation to appear daily before the Privy Council) should have met any three men and spent eight hours or more in retired colloquy with them, to be slain by one at the end . . . What was the business that required discussion from mid-morning to evening? What had they in common for such long and sober discourse?"

But question can be piled upon question. Is it only a coincidence that Ingram Frizer, the one to invite Marlowe to Deptford, should also have been the one to strike the death-blow? William Vaughan, describing the event in *Golden Grove* (1600) distinctly declares that Marlowe "meant to stab with his ponyard one named Ingram, that had invited him thither to a feast . . ." And why should they have all gone to Deptford, when a tavern closer to Scadbury, where Marlowe was believed to be staying, and Frizer was employed, and Poley had probably fetched up, would have been so much more accessible for three of them? Calvin Hoffman comes forward with an answer. A Coroner's report was necessary if a faked murder was to be convincing, and Deptford was within the verge. The Queen's Coroner would have to preside over the investigation and would seal the affair with greater prestige.

Then again, why did the superior Poley, on unofficial leave from his Government mission allow his security to become jeopardized by Frizer sitting alongside him, when he could so easily have intervened and prevented the murder? Why had he allowed himself to become caught up in this "feast" at all, when "letters of great importance concerning her Majesty's special and secret affairs" were perhaps even then waiting so far away to be collected? Why this misguided dalliance when a task of such consequence was waiting to be done? The answer can only be that somebody was making it worth Poley's while to take the risk of so indiscreetly neglecting his official duties.

Finally, Samuel Tannenbaum questions the cause of death. It would have been impossible, he declares, quoting the opinions of several medical men, for death to have followed upon the infliction of such a wound, i.e., one that was only two inches deep. A penetration of six or seven inches into the brain would have been necessary if death were to ensue. Portions of the frontal lobe of the brain, he argues, have been shot away in wartime, and the injured men have survived.

I do not think, in the light of all this, that it is going too far to assume that Frizer, Skeres and Poley were assassins, instructed by Walsingham to inveigle the unsuspecting Shakespeare to Deptford, giving out that he was Marlowe, and there murder him. And since Walsingham would appear to be the key figure in the drama, it will perhaps be useful to build up a more comprehensive picture of the man, from what evidence is available, in order to see whether he was the sort of person who would have risked reputation and perhaps life in an effort to save his friend.

The common ancestor of Thomas and Francis was James, who was born in 1462 and died in 1540. The line then descended to Francis through William, and to Thomas through William's elder brother Edmund, who was by far the most distinguished member of the senior branch. He fought and won his spurs at the Battle of Flodden, attended upon Henry VIII at the Field of the Cloth of Gold and later enjoyed the friendship of the King, who, in 1528, appointed him Lieutenant of the Tower and, in 1539, in recognition of "the good, true and faithful service" he had rendered made him a grant of certain monastic lands. On his tomb are inscribed the words:

Twenty-two years' space
Continuously in his Prince's good grace.

Which, if not fine poetry, at least bear witness to what must have been the patient and self-effacing loyalty of the man; for, as is well known, Henry VIII could be a hard task-master.

During Edmund's term of office at the Tower many illustrious prisoners passed through his hands, most of them bound for the block. Among these were: Bishop Fisher, Sir Thomas More, Thomas Cromwell Earl of Essex, and Queens Anne Boleyn and Katherine Howard. Edmund Walsingham himself died in bed, and one hopes the odour of sanctity, on the 9th February, 1550.

His heir, Thomas, father of the Thomas who is concerning us, was born in 1526 and, eschewing the gaiety of the Court, spent most of his life quietly at Scadbury, where he gave his attention, it seems, mainly to the rearing of an immense brood of children. To him and his fruitful spouse, during their thirty-odd years of married life, were born three sons and seven daughters who reached maturity, and a further two sons and three daughters who died in infancy, bringing the grand total to the imposing figure of fifteen. So that I suppose it might be said that against this particular scion of the house there could be no imputation of homosexuality whatsoever. He died on the 15th January, 1584, and was succeeded by his second son Edmund, his first son Guldeford having predeceased him.

Thomas was the third of his sons who had managed to reach maturity, and his main claim to distinction to-day is the fact that he was the friend of the poets Christopher Marlowe, Thomas Watson and George Chapman. He seems indeed to have had a predilection for the company of poets. Born in the August of 1561, he was two and a half years older than Marlowe, four years younger than Watson and about the same age as Chapman; and since he was a member of so large a family, one is not surprised to learn from Miss de Kalb that in his early manhood he had to work for his living. "In his impecunious years between 1580 and 1589, when he succeeded to his brother Edmund's estates, (Edmund having died), he frequently served her Majesty, under warrant signed by Mr. Secretary (his cousin Sir Francis), as a bearer of despatches to and from Sir Henry Cobham, then Ambassador to France". Marlowe, Poley, Skeres and Walsingham, she tells us, were all in Government service between 1580 and 1593. And there can be no doubt about Walsingham's close association with Sir Francis during the middle 'eighties, for his name is mentioned with Poley's in at least two documents connected with the Babington Plot of 1586. "Balard was arrested at Poley's lodging, immediately after a visit by Thomas Walsingham, 'to whom I had delivered speeches as Mr. Secretary had commanded me the day before'." (Boas in *Marlowe and His Circle*.) And Poley, in a letter addressed to the Earl of Leicester, asserts that, in company with one Thomas Audley, he had gone to Seething Lane "where I attended Mr. Thomas Walsingham for my secret recourse to Mr. Secretary, but all to lost labour then and my distress now." (*Ibid*.)

On inheriting his brother's estate, however, in 1589, Walsingham found that his impecunious days were over. And when his cousin Sir Francis died in the April of 1590, he was able to retire, one can infer, to Scadbury; though he still spent much of his time at Court, being greatly esteemed by the Queen.

It would have been about this time that he married Audrey, daughter of Sir Ralph Shelton of Norfolk; but they had no children until 1600, when a son Thomas was born, who was to become, say the biographers (E. A. Webb, G. W. Miller and J. Beckwith in *A History of Chislehurst*) "an eminently precocious youth. He attracted George Chapman's attention at the age of eight, at thirteen was knighted by James I at Royston, and at fourteen elected M.P. for the Borough of Poole; at fifteen he was married and at sixteen a father." The elder Thomas was knighted by Queen Elizabeth in 1597 after he had entertained her at Scadbury where she planted an oak which still survives and several fig-trees from Marseilles which were to survive until well into the nineteenth century.

This then was the man who we believe saved Marlowe

from the death penalty. Was there a homosexual attachment between him and his protégé, as Calvin Hoffman suggests there was? The evidence to support such a theory is of the most tenuous. There is nothing to go on, except the intensity of their long friendship, vouched for by Blunt, and Marlowe's admission that he favoured such practices.

The homosexual aspect, however, is not vital to the issue. Even a perfectly normal friendship would have justified Marlowe in going to Walsingham, upon feeling the net begin to tighten about him, and ask for assistance; though Walsingham's response might have been less spontaneous.

To deduce the nature of Walsingham's reaction to such a request, one should first consider his relations with the Privy Council whose interests he would be contravening in any attempt to aid Marlowe. These would have been approximately those of his kinsman Sir Francis, to whom, it seems, he had rendered loyal service over a period of nine years. Over matters of national importance Sir Francis had clashed frequently with his colleagues who had often worked actively against him. So that Thomas would hardly have had any feelings of love for the Privy Council, particularly in its present form. For in 1593 Sir Francis had been dead three years; the espionage service had passed to Sir Thomas Heneage, and the influence of Thomas Walsingham had waned. With him it would doubtless have been a case of things are not what they used to be. And that a certain antipathy existed between him and the Council is borne out by their direction to Henry Maunder: "He is to repair to the house of Mr. Thomas Walsingham in Kent, or to anie other place where he shall understand Christopher Marlowe to be remayning, and by virtue hereof to bring him to the Court in his companie, and in case of need to require ayd."

Aid against whom? Obviously Marlowe and anybody assisting him, which, as the Council would have known, did not exclude Walsingham. They thought it possible that Walsingham was *harbouring* Marlowe; and that his attitude might be antagonistic. So that the all-important question becomes: Would Walsingham's desire to protect his friend have developed into the crime one suspects him of committing? Or rephrased: Would his affection for Marlowe have been strong enough to cause him to employ, in order to save him, criminal methods and deliberately to thwart the law? The answer, of course, hinges on the fact that he would not have hesitated to use any methods that he thought necessary. Murders and executions of the most horrible nature were the order of the day, and a resort to such criminal methods would not have been uncharacteristic of him. Long experience of the foreign espionage service, in which spying and counter-spying were the general practice, would have hardened him to that type of action. And he would have had for his example the methods of his illustrious deceased cousin who, in his immense task of ensuring the Queen's safety, had ruthlessly sent thousands to their deaths and had not even hesitated (it is thought) from bringing about the execution of the Queen of Scots by treacherous means. So that in this case considerably less affection has to be weighed against scruple than in a similiar instance to-day. Blunt still reports an abundance of it: "In his lifetime you bestowed many kind favours, entertaining the parts of reckoning and worth you found in him with good countenance and liberal affection."

It remains to consider alternative solutions.

Samuel Tannenbaum would implicate Raleigh, who arranged the murder, he thinks, "to stop Marlowe's mouth" lest he should blab information concerning the school of atheism. But Raleigh, after his spell in the Tower for having courted Elizabeth Throgmorton, had married her and retired to Sherborne where he was "diverting himself with rural pastimes" such as the planting of potatoes; and it is doubtful whether, in perpetrating such a murder, he would have used Thomas Walsingham's henchmen instead of his own.

Miss de Kalb would seem to implicate Walsingham himself, who would have stopped Marlowe's mouth because of secrets deriving from their espionage days, and since Dr. H. N. Gibson repeats the theory in his own terms (playfully), it becomes necessary closely to examine it. "There was a Walsingham plot, but it was a plot to *kill* Marlowe, not to *save* him. Since the arrest, which had taken place in his house, Sir Thomas had feared that Marlowe, if made to talk, might implicate him, and so took prompt steps to have the young dramatist eliminated . . . Of course this is not my real view. I agree with Hotson that the official version is probably (!) the real one."

Nevertheless, Dr. Gibson, without realizing it, has put his finger on the weak point of the argument: the fact that Marlowe might *implicate Walsingham*. Implicate him in what? And the phrase "secrets deriving from their espionage days" is equally empty. Anything that Walsingham could have had to fear from the Privy Council would have been in the nature of high treason or unorthodox religion; and to have charged him with high treason, when he had loyally assisted his cousin, the most loyal man in the Kingdom, for a period of nine years, would have been nothing short of laughable, just as it would have to have accused him of becoming a papist. And for Marlowe to have blabbed homosexuality would only have been further to have indicted himself. Moreover, the fact of the persisting friendship was tacitly accepted by the Privy Council.

As for the murderers themselves, two of them had been in the foreign espionage service; the third, Frizer, he who had struck the death-blow, had not. He can hardly have volunteered to stop Marlowe's mouth for the sake of the other two.

To sum up, much that is recorded in the Coroner's report is true, but parts of it are false. There was no brawl, let alone one provoked by the victim; Frizer's wounds were self-inflicted and the corpse viewed by the sixteen jurors the following day was not Marlowe's, but Shakespeare's. The Coroner, however, was not bribed, as Calvin Hoffman suggests he was, but deceived. For in the official document, though much mention is made of Christopher Morley, there is none of the identification of his body. How did the Coroner satisfy himself that the body lying dead and slain at his feet was indeed that of the dramatist? There seems to have been a complete absence of witnesses who could have helped him to such certainty. Identification must have rested with Poley, Frizer and Skeres; and if they had been instructed by Walsingham to declare that the body of Shakespeare was that of Marlowe, then the Coroner, for want of evidence to the contrary, was bound to have accepted their word.

The murder, I believe, was committed in this manner. Shakespeare was poisoned. First, if his death was not brought about by stabbing, as it apparently was not, since the wound was too shallow, it must have been caused by poisoning; for there were no other marks on the body. Then, Poley was a known poisoner. I quote Dr. Boas in *Marlowe and His Circle*: "Among the depositions on the 7th April, 1595, by one Nicholas Williamson a prisoner in the Gatehouse, is one to the effect that 'if Pooley or Barnard Maude shall come again in to the lowe cuntryes, they are threatened to be apprehended. Creichton chargeth Pooley to have poysoned the Bishop of Diuelinge'." And though Dr. Boas is unwilling to accept this accusation without stronger evidence and suggests that it "refers back vaguely to a suspicion mentioned by J. H. Pollen that in 1585 Poley poisoned in the Tower Richard Creagh, Archbishop of Armagh," the fact remains that there is no smoke without fire, and that in poisoning Shakespeare Poley would only have been following the pattern of other murders. Finally, it was stressed in the Coroner's report that the murderers had walked in the garden, and there is the passage in *Hamlet* concerning the King's murder in an orchard, which could conceivably be a memory of the one at Deptford. I shall show later that, in writing *Hamlet,* Marlowe was attempting to expiate his crime by confession, and that it was with his own conscience that he endowed the king guilty of a brother's murder.

Yes, it seems more than probable that Shakespeare

was poisoned. That is why Poley, abroad on official business, had to be summoned back in haste from the Hague. His services as a poisoner were necessary to the smooth working of the plan. The provincial Shakespeare was powerful, and an attack on him by Frizer and Skeres might have miscarried. And if it had, not only Marlowe, but also Walsingham, would then have been called before the Privy Council to answer for past indiscretions.

A more truthful account of the murder would probably have been something like this. After dining and administering the poison, the three assassins left their victim floundering under its effects on the bed—and walked in the garden. But because of his robust constitution, the poison was slow in working. When they returned, Shakespeare was still alive, still groaning on the bed. Accordingly, being hard men, they sat down and supped, and were waited upon by Eleanor Bull, who was evidently their accomplice. Finally Frizer, through impatience, but more to make it look like the result of a brawl, despatched the dying man with a short jab in the eye with his dagger, which, as a sole cause of death does not satisfy modern medical opinion. Then he inflicted his own wounds, or got one of the others to inflict them; and the three prepared to meet the Queen's Coroner who was going to place the seal of finality on the story of Marlowe's death.

Of course we know more about Marlowe's last day than we do about that of almost any other personality of the period (I am quoting the traditionalists): Walsingham wanted it that way. He wanted it believed, without any shadow of doubt, that Marlowe had been completely expunged. The death is so sure that it is too sure, and such surety must inevitably arouse suspicion. Suspicion is aroused, too, by the disposal of the body. It was thrown into an unmarked grave the position of which was soon forgotten. Surely Marlowe was well enough known to have merited some sort of epitaph, if it were only: Here lies Christopher Marlowe, poet and dramatist. The unfortunate Shakespeare, on the other hand, might well have been buried anonymously. His *Venus and Adonis,* anonymously registered, had still to come out.

And what happened to the murderers? Since Walsingham probably spoke in their behalf, Skeres and Poley were exonerated, and Frizer, who, according to the Coroner's report had struck the death blow, was released with the Queen's Pardon after suffering only a month's imprisonment. He then returned to the employment of Walsingham and, in the words of Dr. Boas, "seems to have shared the good fortunes of his master who in 1597 was visited by Elizabeth at Scadbury and was knighted". Both flourished for a good many years, Frizer living until 1627 and Walsingham until 1630.

So that it is possible that Marlowe, too, lived on; and, apart from any consideration of a deciphered epitaph, a Marlowe surviving the 30th May, 1593, makes a formidable claimant to the Shakespeare authorship; because he had inevitably to continue producing his plays.

Let us see what is likely to have happened next. Calvin Hoffman, I am afraid, goes sadly astray at this point. He supposes that a victim was selected "among the strangers of the port"—a sailor perhaps—and that Marlowe travelled to the Continent and sent back plays which were produced under the name of the still living Shakespeare. But if we are to account for the presence of Marlowe's bones in Stratford-upon-Avon, that could hardly have been the case. Besides, was Walsingham, guilty now of murder and the perversion of justice, likely to have taken an unknown man into his confidence? And with Marlowe supposedly abroad and in safety, what was the purpose of using the name of a living, present non-writer, when any pseudonym would have done? At this point Calvin Hoffman's theory becomes very clumsy.

No, the only possible sequal, if the bones are at Stratford, is that Marlowe *became* Shakespeare. Let us therefore conjecture how the new William Shakespeare would have behaved. When he heard that the murder had been successfully perpetrated, he would have packed only his most precious possessions. He would have sorted his manuscripts, taking up everything that, over a period of months, for one reason or another he had not talked about. The "hinge-poem" *Venus and Adonis,* finished to line 1026, he would certainly have taken up. A copy of the completed portion was already in the hands of the printers. (Those worried by the anonymity of the submission should note that on the title-page of *Tamburlaine,* which had been published in 1590, there was no mention of author.) *Hero and Leander,* only two sestiads of which had been written, he would have abandoned. This unfinished work, relinquished, we may be sure, not without considerable mental anguish, was to underline his tragic "death". (It later passed into the hands of George Chapman). He would have left all his clothes behind, but for those he "stood up in", and everything of the sort that goes to form the fringe or aura of a deceased personality. He would then furtively, possibly at dead of night, have made his way to Shakespeare's lodgings and installed himself, avoiding, from then on, as far as possible, all contact with the riffraff of the everyday round, landlord, tradesmen and so on; those, that is to say, whose illiterate minds were insensitive to subtle shades of distinction, but whose instincts might have discerned some difference. A week or so of feigned illness could have helped him over this difficulty. He would then have emerged, slightly changed because of whatever his "malady" had been. He would have said perhaps that he had been wounded in a duel, and this could have been the truth. For it here becomes necessary to leave the main argument for a moment in order to discuss a problem that has arisen.

7

Marlowe may have been lame.

Calvin Hoffman, basing his theory on an "Elizabethan" manuscript version of a ballad entitled *The Atheist's Tragedy,* which he admits is considered to have been forged by John Payne Collier, believes that he was indeed lame, having broken his leg in "a lewd scene" on the stage of the "Curtain": another reason, he says, for supposing that Marlowe and the author of the works attributed to Shakespeare were one and the same person; for the author of the Sonnets was lame too. In the entire collection his lameness is mentioned three times.

> As a decrepit father takes delight,
> To see his active child do deeds of youth,
> So I, made lame by Fortune's dearest spite
> Take all my comfort of thy worth and truth.
> For whether beauty, birth, or wealth, or wit,
> Or any of these all, or all, or more
> Entitled in thy parts, do crowned sit,
> I make my love engrafted to this store:
> So then I am not lame, poor, nor despis'd,
> Whilst that this shadow doth such substance give.
>
> (Sonnet 37)

> Say that thou didst forsake me for some fault,
> And I will comment upon that offence,
> Speak of my lameness, and I straight will halt:
> Against thy reasons making no defence.
>
> (Sonnet 89)

Moreover these two poems are strangely echoed in the great opening speech of *Richard III.*

> But I, that am not shaped for sportive tricks,
> Nor made to court an amorous looking-glass;
> I, that am rudely stamped, and want love's majesty
> To strut before a wanton ambling nymph;
> I, that am curtailed of this fair proportion,

64

Cheated of feature by dissembling nature,
Deformed, unfinished, sent before my time
Into this breathing world, scarce half made up
And that so lamely and unfashionable
That dogs bark at me as I halt by them;
Why, I, in this weak piping time of peace,
Have no delight to pass away the time,
Unless to spy my shadow in the sun,
And descant on mine own deformity.

Noteworthy in this connection is the fact that, if the author of the Sonnets was indeed lame, then his lameness would have supplied him with a powerful incentive for writing *Richard III*.

But Calvin Hoffman did not have to go to John Payne Collier's perhaps spurious manuscript for proof that Marlowe and the author of the Sonnets were linked by a physical disability. It is quite clear to me, from the opposite and more dependable angle of approach, that William Shakespeare of Stratford-upon-Avon is unlikely to have been lame and cannot, on that account, have written the Sonnets.

He was an actor, and lameness hardly accords with success on the stage—except perhaps in the character parts known to have been played later by "Shakespeare" the dramatist. Even in these days of exaggerated realism, when all is grist to the theatre and television mill, if a census were taken of all actors suffering from so limiting a disability, they would number a minute fraction of the sum total. In Elizabethan times, however, the percentage is unlikely to have existed at all. In society generally, unusually high standards of decorum and beauty were dictated by the renaissance humanism. "In their teaching of rhetorical delivery," writes B. L. Joseph in *Elizabethan Acting,* "humanists were inspired by clearly formulated convictions respecting the nature of man and his place in the universe. They adhered to the normal Christian view of man as unique among the inhabitants of the earth in virtue of his rational soul. Reason had made him the link between heaven and earth in the ordered chain of the universe. Reason, more-

C

over, was the divine part, by means of which human beings knew God; it showed itself in erect stature, grace of movement, beauty of body, and . . . in speech."

Later he quotes the Dutchman, Lemnius, writing on the "heroic" appearance (translation Thomas Newton):

". . . in the countenaunce, which is the image of the mynde, in the eyes, which are the bewrayers and token-tellers of the inward conceiptes: in the colour, lineaments, proportion and feacture of the whole body, ther appeareth a kind of heroicall grace and amiablenes, in so much that the very viewe and sight therof allureth and draweth everyone by a certayne secrete sympathy or consent of nature to love it without anye hope of profite or commodity therby to be reaped or received."

There was besides a highly specialized rhetorical technique to be observed by orators, lawyers and clergymen, and by actors with whom the first three categories were equated. Precise rules governed the use of the voice, and the action was so suited to the word, the word to the action, that Titus Andronicus, on being asked to speak by Tamora, after his hand has been lopped off, replies:

> No, not a word. How can I grace my talk,
> Wanting a hand to give that accord?
> Thou hast the odds of me, therefore no more.

Indeed, to judge from the illustrations given in John Bulwer's two treatises on the use of the hand, arm and fingers in rhetorical delivery (*Chirologia* and *Chironomia,* both published in 1644), the hands in the acting of the period would seem to have been placed with the meticulous precision of those of a Balinese dancer. And this applied to the whole body. "Details concerning a Christmas play," writes Mr. Joseph, "are given in a 'dictate'—written in Latin—which has survived in a notebook, belonging originally to William Badger, a pupil at Winchester from 1561 to 1569," and he quotes: ". . . there should be in the voice a certain amount of elevation, depression and modulation, in the body decorous movement without prancing around, sometimes more quiet, at others more vehement, with the supplosion of the feet accommodated to the subject." Whereas Abraham Fraunce, writing in 1588, has the following to say: "Let the bodie therefore with a manlike and grave motion of his sides rather followe the sentence than expresse everie particular word. Stand upright & straight as nature hath appoynted: much wavering and over-curious and nice motion is verie ridiculous . . . For the feete; it is undecent to stand waggling now on one foote, now on another. To strike the ground with the foote was usuall in vehemencie of speach. To stirre a step or two is tollerable, so that it be seldome."

"For player and orator alike," says Mr. Joseph, "voice and body must function as an instrument transmitting sensitively the quality of *elecutio,* the style in which the literary record mirrored the exact quality of the subject as that existed in the author's mind."

There seems, therefore, to have been little room for lameness in so exacting a technique. Even character would probably have been acted, and any deformity superimposed upon the *tabula rasa* of a perfect body. Mr. Joseph writes: "Elizabethan acting probably lent itself to parts involving imposture and disguise. To assume the salient features of another's 'action' would not be too difficult; and in the case of disguise, change of clothes would be accompanied by change of voice and bearing complete enough to suggest a new personality."

The lameness of Marlowe, it follows, would have been tolerated by the Burbages in character acting only because he was a successful dramatist and, as I shall show, he had to act, since the supplanted Shakespeare had been an actor.

Strangely enough, the fact that Shakespeare the actor is unlikely to have been lame is supported by a writer of the period. It will be remembered that, although Henry Chettle had only heard of his uprightness of dealing and facetious grace in writing, he had actually had direct experience of his civil demeanour and excellence in the quality he was professing. So that at the end of 1592, when *Kind-Harts Dreame* was published, Shakespeare does not appear to have been lame. Had he been, I cannot help feeling that Chettle, after observing a disability so discordant in a technique so precise, would have hesitated to use the word 'excellence', which, after all, allows of no degrees. We can be fairly confident, then, that any lameness that existed could have been acquired by William Shakespeare of Stratford-upon-Avon only between the end of 1592 and the date of composition of Sonnet 37, which I myself would place in July 1595, but most Stratfordians considerably earlier, some even as early as 1588. And William Shakespeare of Stratford-upon-Avon is believed to have produced an immense amount of work in the years 1593, 1594 and 1595. He would have had no time for the sustaining of and recovery from an injury so severe that it was attributed to "Fortune's dearest spite".

When, then, did the author of the Sonnets suffer this hurt? I believe that it was in the September of 1589 during the course of the Hog Lane duel. For that would explain why Marlowe, contrary to character, at a certain point in the duel withdrew from it and allowed his friend Thomas Watson to take over, a twist of the plot which I have always thought to be rather unconvincing. If, however, he had sustained a wound in the thigh, it immediately becomes plausible. He would then have had to withdraw. And if the wound had become septic during his twelve days in prison, it could have caused him considerable torment and eventually brought about his lameness. Raleigh was lame from just such a wound as this.

For Stratfordians the inconsistency of their playwright's lameness should be embarrassing, since they have either to explain how it was possible for him to be an actor and lame at the same time, during a period when actors had to be precise in movement and more than usually agile—some of them danced jigs; or they have to redate the Sonnets. They have then to explain how, within the limits I have laid down (which can be narrowed until they disappear), he could have acquired his injury and recovered from it while producing an immense volume of work.

For me this probable lameness of Marlowe's is embarrassing too, but in a different way; for it concerns the imposture. If it were at all pronounced, it would, in the early part of the deception, certainly have had to be concealed, not so much on account of Shakespeare's friends, who would have noticed a defect which, after a short period of seclusion, could in those days be easily explained, as on account of his own associates, who might well have recognized this giveaway characteristic in the new Shakespeare. Thereafter, for fear of coming under the notice of these people, he would have avoided the literary taverns and other haunts where he was likely to meet them. The situation, however, was not quite so difficult as it sounds, for several reasons. First, he had now of necessity to enter the more lowly world of the Elizabethan actor and would automatically have frequented a different environment. Secondly, in those days of barely restrained duelling and primitive surgery, lameness was probably more common than it is to-day and therefore less worthy of note. And thirdly, there was the all-important factor of the plague. He was not likely to be seen by his associates, simply because most of them had fled into the country. He was on that account relatively safe until the month of September when they would all be returning. And perhaps by then nobody would remember *exactly* what anyone so little known as Shakespeare, or so generally disliked as Marlowe, had looked like—even whether he limped or not. And, strangely enough, when the time came for his friends to return, his "death" was hardly noticed. He simply slipped out of the Elizabethan scene. There were no references to his unnatural murder in the literature of the period—until years had elapsed; and then there was the most extraordinary confusion as to the manner of it. During the weeks, however, that immediately followed his supposed death, the imposture must have seemed an awe-inspiring gamble, and one can imagine him, during those lonely months when the plague still stalked the streets, wandering dejectedly about the city, guilt-ridden and racked by doubts as to whether his deception was going to succeed or not. One can picture him spending long hours in self-scrutiny and determining in future to be less violent, less headstrong and less indiscreet in the expression of his opinions: the soul-searching in which he then indulged was possibly so profound that it resulted in a complete change of heart akin to a religious conversion. One can see him avoiding moments of embarrassment, skulking with his slight limp round corners and scanning faces for the twinkle of recognition that would betoken the arrival of one of Shakespeare's vulgar friends, the glare of outrage that would signify the approach of one of his creditors, or the coquettish lascivious look that would indicate the advance of one his mistresses. Each fresh encounter would present its own new and perhaps terrifying challenge. In this moment of fierce crisis his sense of humour seems to have come to his aid. For it is a strange coincidence that *The Comedy of Errors,* a play about twins and mistaken identity in which friends, creditors, mistresses and even wives are deceived, should have been written at about this time. It was performed at the Gray's Inn revels (according to the *Gesta Grayorum*) on the night of the 28th December, 1594, and would have been in the crucible of Marlowe's invention about a year earlier. Nevertheless it is his guilt-racked conscience that is the predominating feature of the plays he wrote just then. For there can be no doubt that he was indeed racked by guilt, that his conscience was to torment him for the remainder of his life, and that it was to do so with a double intensity, because, on account of the likeness that had existed between him and Shakespeare, he was to look upon his crime as the murder of a brother. There were to be frequent references to the murder of Cain. I quote Dr. Rowse: "Of all Shakespeare's 'sources' the Bible and Prayer Book come first and are the most constant. Altogether there are definite allusions to forty-two books of the Bible including the Apocrypha. The story of Cain gripped his imagination.

He refers to the story of this 'primal' murder not less than twenty-five times. Others seized on him with less tenacity." Though Judas is referred to twenty-one times.

The period after the murder gave rise to the writing of *Richard III*, "a play so Marlovian in inspiration," says Dr. Rowse, "that one is inclined to think of it as written in the year of his (Marlowe's) death." Truly a most significant comment in the light of an argument on behalf of Marlowe! Later he writes: "The atmosphere of the play is haunted with guilt and night terrors, there are no less than four dreams, while the word 'blood' runs as a leit-motif through it." From this he draws the implausible conclusion that "Shakespeare" had *evidently* recently read Nashe's *Terrors of the Night* which, though not yet published, was being circulated everywhere at the time in manuscript. But from what we now know of Marlowe's guilt, he would hardly have had to draw for material on Nashe's *Terrors of the Night*, when his own experiences would have been so much more vivid. Shut up for a period in his victim's room, he must have been incessantly harassed by the sight of the dead man's belongings.

Written, too, was *The Rape of Lucrece*, in which Dr. Rowse also finds evidence of a deep emotional disturbance. "It is but an earlier manifestation of that tragic disgust and revulsion which appear in *Hamlet, Lear* and *Timon*, and underlie so much of Shakespeare's later work."

And that the crime of the poem was looked upon as not so much rape as murder can, I think, be inferred from Macbeth's speech outside the bed-chamber of Duncan just before the commission of his own fell deed.

> Now o'er the one half-world
> Nature seems dead, and wicked dreams abuse
> The curtain'd sleep; witchcraft celebrates
> Pale Hecate's offerings; and wither'd murder,
> Alarum'd by his sentinel, the wolf,
> Whose howl's his watch, thus with his stealthy pace,
> With Tarquin's ravishing strides, towards his design
> Moves like a ghost.

Titus Andronicus also emerged at that time. It was published in 1594. But I have a feeling that it was written in the period preceding the murder. Again I quote Dr. Rowse: "We observe that his (the author's) own inner nature and sympathies are not engaged, that the tragedy has a curiously external attitude to its horrors, a kind of barbaric classicism not really natural to him"—To be found also in *Tamburlaine*? "There is a curious disjunction between the horrors of the action and the country observations that are scattered all through—as if it were a school piece written in the country, in absence from London during the closing of the theatres." This is interesting, because Marlowe at the time may well have been staying at Scadbury.

Towards the end of the summer, deaths from the plague decreased. Those who had fled the city came filtering back—to find the despised atheist Marlowe dead and a new literary name emerging. About September *Venus and Adonis* was published with such success that during the next few years it was to be reprinted several times. Its author William Shakespeare, hitherto known mainly as a rather "ham" actor, became suddenly very much discussed—particularly as his patron happened to be the brilliant young Earl of Southampton. How strange, everybody was saying, that this duckling of so little ability should have matured into the Swan of Avon! But the danger was still not past. It was to be years before he was secure in his new personality.

8

Before proceeding to a discussion of how it was possible for Marlowe to sustain his imposture for such a length of time, that is to say, for the remaining twenty-three years of his life, I propose to step aside momentarily to consider a theory I have been led to regarding his whereabouts during the two "silent" years.

As we have seen, both Parts of *Tamburlaine* seem to have been written by the autumn of 1587, and both appear to have been performed by the 10th November. From then on, for the next two years, there is a hiatus in the records. Nothing was done to cause attention; but, more revealingly, nothing was written. Then, on the 18th September, 1589, Marlowe leaps back into the limelight. After fighting a duel in Hog Lane, he was arrested on suspicion of homocide and imprisoned in Newgate, to be released two weeks later on bail. What was he doing between the last weeks of 1587 and the middle of September, 1589? But, more pertinently, what had happened in his life to change him from the polite young man, who in all his actions had behaved orderly and discreetly, rendering her Majesty such service that he deserved to be fittingly rewarded for his faithful dealing, into the desperado and sceptic that he had become by the latter date and was to remain until 30th May, 1593? Answers to these questions can be no more than conjectures; but conjectures so plausible that they are worth examining in detail.

Philip Henderson in *And Morning in His Eyes* writes: "The genius, the originality, the general philosophical and aristocratic temper of Marlowe's mind procured him the friendship of wealthy men, which easily raised him above the degrading level of drudgery of the usual Elizabethan free-lance. His friendships with Raleigh and Thomas Walsingham, for instance, were evidently something very different from the ordinary relations existing between writer and patron. From which we may safely conclude that Marlowe was seldom compelled to work for a living."

I do not think, however, that we may safely conclude any such thing. Nothing will persuade me that Marlowe, during these two silent years was content to sit back and "sponge" on his patrons. He was too independent at this phase of his career, too self-sufficient to accept money for no work done. It is not unnoteworthy that his literary inventions were never, so far as is known, dedicated to a patron. I would look elsewhere, therefore, for his means of support during the years 1588 and 1589. It is a safer conclusion, surely, that he was out gaining the experience of life that, during his later years of intense production, was to stand him in such good stead.

In a fascinating little book entitled *Shakespeare and the Sea* Lieutenant Commander A. F. Falconer lists the many references in the Shakespeare plays to the sea and nautical life. The dramatist, he emphasizes, is remarkable for the extent and accuracy of his nautical knowledge. Most relevant, however, is his discussion of the *Henry VI* plays.

"The nautical rhetoric of Queen Margaret in *Henry VI*, with its shrouds, tacklings, anchors, cables, hatches, helms, masts and sails, has been thought strange in a queen, a lapse perhaps while Shakespeare is finding his way in early work. But there is a sound reason for it." This would appear to be that Margaret has just crossed the Channel in her return from France. Nevertheless "what appears in *Henry VI* gives the impression of one who has recently left the sea and whose thoughts keep turning to it . . . Much has been written about the gap in what is known in Shakespeare's life and, despite attempts to suggest how the years 1584-90 may have been passed, they cannot be accounted for satisfactorily. One thing can be taken as certain, it was during this period that Shakespeare came to know the sea and the navy."

Now in my own mind there is no doubt whatever that Christopher Marlowe wrote the Shakespeare plays; and even the most rabid Stratfordian alive can be brought to admit (perhaps with relief) that a certain part of the trilogy to-day entitled *Henry VI,* since he believes it to have been written in approximately 1591 and therefore before the Deptford murder, was the work of Marlowe. So that the passage quoted above may refer to an author called Shakespeare, and it may not. The lengthy extract, however, which contains the "nautical rhetoric of Queen Margaret" (3 *Henry VI,* Act V, Scene iv) is also to be found in embryonic form in *The True Tragedy of Richard Duke of York,* which Tucker Brooke, and others, believe was indeed written by Marlowe. It runs as follows:

> Once more have we spread our sails abroad,
> And though our tackling be almost consumed,
> And Warwick as our mainmast overthrown,
> Yet warlike lords raise you that sturdy post,
> That bears the sails to bring us unto rest,
> And Ned and I as willing pilots should
> For once with careful minds guide on the stern
> To bear us through that dangerous gulf
> That heretofore hath swallowed up our friends.

By itself this fact of the sea references in *The True Tragedy* and *Henry VI, Part III,* whose strange relationship will be discussed in a later volume, would perhaps mean little, if it could not be coupled with the circumstance that *The Jew of Malta,* written undoubtedly by Marlowe in 1589/90, that is to say, next (but one) after *Tamburlaine* and after the two-year hiatus, also abounds in sea terms. I quote at random.

> Our fraught is Grecians, Turks and Afric Moors;
> For late upon the coast of Corsica,
> Because we vailed not to the Turkish fleet,
> Their creeping galleys had us in the chase:
> But suddenly the wind began to rise,
> And then we luffed and tacked, and fought at ease:
> Some have we fired, and many have we sunk;
> But one amongst the rest became our prize.

See how stand the vanes—
East and by south: why, then, I hope my ships
I sent for Egypt and the bordering isles
Are gotten up by Nilus' winding banks;
Mine argosies from Alexandria,
Loaden with spice and silks, now under sail,
Are smoothly gliding down by Candy-shore
To Malta, through our Mediterranean sea.

A fleet of warlike galleys, Barabas,
Are come from Turkey and lie in our road.

Sir, we were wafted by a Spanish fleet,
That never left us till within a league,
That had the galleys of the Turk in chase.

First we will raze the city-walls ourselves,
Lay waste the island, hew the temples down,
And, shipping off our goods to Sicily,
Open an entrance for the wasteful sea,
Whose billows, beating the resistless banks,
Shall overflow it with their refluence.

I therefore ask: Can it be imagined that, in the vital
year 1588 when England's destiny hung in the balance,
the dynamic tempestuous Marlowe, who had already
worked for Sir Francis Walsingham in Europe, could
have stayed at home? Nor does one have to look to a
friendship with Raleigh to find out what his course of
action is most likely to have been. At the beginning
of 1588, just after his triumph with the two *Tamburlaine*
plays, and perhaps on account of the jealousy they had
aroused in his rivals, it is not improbable that he will
have travelled to the coast to seek employment as a
gentleman adventurer, or even a mariner, in any of the
ships just then preparing for an expected Spanish inva-
sion. Add the coincidences that the patron of the
Admiral's men, the troupe that had produced the two
Parts of *Tamburlaine,* was the Lord High Admiral himself, Charles Lord Howard of Effingham, who stood in
command of the Queen's sea defences, and that Sir
Walter Raleigh, who is known to have included Marlowe in his School of Night, was in charge of the organization of the Queen's land defences, and it becomes very

difficult to believe that the dramatist, during that critical year, sat inactive in London and accepted money from wealthy men, though writing no plays.

There is a further coincidence: the Lord Admiral's flagship was named, at any rate during the early months of the year, the Ark Raleigh (Raleigh's Ark). She was thus referred to frequently by Sir John Hawkins, though Howard himself always spoke of her simply as the Ark. She was not renamed the Ark Royal until later in the campaign. Launched on the 12th June, 1587, at Deptford Strand, this galleon had been built by Richard Chapman for Sir Walter Raleigh who sold her to the Queen for £5,000, which amount was never paid in cash, but was, on Raleigh's fall in 1592, deducted from his debt to the Crown. It is therefore interesting to speculate that the adventurous Marlowe, but twenty-four years old at the time, and undoubtedly connected through his plays with the Lord Admiral, and possibly already by bonds of friendship with Sir Walter Raleigh, should have approached one of these influential men and come to rest in the splendid ship that linked them. The point will perhaps never be proved. No musters of the fleet have yet been found, and the collected State Papers mention only the names of captains and, in the case of the largest ships, a few officers.

Marlowe then, if there is any truth in what we are assuming, will have set off for the wars with his head full of romantic chivalrous ideals—only to be disillusioned. For the horrors of the escapade, which are well-known, would have weighed heavily upon him: the long months of waiting before, on the 19th July, the Armada was sighted near the Scilly Isles; the appalling privations that the men in the ships suffered: the bad victuals, sour beer, filthy conditions, lack of adequate living space and finally, as was only to be expected, disease. Howard himself describes it in a letter to Lord Burghley written on the 10th August.

> Sicknes and Mortallitie begin wonderfullie to growe amongste us . . . The Elizabeth, which hath don as well as eaver anie ship did in anie service, hath had a great infectione in her from

the beginning soe as of the 500 men which she carried out, by the time she had been in Plymouth three weeks or a month there were ded of them 200 and above, soe as I was driven to set all the rest of her men ashore, to take out the ballast and to make fires in her of wet broom 3 or 4 daies together, and so hoped therebie to have cleansed her of her infectione, and thereuppon got new men, verie tall and hable as eaver I saw and put them into her; nowe the infectione is broken out in greater extremitie than eaver it did before, and they die and sicken faster than ever they did, so as I am driven of force to send her to Chatham . . . Sir Roger Townsend of all the men he brought out with him hath but one left alive . . . it is like enough that the like infectione will growe throughout the most part of the fleet, for they have bin soe long at sea and have so little shift of apparell . . . and no money wherewith to buy it.

On the 22nd August he wrote informing the Privy Council that "the most part of the fleet is grevouslie infected and die dailie . . . and the ships themselves be so infectious and so corrupted as it is thought to be a verie plague . . . Manie of the ships have hardly men enough to waie their anchors."

M. Oppenheim in *The Administration of the Royal Navy* (from which I have taken the extract) suggests that the disease was not the plague, or typhus, as has been thought, but an acute enteritis, caused by the sour beer, acting on frames enfeebled by bad and insufficient food, and still further weakened by the scorbutic taint to which all classes, but especially seamen, were subject in the middle ages. Whatever it was we may be sure that Marlowe, more sensitive than most to the sufferings of his fellow men, would (if he were indeed present) have been harrowed by all he saw about him.

So much for the year of the Armada! What of the one that followed? There was the expedition to Portugal undertaken by Drake and Norris. Thousands were drawn to it by the hope of plunder. And thousands were signed on. Drake was obliged to apologize for the numbers he was taking with him: "By repair of many gentlemen and divers companies of voluntary soldiers offering to be employed in this action, whom, both for their satisfaction and the advancement of the service, we could in no sort refuse to entertain." Accordingly, whereas it had been the original intention to embark a force of some ten thousand men, in the end over twenty-three thousand sailed. Again there were months of waiting. On the 30th December, 1588, the Queen gave orders that the troops to be pressed in England be brought to their ports of embarkation by the 20th January, 1589. By the middle of March the whole force was assembled at Dover and other south eastern ports. The ships arrived in Plymouth on the 19th. And again there was an appalling shortage of victuals. The country round about was ransacked for food but could not provide for so large a multitude. In addition niggardly economies were being practised, some said at the Queen's direction. Biscuit, beer, meal, oatmeal, pease, dry fish, cheese and beef were ordered; but to save expense, the beef was replaced by fish; the oil, pease and beer were cut out altogether. The ships sailed with their huge compliments early in April —with only three weeks' victuals aboard. The expedition, as is well known, was a failure. Corunna was besieged, Lisbon attacked, Vigo burned; but the remnants of the Armada lurking in Santander were avoided. The Queen remarked cuttingly of her sailors that "They went to places more for profit than for service." And again the ships were smitten by disease. It is estimated that three-quarters of their compliments died.

That Marlowe sailed with the expedition must remain the merest assumption, but it is one that fills in most neatly the remainder of the two silent years. For the ships that survived were nearly all back by the end of June, and on the 18th September the dramatist was arrested for his part in the Hog Lane duel.

9

I am now faced with the task of explaining how it was possible for Marlowe, posing as Shakespeare, to avoid detection for a period of twenty-three years; and it sounds a formidable one; but it is not nearly so formidable as it would at first appear to be. It is closely linked with the important question: What of the Burbages? How was it possible for them to be taken in? A glance at their history will help us to form an answer.

So great a nuisance had the bands of strolling players become by the beginning of the 1570's that an Act of Parliament was passed requiring them, if they were to practise their profession, to procure a licence from a peer of the realm or person of high degree; otherwise they would be pronounced to be of the status of rogues, vagabonds or sturdy beggars and would be liable to incur the penalties prescribed by the Act for Restraining Vagabonds. Those players who came under the patronage of such a high-ranking person were known thereafter as his men or servants and affected his livery or badge. The principal peers to extend their patronage to troupes of players at this period were the Earls of Leicester, Pembroke and Worcester. Other important companies were founded later in the decade by Lord Strange, heir to the Earl of Derby, and Charles Lord Howard of Effingham; whereas the Queen herself founded a company in 1583. No woman, it should be noted, featured in any of the performances. The parts of women were played by boys.

James Burbage was born about the year 1530. His early history is summed up succinctly by C. W. Wallace in the quotation: "By occupacion a joyner and reaping but a small lyving by the same, he gave it over and became a commen player in playes." More definitively, he joined the Earl of Leicester's men in 1572 and maintained his connection with them over a period of years. In 1576, since plays attended by the general public had so far been performed mainly in inns by arrangement with the innkeeper (to whose benefit it was to provide entertainment for his guests) and since there had been perpetual conflict between the players and the City authorities, Burbage decided to build a theatre in an area outside the City walls where the players would be free of the hampering restrictions of the Lord Mayor and his Councillors. On the 13th May of that year he signed the lease of a plot of ground in Holywell in the parish of St. Leonard's Shoreditch, and there, with the financial assistance of his brother-in-law John Brayne, built the first London playhouse. He called it quite simply the "Theatre"; first because he was a simple man and his mind, apparently, did not run to great feats of invention; and, secondly, because there was no other. He was a stubborn fellow, violent in temper and inclined to be shady in business dealings. He had a wife who closely resembled him in character, and two sons, Cuthbert and Richard, who were both to become famous on the stage, the one as a manager, the other as the great player friend of "Shakespeare".

The entire history of the "Theatre" (the lease taken out was only for twenty-one years) is made up of a constant squabble between Burbage and Brayne over their earnings: lawsuit followed lawsuit as Brayne, who frequently suspected that he was being "done" by Burbage, took his brother-in-law to Court; and when Brayne died in 1586, between Burbage and Brayne's widow who fought equally truculently on her own behalf.

Shortly after the erection of the "Theatre", another playhouse called the "Curtain" was built just to the south of the first, and this acted as a sort of overflow house. Both were very popular, and on fine nights the City crowds would go pouring across the meadows for the entertainment provided. If there was any rivalry between them, it was resolved in 1585 when the "Theatre" and the "Curtain" passed under joint management.

It was not until two years later that a serious threat to Burbage's prosperity loomed over the horizon in the form of a competitor. A new playhouse was being built on the south bank of the river. Bankside, at this time, was a disreputable area, the entertainments it offered being of the grossest. Here was the Paris beargarden, where bear- and bull-baiting were shown to the public. Here were the stews. And here, not surprisingly, just to the east of Lambeth Marsh, the Clink prison added its noisome stench to the already unwholesome atmosphere. In the midst of this dunghill, however, there was now to bloom a fragrant flower. On the 10th January, 1587, Philip Henslowe entered into an agreement with one John Cholmley, citizen and grocer of London, to build a playhouse on a rose-garden plot that he had bought two years earlier. This was to become known as the "Rose". Henslowe was a many-sided personality. A leather merchant by trade, he dabbled also in pawn-broking and the profitable brothel-keeping of the area; and he was now to undertake an artistic venture. Primarily, however, he was a shrewd man of business, and it can be imagined with what spleen Burbage watched the building of the new playhouse. Though he had little to worry about for the first five years. Hardly anything is known of the activities of the "Rose" until 1592, so that one can assume that in most respects it was a failure.

Now a feature that all scholars who have dealt with the complex history of the Elizabethan stage (or at any rate all those I have read) seem to have underestimated is the immense rivalry that existed between the Burbages and Philip Henslowe and, later, between the Burbages and Edward Alleyn. They may have mentioned the Burbages in their "Theatre" on the north bank of the Thames and Henslowe in his "Rose" on the south bank (in much the same way as they might say "That is a gate and this is a barn"); but the human relationship that existed between the two proprietors has been left unstressed; and it is this relationship, this rivalry in all its bitterness, that concerns me; for rivalry is a powerful motivating force.

If one can believe contemporary reports, the Burbages were awe-inspiring in action. The following scene (taken from E. K. Chambers' *Elizabethan Stage*) is simply a part of their quarrel with Mrs. Brayne.

In 1590 the Court seemed inclined to grant a sequestration of half the profits; but instead made an order that the arbitrament of 1578 should be observed. On the strength of this Mrs. Brayne and (an associate) Robert Miles came to the "Theatre" on more than one occasion, and claimed to appoint collectors, including one Nicholas Bishop, who was asked to stand "at the door that goeth uppe to the galleries of the said Theater to take and receyve for the use of the said Margarett half the money that shuld be gyven to come uppe into the said galleries at that door". They were, however, refused access, and on 16 November 1590 there was a row royal, of which independent witness was borne by (the actor) John Alleyn (brother of Edward) of the Admiral's men, who were then playing at the "Theatre". James Burbage, "looking out at a wyndoe upon them", joined his wife in reviling them as a murdering knave and whore, and expressed his contempt for the order of Chancery; Cuthbert, who came home in the middle of the fray, backed him up; while Richard, "the yongest sone of the said James Burbage (appearing for the first time in history), with a broome staff in his hand, of whom when this deponente asked what sturre there was, he answered in laughing phrase hew they come for a moytie. But quod he (holding uppe the said bromes staff) I have, I think, delivered him a moytie with this and sent them packing." He then threatened Nicholas Bishop, one of Mrs. Brayne's agents, "scornfully and disdainfullye playing with this deponentes nose, and saying that yf he delt in the matter, he wold beate him also, and did chalenge the field of him at that tyme". James said that at their next coming his sons should provide pistols charged with powder and hempseed to shoot them in the legs. Both Cuthbert and James were summoned on 28 November for contempt before the Court, which instead of dealing with this charge proceeded to take the whole case into further consideration. This was something of a triumph for Burbage, who continued to resist the order, and repeated with oaths that twenty contempts and as many injunctions would not force him to give up his property. This was heard by John Alleyn in the "Theatre" yard about May 1591, and about eight days later "in the Attyring housse or place where the players make them ready", on the occasion of a dispute with the Admiral's men about some of "the dyvydent

money between him and them" which he had detained, Burbage
was equally irreverent before Alleyn and James Tunstall about
the Lord Admiral himself, saying "by a great othe, that he
cared not for iij of the best lordes of them all".

These are the Burbages defending their rights in their
beloved "Theatre". From which I dare to deduce that
they lived and breathed the "Theatre". It was their life's
blood.

Now, one of the outstanding problems of the history
of the English stage at this period is the whereabouts
of William Shakespeare. For until the late summer or
autumn of 1593, when *Venus and Adonis* was published,
he is (to the immense frustration of scholars) nowhere
mentioned by name. Even in *A Groates-Worth of Witte,*
his identity has to be inferred from Greene's use of the
word Shake-scene. Generations of scholars have therefore ransacked the provincial and other archives in the
hope that the magic name will turn up and confer upon
the fortunate finder a flickering immortality as having
been the first to establish the fact that in such and such
a year William Shakespeare the actor was one of the
Queen's, or Lord Strange's, or the Admiral's men. Alas,
they have searched in vain. Shakespeare's name nowhere
(but nowhere) appears. And so huge is the mass of
material they have sifted over that their findings are
like the deposited shells of countless sea creatures on
the ocean bed, and their writings are an impenetrable
jungle of dry-as-dust facts.

Thus Sir Edmund Chambers in dealing with the
earliest known wanderings of Lord Strange's men:
"The 3rd Earl had a company in Henry VIII's reign.
His successor had one as Lord Strange, which is only
recorded in the provinces, in 1563-70. Four years later
he had again a company as Earl of Derby. The earliest
mention of it is at Coventry in 1577-8, at Ipswich on
28 May 1578, at Nottingham on 31 August 1578, at
Bristol in the same year, and at Bath in 1578-9. In the
last three months of 1579 it was at Leicester; and during
the following Christmas it made its first appearance at
Court with a performance of *The Soldan and the Duke*

of ———— on 14 February 1580. In 1579-80 it was at Stratford-on-Avon, Exeter and Coventry, on 1 January 1581 at Court, in 1580-81 at Bath, Leicester, Nottingham, Exeter, and Winchester, in 1581-2 at Nottingham, Winchester, and Abingdon, in October to December 1582 at Leicester, and in 1582-3 at Bath, Norwich and Southampton." And so on for many pages.

And in dealing with the Queen's men: "Provincial visits of Queen's men are recorded in November 1605 at Dover; in 1605 at Leicester; in 1605-6 at Bath, Coventry, Saffron Walden, and Weymouth; on 25 July 1606 at Ipswich; on 4 September 1606 at Ludlow; in 1606 at York; in 1607 at Bath (twice), Coventry, Exeter, and Ipswich; on 14 August 1607 at Oxford . . ." Thus the monotonous recital continues, page after page of it. Of what value can this sort of information be to anyone? Even if such bald facts were developed with the descriptive power of a Hazlitt, a performance of Lord Strange's men on the 25th July, 1606, at Ipswich would still not come to life.

The territory is moreover littered with the bones of felled scholars. Scholars who have gone down in the bitter struggle that has raged in this fruitless pursuit of Shakespearean spoor: scholars who have been annihilated in their efforts to find the actor—before Marlowe clothed his name with glory; for he was a nonentity. Percy Simpson admits (in *Shakespeare's England*): "Of Shakespeare's acting we have only a meagre record, and there is nothing to suggest—as contemporary references to Edward Alleyn and Richard Burbage do—that he was in the front rank of actors. The only indication that he ever played an important part is given in the Folio text of Jonson's *Everyman in his Humour* (1616), where his name heads the actor list; and the only parts which have been definitely assigned to him—Adam in *As You Like It* and the Ghost in *Hamlet*—are rather disappointing."

The frustration of scholars has therefore been intense. Murray is driven to inferring parts for Shakespeare. Since the name does not figure in any of the early cast

lists, he places him against minor unallotted characters
—using square brackets. Whereas some scholars, of the
more avid type, have actively cheated; and it is these
who have been struck down—acrimoniously; for the
learned can dispense an unrivalled bitterness. I quote
from Sir Edmund Chambers: "Mr. Fleay's blundering
conjectures must be distinguished from the deliberate
fabrications of Collier, who published in his *New Facts*,
11, from a forged document amongst the *Bridgewater
MSS*, a certificate to the Privy Council under the date
'Nov. 1589', from 'her Majesty's poor players: James
Burbage, Richard Burbage, John Laneham, Thomas
Greene, Robert Wilson . . . William Shakespeare,
William Kempe, William Johnson,' etc." But there can
be no doubt about it. This sort of naughtiness deserves
the scorn it receives. I repeat: There is no mention of
Shakespeare's name *anywhere* in the archives until it
crops up, for the first time, on the dedication page of
Venus and Adonis.

Now, in making one's way through this immense
quantity of scholarly pap in order to penetrate to the
skeleton, one finds that a great deal of simplification
is necessary. Of the thirty-eight companies listed and
dwelt upon by Sir Edmund Chambers (twenty-four
adult, eleven boy and three foreign) all of thirty-five,
for one reason or another, can be pared away. And of
the three that remain, one need be awarded only the
barest mention. It is the Queen's men. Formed in 1583,
it fell out of vogue with the death of its famous comed-
ian Richard Tarlton five years later. During the interim
period it seems to have played, when not in the provinces, sometimes at the "Theatre", sometimes at the
"Curtain" and sometimes in the City inn-yards.

The other two concern us intimately. First, Lord
Strange's men. This was the company of Fernando
Stanley, Lord Strange, son and heir of the fourth Earl
of Derby. Its origins need not interest us. All we need
know about it is that it absorbed an important part of
the Earl of Leicester's men, when that Company disinte-

grated on the death of its patron in September, 1588. In 1590 it joined Burbage at the "Theatre".

Secondly, the Admiral's men. This was the company of Charles Lord Howard of Effingham. Originally named Lord Howard's men, it was renamed the Admiral's men when its distinguished patron (cousin of the Queen) was advanced to the post of Lord High Admiral in 1585. It numbered among its actors Edward Alleyn, the most considerable performer of his time. "Not Roscius nor Aesope, those admired tragedians that have lived ever since before Christ was borne, Could ever perform more in action than famous Ned Allen." (Nashe.) The Admiral's men joined forces, while still retaining their individuality, with Lord Strange's men at the "Theatre" some time in 1590.

In one of these companies the unnoted actor Shakespeare lurked. John Tucker Murray (in *English Dramatic Companies*) makes desperate efforts to locate him. "Leicester's Men, from 1585-6 to 1588 acted in the Provinces, visiting among many other towns and cities Stratford-upon-Avon. During these years we have no records of them at London or at Court. It seems not unlikely that Shakespeare joined these men during their visit to Stratford-upon-Avon in 1586-7 . . . On September 4th, 1588, the Earl of Leicester died. As he left no heir and the Earldom became extinct until the new creation of 1618, the company was forced to seek a new patron. What seems to have occurred is, that several of the principal actors in the company joined Lord Strange's men." The use of the word 'principal' is another instance of the unreasoning desire of Stratfordians to remove from their idol anything that can be interpreted as a fault: here it is the idea of mediocrity. But where are the records that will place this actor with Alleyn, one of whose "rave" notices I have quoted above, and others? Actually, in view of the tragic rôle for which he was cast, his status does not matter. Let us assume, therefore, that he did in fact become one of Lord Strange's men, transferring, on the dissolution of Leicester's men, not as a principal, but as a minor,

actor. Murray, at all events, modifies his initial statement later. "He was almost certainly one of the men
who went over to Lord Strange's company in September
1588, and with this company, under its various patrons,
he was connected until his retirement from the stage."
He retired from the stage, we are now fairly sure, on
the 30th May, 1593.

At any rate, what concerns us at the moment are the
histories of Lord Strange's men and the Admiral's men
as they affect the Burbages and Philip Henslowe; and
here we have to tread very cautiously indeed, for the
story has gaps and is of the most complex.

Some time in 1591 (according to Kyd), Marlowe
quarrelled with Lord Strange: "My first acquaintance
with this Marlowe, rose upon his bearing name to serve
my Lord although his Lordship never knewe his service,
but in writing for his plaiers, ffor never cold my Lord
endure his name, or sight . . ." But this, dare I call it,
estrangement does not seem to have prejudiced the
patron against the professional dramatist. The rights
to a further two plays were acquired for the company
and the leading parts were created by Alleyn. He had
already played Tamburlaine in both Parts of the drama:
he was now to play Barabas in *The Jew of Malta* and
Faustus in *The Tragical History of Doctor Faustus*.

Towards the middle of 1591 Burbage quarrelled with
the Admiral's men over a part of "the dyvydent money
between him and them" which he appears to have re-
tained. The Lord Admiral's men were at this time in
serious financial difficulties. I quote Sir Edmund Chambers: "I suspect that in 1589 or 1590 they were prac-
tically dissolved, and this view is confirmed by the fact
that their most important play was allowed to get into
the hands of the printers." *Tamburlaine* was entered
in the Stationers' Register on the 14th August, 1590.
"Alleyn, with the help of his brother (John), bought up
the properties and allied himself with Lord Strange's
men, and so far as the Admiral's continued to exist at
all for the next few years, it was almost entirely in and
through him that it did so." But Alleyn, who from then

on was to show remarkable business acumen, was also occupied in another direction. As a result of the quarrel that his old company had had with Burbage he approached Philip Henslowe, leather merchant-cum-pawnbroker-cum-brothelkeeper, but more advantageously proprietor of the so far unsuccessful "Rose" on Bankside, and agreed to appear at his rival playhouse. Because late in 1591 or at the beginning of 1592 Henslowe, we know from his famous Diary, began refurbishing the "Rose". Carpenters, workmen and labourers, painters and one thatcher were as busy as bees doing everything needful to "my playe howsse" to make it worthy of the illustrious troupe of players that was about to appear in it. And then, early in 1592, Alleyn and Lord Strange's men, together with the remnants of the Admiral's men, crossed the River (doubtless to Burbage's mortification) and installed themselves in the newly decorated playhouse, where they were highly successful with a number of plays to which they now had exclusive rights. Moreover, about this time Alleyn married Joan Woodward, Henslowe's stepdaughter, thus strengthening his business ties with Henslowe and further weakening any that remained with Burbage. For the next five years he was to be closely linked with the "Rose".

The season lasted until the 22nd June, when Lord Strange's men were driven into the provinces by the plague. On their return to London late in the year there were complications about obtaining a permit to open. They began playing on the 29th December and continued until the 12th February, 1593, when the "Rose" again closed on account of the plague, and now it was to remain closed for the remainder of the year. To meet expenses the company was again forced into the provinces, and at this point there occurs an event of great interest. It will be remembered that John Tucker Murray stated that Shakespeare "was almost certainly one of the (Earl of Leicester's) men who went over to Lord Strange's company in September 1588, with which company he was to continue until his retirement from the stage." On the 6th May, 1593, that is to say three weeks before the Deptford murder, the Privy Council granted Lord Strange's men a travelling licence in which the principal players of the troupe were named: "Edward Alleyn, William Kemp, Thomas Pope, John Heminges, Augustine Philips and George Bryan."

William Shakespeare's name is still missing. "He was too busy to go," explains Murray with glib plausibility. "He was working on his *Venus and Adonis*." Alas, poor man, still nameless, he was remaining in London despite the plague, because he had not the money to go into the country. And he was getting ready to keep an appointment with death.

We come now to the circumstance upon which this entire chapter hinges. Yet in spite of the fact that it is the clue to the whole situation, it is hardly mentioned by scholars at all. Stated quite simply, it is this. The Burbages' "Theatre" was now empty. J. Q. Adams in *Shakespearean Playhouses* is the only one to hint at it. "In 1590," he says, "the 'Theatre' was being used by the Admiral's men. This excellent company had been formed early in 1589 by the separation of certain leading players from Worcester's men, and it had probably occupied the 'Theatre' since its organization." But by "February 6, 1592, they had certainly left it." And here is the all-important point. "The next company that we can associate with the 'Theatre' was the famous Lord Chamberlain's men," that is to say, the company with which William Shakespeare is undoubtedly known to have been associated. But the Lord Chamberlain's men was not formed until the middle of 1594 (long after the murder at Deptford). "The first notice of the new organization," says Sir Edmund Chambers, "is in June" of that year, "when 'my Lord Admeralle men and my Lorde Chamberlen men' played from the 3rd to the 13th of the month, either in combination or separately on allotted days, for Henslowe at Newington Butts." This was another of Henslowe's playhouses. And the name William Shakespeare still does not occur. Indeed it does not appear on an actor's list until Christmas 1594, when on the 26th and 28th December "Shakespeare" joined Kemp and Burbage before the Queen; that is to say, until after the newly formed Lord Chamberlain's men had taken up residence at Burbage's "Theatre".

But I am progressing too fast and must retrace a little.

Fernando Stanley, Lord Strange, was, as I have already mentioned, son and heir of the fourth Earl of Derby. On the 25th September, 1593, the fourth Earl had died, and Fernando Stanley—he who, according to Kyd, could never endure the name or sight of Marlowe —had succeeded to the title, so that Lord Strange's men had been rechristened the Earl of Derby's men. This may not of itself seem very important. More arresting is the odd sequal. On the 16th April, 1594, Lord Strange himself (now the Earl of Derby) died—in peculiar circumstances. I am drawing no sinister inference from this event. I am saying quite simply that thereafter Lord Strange (or the Earl of Derby) was no longer in a position, so far as his bête noire Marlowe (or Shakespeare) was concerned, to be aware of any deception. But also relevant is the fact that, under the patronage of the Dowager Countess of Derby, the Earl's company failed, and Edward Alleyn, apparently loyal to his earlier sympathies, reformed his troupe into a separate Lord Admiral's company.

The short season, from the 3rd to the 13th June, of the new Lord Chamberlain's men at Newington Butts was not a success. The playhouse, about which little is known, appears to have been too far from the City to draw the crowds. Among the plays given were *Titus Andronicus* (twice), *Taming of a Shrew* and an early *Hamlet,* but Henslowe's takings were low. On the 13th June he drew a line under the enterprise where it is recorded in his Diary, consigning it, presumably, to the scrap-heap. Thereafter all performances noted in the Diary were given by the Admiral's men, probably at the "Rose": the contract of the Chamberlain's men was not renewed. The company joined Burbage at the "Theatre", and very soon we find *Richard III* and *The*

Comedy of Errors being added to their repertoire.

I have only these points to make. At the beginning of 1592 the situation of the business-minded, inclined-to-be-shady James Burbage is quite clear. The "Theatre" for which he lived was empty. His leading actor had deserted him, so had his troupe of players; and he had no properties. When news came to him from across the water of the triumphs his rivals were having with the "money-spinners" they had taken away, he must have grinned in impotent rage. Then in 1593 all places of entertainment on account of the plague were closed. His plight by the end of that year must have been critical. What, then, would his reaction have been if, at the beginning of 1594, Marlowe, weary of skulking about the streets and fleeing from his own and Shakespeare's friends, and laden with the fruits of his brilliantly inventive mind, had gone to him and told him what had happened? Would this shady fellow, desparate for new properties with which to keep his "Theatre" alive and solvent, have thrust him forth? Would he have denounced him? Or would he have taken him in? He would of course have taken him in. Far from denouncing him he would have shielded him for the sake of the golden eggs that were yet to be laid. (There could have been greasepaint for the odd jaunts abroad, for that the players made abundant use of it is borne out by Greene who, in *A Groates-Worth of Witte,* refers to them as "painted monsters".) Far from denouncing him, he might even have resorted to blackmail to ensure the fact that the dramatist remained exclusively his. For Marlowe was now Burbage's most valuable possession. Not even the "Theatre" could be rated higher; for it, too, was now dependent on Marlowe. He had at the same time to display him. For Shakespeare had been an actor and, whereas it had been Walsingham's task to prove that Marlowe was dead, it was Burbage's to demonstrate that "Shakespeare" was still alive. Burbage would have seen that clearly. A year later, therefore, "Shakespeare" was put on show. On the 26th and 28th December, 1594, William Shakespeare is mentioned as an actor for the first time. We find him appearing, as I have stated, with Richard Burbage and William Kemp before the Queen. Neither plays nor parts are listed; so that he may have been heavily disguised in character. ("The only parts that have been definitely assigned to him (are) Adam in *As You Like It* and the Ghost in *Hamlet.*") This was an act of daring which tacitly declared to Elizabeth: "The felonious Marlowe a copy of whose odious opinions was sent to you at Whitsun 1593 is dead. This is Shakespeare." Henceforward James and Richard Burbage, "Shakespeare", Heminges and later Condell (perhaps unaware of the deception, since they seem not to have been associated with "Shakespeare" before) and the rest were to live in the closest degree of amity. "There is much to show," says G. B. Harrison in *Elizabethan Plays and Players,* "that the Chamberlain's men were a company of friends closely united."

10

"Marlowe could still never have written Shakespeare,"
scholars will insist; and they will quote their favourite
objection: "Stylistically they are so different. If you
prove that Marlowe wrote Shakespeare, you will then
have to find out who wrote Marlowe."

But this argument is based on a fallacy, for it places
the earlier and the later plays side by side. Several con-
siderations can be brought forward to refute it. First,
there is the pitiful confusion among scholars as to whose
hands the plays of what might be called the "blending"
period are to be attributed. As evidence of this I quote
Sir Edmund Chambers, who is perhaps the most dependable authority: "Discussions of authorship have
been much complicated by the revision theory. Most
of those who have found the hands of Marlowe, Kyd,
Peele, Greene, Lodge, and Nashe, as well as of Shakespeare, in the plays (the three Parts of *Henry VI*) have
held it . . . A partial exception is Fleay, who recognized
the surreptitious character of Q, and in 1886 modified
an earlier view by assigning 3 *Henry VI* substantially
to Marlowe, and dividing 2 *Henry VI* between Greene,
Peele, Kyd, Marlowe and Lodge. Shakespeare he only
brought in about 1600, as revising 2 *Henry VI* considerably and 3 *Henry VI* slightly . . . Clifford's speech in
2 *Henry VI* (v.2.31-65) seems to me clearly of later style
than the rest. It is certainly Shakespearean, although
the unfortunate Miss Lee, pressed by Furnival to be
precise in her attributions (thus bitter can scholars
become!) gave it to Marlowe, in spite of the internal
pausation . . . Pollard, a revisionist, thinks that the character of Richard has undergone transformation; that he
was originally conceived by Marlowe as a valiant hunch-
back, and afterwards altered by another writer, with a

prospective *Richard III* play in his mind, into an ambitious hypocrite."

As regards *Richard III*, "Coleridge once, but not consistently, doubted the genuineness of the play. But the scepticism of some recent writers seems to be traceable to the influence of Fleay, who in 1875 thought that it was left unfinished by Peele and completed and revised by Shakespeare, in 1881 substituted Marlowe alone, but did not 'think it possible to separate Shakespeare's work from Marlowe's' . . . (On the other hand) Robertson is a thorough-going sceptic. For him the play is Marlowe's, with 'primary collaboration' by Kyd in certain scenes." Indeed, "he transfers the primary responsibility for *Richard III, A Comedy of Errors, Richard II* (and even) *Henry V* and *Julius Caesar* to Marlowe, charging Shakespeare with a 'passion for plagiarism', with 'tranced' or 'slavish' mimicry, with 'abject parodies'."

He sums up the situation succinctly: "The history of Shakespeare's writing is one of the gradual development of a characteristic style or series of styles. In its natural flights it is often unmistakable. Its beginnings belong to a period in which the difficulties of style discrimination are at their maximum. The dramatists of the 'eighties may be reasonably called a school . . . Marlowe is the dominant figure . . . This school was Shakespeare's early environment and his first plays were inevitably in its manner. The influence of Marlowe is discernable until well on in his career."

Thus do scholars split hairs over problems that do not exist. In the light of what we now know (or at any rate suspect) there is considerable irony in the situation. For all those quoted above are right; and if they could only be made to realize that the two principal authors they are discussing were two phases of one career, their differences would be immediately resolved.

Secondy, there was a flowering, due to the natural development of genius. The thunder of what Jonson later called "the mighty line" gave way to the more lyrical quality of the early "Shakespearean" verse. In 1593-4 the two long poems *Venus and Adonis* and *The Rape of Lucrece* had been produced, and the writing of these must have contributed powerfully to the dramatist's mastery of his medium. The strongly stressed rhythm, chief characteristic of the mighty line, yielded to sound, and many uglinesses went: such lines as

> And there in mire and puddle have I stood
> This ten days' space.

and :

> Pliny reports, there is a flying-fish
> Which all the other fishes deadly hate,
> And therefore, being pursued, it takes the air:
> No sooner is it up, but there's a fowl
> That seizeth it.

could not later have been written.

A magic came into the verse, which must have been acquired by dint of much hard labour: a richness and a musical sweetness of sound, springing from alliteration. This is first apparent, I have to admit, in *Venus and Adonis;* but it could not have been effortlessly inherited. No one, delivering himself of the first heir of his invention, could have written:

> Lo, here the gentle lark, weary of rest,
> From his moist cabinet mounts up on high,
> And wakes the morning, from whose silver breast
> The sun ariseth in his majesty;
>   Who doth the world so gloriously behold,
>   That cedar-tops and hills seem burnished gold.

This, coming towards the end of the poem, is momentary perfection.

Thirdly, there was the fact that Marlowe had been through a period of great emotional crisis which had involved him in abnormal mental strain. His execution had for a time seemed certain; and this, I am sure, would have had a mellowing, sobering effect upon him. He became, after his contrived escape, more subdued, more cautious, more contemplative, more philosophical. Indeed, as I have said before, there may even have been a complete change of heart akin to a religious conversion. His style would have changed in consequence.

11

The subject I have now to embark upon is one that is distasteful to many people. In an investigation such as this, however, no effort can be spared in the attempt to arrive at truth. I claim the right, therefore, to discuss this censured topic at length and with scientific candour.

The Sonnets attributed to Shakespeare are the most intimately personal expression of feeling left behind by the poet-dramatist; and in them, more than in any of his other works, we may well expect to find a revelation of his soul. They are all addressed, as is widely known, to a young man of exceptional physical beauty. To the *only* begetter of these insuing Sonnets, runs the dedication; and there has been much scholarly argument as to the nature of the association lauded. Those against the theory that it was a homosexual attachment claim that the extravagant expression of love found everywhere in the poems can be explained away by the mode of address fashionable among men of the Elizabethan era. And to clinch the argument a well-known writer on Shakespeare has coined a cliché to the effect that those declaring the Sonnets to be homosexually inspired are simply homosexuals trying to annex the poet-dramatist for themselves.

Now, since it is an important factor in my thesis to show that the Sonnets are indeed an expression of homosexual love, I must first refute the objections. I begin with the well-known writer's cliché, rebutting it thus: Critics claiming that the homosexual element in the Sonnets is imagined by homosexuals wishing to annex the poet-dramatist for themselves should be on their guard lest the wish to do likewise should rob them of their own impartiality. The argument cuts both ways and ultimately proves nothing.

The demonstration from a mode of address similarly miscarries, for it reduces the content of the poems to a mannerism, which it certainly is not. The emotion expressed lies in the essence of the poetry and springs unmistakably from the heart. Almost every line of the Sonnets (I am referring to the first one hundred and twenty-six addressed to the young man and not to the final twenty-eight most of which pay court to the Dark Lady) breathes passion, so that the poems together constitute the greatest outpouring of love (normal or abnormal) ever penned.

This is of course a "facer" for people so ruled by their senses that they cannot be impartial about the work of homosexuals and would relegate to the scrap-heap even the sublime First Pietà of Michelangelo (both figures of which are thought to have been homosexually inspired, since the model for the Madonna was a boy) before which, by a strange quirk of irony, thousands of the faithful daily bend the knee in Saint Peter's Cathedral in Rome. Mr. Walter Thomson, writing in 1938, tables the following misgivings on the subject (the oddness of the style is due to the use of the journalistic plural throughout): "On this question our withers have not remained unwrung. When the 20th Sonnet and its implications were brought to our notice, we were disturbed and for nearly a year we lost our keenness for Shakespeare, which was no insignificant deprivation. In our state of ignorance we slipped into a morass in which we were puzzled and unhappy." (In other words, we were off our food.) Fortunately for his peace of mind he was rescued from his unenviable predicament by "an excellent little book on the Sonnets written by Mrs. Carmichael Stopes" (not to be confused with her daughter the Marie of birth-control fame) who was able to explain to his satisfaction that in Shakespeare's day the word " 'passion' bore the meaning of poem as well as other meanings", and thus cleared up the stumbling-block of the first two lines:

A woman's face with Nature's own hand painted,
Hast thou the Master Mistress of my passion.

Eric Partridge, writing in *Shakespeare's Bawdy,* is equally upset by the suggestion that Shakespeare may have been homosexual, and comes forward with an argument of some power. "Like other heterosexual persons, I believe the charge against Shakespeare; that he was a homosexual; to be, in the legal sense, 'trivial': at worst, 'the case is not proven'; at best—and in strict accordance with the so-called evidence, as I see it—it is ludicrous . . . Shakespeare alludes to homosexuality very seldom and most cursorily . . . Of feminoid males or, in everyday language, effeminates, whether they be actual or merely potential intersexuals or inverts, Shakespeare makes much the same sort of kindly-contemptuous or unmawkish-pitying remark as the average tolerant and understanding person of the present generation would make."

This I can refute only by begging the question. If one accepts the fact that Shakespeare was Marlowe, one expects the subject to be treated thus. Having once fallen so seriously foul of the law, the author was hardly likely to continue to draw attention to his abnormal proclivities, as he had been so recklessly doing. The obsessive homosexual interest, so evident in, for example, *Edward II,* had later, in those works destined for performance and publication, to be muted. It appeared, therefore, in the guise of the great friendships: those of Valentine and Proteus, Romeo and Mercutio, Antonio and Bassanio, Hamlet and Horatio, Brutus and Cassius, Achilles and Patrolus; and in the turning of girls into boys. Boys, it is pertinent to note, were rarely turned into girls.

There were, nevertheless, despite Mr. Partridge's opinion to the contrary, several major lapses. *Venus and Adonis* was written from the emotional standpoint of the woman. The goddess's lustful mind is throughout intimately described; her body hardly at all. Whereas the marvellous beauty of Adonis is dwelt upon in minute detail.

At this Adonis smiles as in disdain,
That in each cheek appears a pretty dimple:
Love made those hollows, if himself were slain,
He might be buried in a tomb so simple;
  Foreknowing well, if there he came to lie,
  Why, there Love lived, and there he could not die.

These lovely caves, these round enchanting pits,
Open'd their mouths to swallow Venus' liking.
Being mad before, how doth she now for wits?
Struck dead at first, what needs a second striking?
  Poor queen of love, in thine own law forlorn,
  To love a cheek that smiles at thee in scorn!

And later :

Once more the ruby-colour'd portal open'd,
Which to his speech did honey passage yield;
Like a red morn, that ever yet betoken'd
Wreck to the seamen, tempest to the field,
  Sorrow to shepherds, woe unto the birds,
  Gusts and foul flaws to herdsmen and to herds.

And his reluctance, and Venus's ultimate defeat, are
savoured as though the poet were unwilling to relinquish
the lovely youth to a passion so defiling. It is one of his
own less successful enterprises, perhaps, that he is unveil-
ing: hence the peculiar naïveté of Adonis's protesta-
tions :

"Give me my hand, why dost thou feel it!"

"You hurt my hand with wringing; let us part,
And leave this idle theme, this bootless chat."

"Fie, fie, you crush me; let me go;
You have no reason to withold me so."

And hence the fact that at the end of the poem the
poet is constrained to moralize bitterly: They who love
best shall not their loves enjoy.

The oddest thing about *Venus and Adonis*, however,
if I may mention simply in passing so important a
factor in my thesis, is the use of a large number of
images, and combinations of words, which run "un-

naturally" parallel to many used by Marlowe in *Hero and Leander*: so unnaturally parallel, indeed, that one wonders if it could have been humanly possible for two separate minds, working independently, to achieve such similarity of expression. At the risk of appearing discursive, I list the most outstanding of them here. Those from *Hero and Leander* are for the most part in the order in which they occur: those from *Venus and Adonis* are printed in italics for easy identification and are followed by the number of the verse from which they are taken.

Her veil was artificial flowers and leaves
Whose workmanship both man and beast deceives.

H & L.

Even so poor birds, deceived with painted grapes,
Do surfeit by the eye and pine the maw.

V & A, v.101.

Many would praise the sweet smell as she past,
When 'twas the odour which her breath forth cast.

H & L.

For from the stillitory of thy face excelling
Comes breath perfumed, that breedeth love by smelling.

V & A, v.74.

She bows her head, the new-sprung flower to smell,
Comparing it to her Adonis' breath.

V & A, v.196.

Those orient cheeks and lips, exceeding his
That leapt into the water for a kiss
Of his own shadow.

H & L.

Narcissus so himself himself forsook,
And died to kiss his shadow in the brook.

V & A, v.27.

The men of wealthy Sestos every year,
For his sake whom their goddess held so dear,
Rose-cheek'd Adonis, kept a solemn feast.

H & L.

Even as the sun with purple-colour'd face,
Had ta'en his last leave of the weeping morn,
Rose-cheek'd Adonis hied him to the chase.

V & A, v.1.

The unusual adjective 'rose-cheek'd', here applied to Adonis, is made more unusual still by being spelt 'rose-cheekt' in the first editions of both poems. The odds against its being fortuitously selected to describe the same youth by two authors working independently, and spelt by each in the same manner, must be indeed enormous.

There Hero sacrificing turtle's blood,
Vail'd to the ground, veiling her eyelids close.

H & L.

Here overcome, as one full of despair,
She vail'd her eyelids.

V & A, v.160.

Thence flew Love's arrow with the golden head.

H & L.

Love's golden arrow at him should have fled.

V & A, v.158.

He started up; she blushed as one asham'd.
(Hero has been accosted.)

H & L

He burns with bashful shame . . .
(Adonis is being importuned.)

V & A, v.9

Pure shame and awed resistance made him fret.

V & A, v.12.

Forgetting shame's pure blush and honour's wrack.
(Venus)

V & A, v.93.

A stream of liquid pearl, which down her face
Made milk-white paths . . .

H & L.

And, as she wept, her tears to pearl he turn'd.

H & L.

Whereat her tears began to turn their tide
Being prison'd in her eye like pearls in glass.

V & A, v.164.

Till in his twining arms he lock'd her fast.

H & L.

And from her twining arms doth urge releasing.

V & A, v.43.

By this, sad Hero, with love unacquainted,
Viewing Leander's face, fell down and fainted.
He kiss'd her, and breath'd life into her lips.

H & L.

For on the grass she lies as she were slain,
Till his breath breathed life in her again.

V & A, v.79.

For as a hot proud horse highly disdains
To have his head controll'd, but breaks the reins,
Spits forth the ringled bit, and with his hoves
Checks the submissive ground . . .

H & L.

Imperiously he leaps, he neighs, he bounds,
And now his woven girths he breaks asunder;
The bearing earth with his hard hoof he wounds,
Whose hollow womb resounds like heaven's thunder;
  The iron bit he crusheth 'tween his teeth,
  Controlling what he was controlled with.

V & A, v.45.

Love is too full of faith, too credulous,
With folly and false hope deluding us.

H & L.

O hard-believing love, how strange it seems
Not to believe, and yet too credulous!

V & A, v.165.

With both her hands she made the bed a tent.

H & L.

Making my arms his field, his tent my bed.

V & A, v.18.

Stranger perhaps is Leander's speech to the reluctant
Hero:

Abandon fruitless cold virginity,
The gentle queen of love's sole enemy.
Then shall you most resemble Venus' nun
When Venus' sweet rites are perform'd and done.

H & L.

Which ties up with Venus's advice to the reluctant Adonis:

Therefore despite of fruitless chastity,
Love-lacking vestals and self-loving nuns,
That on the earth would breed a scarcity
And barren dearth of daughters and of sons,
Be prodigal.

V & A, v.126.

Strange, too, is the tiny synopsis of the plot and description of the scene of *Venus and Adonis* given by Marlowe in detailing Hero's clothing in *Hero and Leander*:

Her wide sleeves (were) green, and border'd with a grove,
Where Venus in her naked glory strove
To please the careless and disdainful eyes
Of proud Adonis, that before her lies.

And that Venus was intimately connected with Hero in Marlowe's mind is made clear in his description of her beauty:

Some say, for her the fairest Cupid pin'd,
And, looking in her face, was strooken blind.
But this is true; so like was one the other,
As he imagin'd Hero was his mother; (i.e., Venus.)
And oftentimes into her bosom flew,
About her naked neck his bare arms threw,
And laid his childish head upon her breast,
And, with still panting rock, there took his rest.

Which may be compared with the penultimate verse of *Venus and Adonis*. Venus is speaking to the flower into which Adonis has been metamorphosed:

Here was thy father's bed, here in my breast;
Thou art the next of blood, and 'tis thy right:
Lo, in this hollow cradle take thy rest;
My throbbing heart shall rock thee day and night.

This a formidable array. It may be objected that such lines as "With both her hands she made the bed a tent"

and "Making my arms his field, his tent my bed", have
no similarity of meaning. But, if Marlowe wrote both
poems, as I believed he did, it is just these which show
his unconscious mind at work. "Shakespeare" was com-
posing just then, according to Dr. Rowse, at enormous
speed, and words have a curious tendency to cling
together.

The circumstances of the composition and publication
of the two poems adds force to the argument. *Hero and
Leander* was not published until 1598, that is to say,
until five years after the completion of *Venus and
Adonis;* and *Venus and Adonis* was not published till
the September of 1593, that is to say, until after the
murder at Deptford; so that ostensibly, if there were two
authors, neither could have seen the other's work. And
the parallels (all of them coincidences which have to be
multiplied, not added) become all the more curious
when one remembers that the two poems are thought to
have been composed contemporaneously; the one by
Marlowe who was forced to remain in London because
of the Privy Council's decree; the other by Shakespeare
who is held traditionally to have been out of London
because of the plague. Although, even if there were two
authors and they had both been in the city, there is
little to suggest that they would have had access to each
other's manuscripts, since the traditional Shakespeare
at that time, having not yet published "the first heir of
his invention", would probably have been far beneath
the notice of Marlowe. (Had he not aroused the scorn
of Greene?) And then, even if they *had* known each
other would one have been so unashamedly guilty of
thus plagiarizing the work of the other? But according
to the scholars they did not meet. Dr. Boas declares in
Christopher Marlowe that "there is not a jot of evidence
pointing to personal intercourse between Marlowe and
Shakespeare". How could there be, when a meeting between Marlowe and Shakespeare the actor would not
have been of sufficient importance to be recorded; and
Marlowe and Shakespeare the poet were, if my theory
is correct, one and the same person.

Then there is the interesting suggestion made (and accepted as truth) by Dr. Rowse, in his recent book on Marlowe, that Leander was a portrayal of the Earl of Southampton. How odd that Shakespeare was dedicating his *Venus and Adonis* to the same youth! How odd, too, that Dr. Rowse should not feel compelled, from such a coincidence, and from the abundance of "unnatural" parallels, some of which he has noticed, to envisage, as I do, the possibility that both poems were the invention of one mind. And if Marlowe wrote *Venus and Adonis*, he wrote also the plays attributed to Shakespeare; for there can be no doubt that these and the poem published under the name of Shakespeare were the work of the same hand.

Hero and Leander also has ties with *The Two Gentlemen of Verona*. There are two references to Leander in the play: the first occurs as soon as the curtain goes up:

> That's on some shallow story of deep love:
> How young Leander crossed the Hellespont.

Which is developed. The second comes in the third act:

> Why, then, a ladder, quaintly made of cords,
> To cast up with a pair of anchoring hooks,
> Would serve to scale another Hero's tower,
> So bold Leander would adventure it.

And this quotation links up with the lines in the poem:

> As he had hoped to scale the beauteous fort
> Wherein the liberal Graces lock'd their wealth;
> And therefore to her tower he got by stealth.

Though not with the continuing story; for:

> Wide-open stood the door; he need not climb.

There is a further tie: one of the two gentlemn is called Proteus. The rapidly working poetic brain has seized upon this name as being suitable, after using it in the description of the temple of Venus in *Hero and Leander*:

The walls were of discolour'd jasper-stone,
Wherein was Proteus carv'd . . .

This frequent harking across to *Hero and Leander*, the manuscript of which he probably had at his elbow, would point to the author's only-fitting obsession with the legend; and to the fact that the poem and the play were being composed contemporaneously; so that the date of *The Two Gentlemen of Verona* would be late 1592 or early 1593, as the scholars believe it to be.

But to return to the homosexuality theme. A trace of this aberration is to be found also in *Othello*. Iago is speaking:

> I lay with Cassio lately
> And being troubled with a raging tooth,
> I could not sleep.
> There are a kind of men so loose of soul,
> That in their sleeps will mutter their affairs:
> One of this kind is Cassio:
> In sleep I heard him say 'Sweet Desdemona,
> Let us be wary, let us hide our loves;'
> And then, sir, would he gripe and wring my hand,
> Cry 'O sweet creature!' and then kiss me hard,
> As if he plucked up kisses by the roots,
> That grew upon my lips: then laid his leg
> Over my thigh, and sigh'd and kiss'd, and then
> Cried 'Cursed fate that gave thee to the Moor!'

If this were the invention of a normal man, surely some expression of revulsion would be put into Iago's mouth. He would at least be made to say, with a rough laugh, that he had brushed Cassio off. But, no, he is allowed to tell the false tale seriously, as if what he is ostensibly relating were the most natural thing in the world, and to dwell upon its homosexual content with a sort of relish: because, I suggest, the author is identifying himself with Iago and enjoying the situation vicariously. It adds force to Iago's deceit, Mr. Partridge would perhaps counter: it helps conjure up in Othello's mind a picture of Cassio's supposed adultery. But does it? Surely for Cassio to have confessed his love in his sleep would have been enough. And can it truly be believed that Othello, in looking at the rugged Iago, could ever have thought of him as Desdemona and become even more jealous on that account? Surely his ejaculation, "O monstrous! monstrous!", coming from a normal man, could be applied more fittingly to the suggested scene of abnormal intercourse, which, to give the author pleasure, has been forced into the context.

Then there is the peculiar relationship, in *As You Like It*, of Rosalind, when dressed as a boy, and Orlando. This is one of the many instances of the delight the author took in transforming his women into boys ("You must needs have breeches with a codpiece, madam"); in returning them, since they were always played by boys, to a costume more natural to them; in restoring them to what he himself called "the lovely garnish of a boy". Fundamentally the situation is of the most innocent; superficially (and basically) it is highly suggestive. After all, Orlando does not know that Ganymede is his beloved Rosalind dressed as a boy. (The audience, on the other hand, know that in her normal attire she is a boy dressed as a girl.) He listens seriously to the supposed youth when he relates how he has cured a lover of his madness:

He was to imagine me his love, his mistress; and I set him every day to woo me: at which time would I, being but a moonish youth, grieve, be effeminate, changeable, longing and liking; proud, fantastical, apish, shallow, inconstant, full of tears, full of smiles; for every passion something and for no passion truly anything, as boys and women are for the most part cattle of this colour: would now like him, now loathe him; then entertain him, then forswear him; now weep for him, then spit at him; that I drave my suitor from his mad humour of love to a living humour of madness; which was, to forswear the full stream of the world and to live in a nook merely monastic. And thus I cured him; and this way will I take upon me to wash your liver as clean as a sound sheep's heart, that there shall not be one spot of love in't . . . I would cure you if you would but call me Rosalind and come every day to my cote and woo me.

To which strange proposition Orlando, still ignorant of the fact that Ganymede is a girl and not a boy, replies:

Now, by the faith of my love, I will: tell me where it is.

The give-away phrase is of course "as boys and women are for the most part cattle of this colour" which ties up so neatly with Marlowe's "Those who love not tobacco and boys are fools". And why was the name Ganymede, with its secondary meaning of catamite, chosen? The relationship between Jove and Ganymede had fascinated Marlowe, who had dealt with it dramatically in *Dido Queen of Carthage,* and referred to it several times in *Hero and Leander*: at the point where Neptune, dazzled by the beauty of Leander, amorously assails him as he is swimming the Hellespont:

Whereat the sapphire-visag'd god grew proud,
And made his capering Triton sound aloud,
Imagining that Ganymede, displeas'd,
Had left the heavens; therefore on him he seiz'd.

And again twice.

It had also, apparently, fascinated Marlowe's friend (and co-protégé of Walsingham) Thomas Watson, who in 1581 (when he was twenty-four) had dedicated his translation from Greek into Latin of the *Antigone* of Sophocles to Philip Howard, Earl of Arundel, in these terms:

Receive, O Earl, this youthful verse . . . then shall I be called happy enough to be your poet, and to become, with Ganymede, the attendant of Jove.

The use of the name here might possibly suggest the desire for an abnormal relationship (with all its concomitant benefits) and could indicate the nature of the one later to spring up between Watson and Walsingham, and even Walsingham and Marlowe; though that is by the by. It is the choice of the name Ganymede by Rosalind (and her creator) that is concerning us, and

I shall confine myself to saying that for the author of *As You Like It* I believe the situation again to have been a homosexual fantasy from the writing of which he was deriving vicarious enjoyment. Moreover, the play is dated between the years 1597 and 1600, and the above-quoted passage may well have been a description of the behaviour of the beautiful youth of the Sonnets (which we are about to discuss), and the "madness" referred to that which the poet himself had suffered. If Leander was indeed a portrait of the Earl of Southampton, as Dr. Rowse believes he was, and was compared, not once, but three times, to Ganymede in the poem, might not Rosalind in male attire, having become the indefinable half-sex, and now named Ganymede, be his counterpart in *As You Like It* too?

Sir Edmund Chambers in *William Shakespeare* appears to be *for* the theory of homosexuality. He says: "To whomsoever written, William Herbert, or Henry Wriothesley, or an unknown, or a group of unknowns, the Sonnets give us a glimpse of a soul-side of Shakespeare imperfectly revealed by the plays. A perturbed spirit is behind the quiet mask. Here is a record of misplaced and thwarted affections, of imperfections and disabilities, inseparable perhaps from an undesired way of life, which clog a mind conscious enough of its power."

Most impartial critics, however, have for long been ready to admit that the Sonnets, even if their author was not wholly homosexual, are indeed of homosexual inspiration. What normal man would write to another:

Not from the stars do I my judgment pluck . . .
But from thine eyes my knowledge I derive.

(Sonnet 14.)

Or avow:

If I could write the beauty of your eyes,
And in fresh numbers number all your graces,
The age to come would say this Poet lies,
Such heavenly touches ne'er touched human faces.

(Sonnet 17.)

What normal man would bewail a parting from his friend thus:

> How heavy do I journey on the way,
> When what I seek (my weary travel's end)
> Doth teach that ease and that repose to say
> Thus far the miles are measured from my friend.
> The beast that bears me, tired with my woe,
> Plods dully on, to bear that weight in me,
> As if by some instinct the wretch did know
> His rider loved not speed being made from thee.
>
> (Sonnet 50.)

Or declare to another:

> Thy love is better than high birth to me,
> Richer than wealth, prouder than garments' cost,
> Of more delight than hawks or horses be:
> And having thee, of all men's pride I boast.
>
> (Sonnet 91.)

Or affirm:

> For nothing this wide Universe I call,
> Save thou my Rose, in it thou art my all.
>
> (Sonnet 109.)

Or asseverate:

> You are my All the world . . .
>
> (Sonnet 112)

Surely any friendship that exists between two normal males is a more casual thing. Men rarely recognize one another's beauty, let alone extol it: far less are they stirred by it. The very polarity of sex makes a true affinity between two normal males impossible. Inseparableness, we know in these psychoanalytical days, must always be suspect.

Let us apply, then, what is undoubtedly a scientific fact to the leading actors of our story.

If I could be sure that William Shakespeare had been sexually one hundred per cent normal, I would be in a very strong position indeed. Unfortunately, in the light of what is constantly being printed in all sections of the

Press to-day, I cannot. I can only say that a country dweller who at the age of eighteen married a girl he had "got into trouble"—a child, we know from the Stratford records, was born six months after the marriage—and who had, in all, three children by her before he was twenty-one (the second and third were twins), seems to have been firmly set on the path of normality. For homosexuality, psychologists tell us is a symptom of arrested sexual development; so that for Shakespeare to have become homosexual, after so promising a beginning, would have betokened a reversion to an earlier stage of his sexual life; and for him to have yielded to such a retrogressive temptation at a time when deviations of the sort (being misunderstood) were likely to be awarded the death penalty, and when he was already deriving ample satisfaction from the normal and legal outlet, would have been both foolish and dangerous. I shall nevertheless content myself with saying that for William Shakespeare to have become homosexual, or even bisexual, after his arrival in London seems to me highly improbable.

With Marlowe it was otherwise. He had openly declared his interest in, and predilection for, homosexual activities ("Those who love not tobacco and boys are fools.") and had shown evidence of his tastes in his writings. Consider the following:

I must have wanton poets, pleasant wits,
Musicians, that with touching of a string
May draw the pliant king which way I please:
Music and poetry is his delight;
Therefore I'll have Italian masks by night,
Sweet speeches, comedies, and pleasing shows;
And in the day, when he shall walk abroad,
Like sylvan nymphs my pages shall be clad;
My men, like satyrs grazing on the lawns,
Shall with their goat-feet dance the antic hay;
Sometime a lovely boy in Dian's shape,
With hair that gilds the water as it glides,
Crownets of pearl about his naked arms,
And in his sportful hands an olive-tree,
To hide those parts which men delight to see,
Shall bathe him in a spring; and there, hard by,

One like Actaeon, peeping through the grove,
Shall by the angry goddess be transform'd,
And running in the likeness of an hart,
By yelping hounds pull'd down, shall seem to die:
Such things as these best please his majesty.

(Gaveston in *Edward II*)

Consider, too, the section of the second sestiad of *Hero and Leander,* already quoted, in which the god Neptune sexually caresses the youthful Leander when, "stripped to the ivory skin", he is swimming the Hellespont. The subject is also freely dealt with in *The Massacre at Paris,* in which the homosexual French King, Henri III, is shown among his minions, and in *Dido, Queen of Carthage.*

So that it would seem evident that the author of the Sonnets and the remainder of the Shakespeare canon sexually resembled Marlowe, but differed from the man from Stratford: which is tantamount to saying that, if William Shakespeare were sexually normal, then he could not have written the works attributed to him.

It is still true that the author of the canon lavished a good deal of attention upon his female characters. His women were keenly observed and marvellously drawn; though always with the idea of a boy player in mind. No portrayal of physical contact was included, since it would have offended the sensibilities of the Elizabethan audience.

Marlowe, too, understood the heterosexual viewpoint. Observe for instance, Tamburlaine's beautiful, but passionless, speech to Zenocrate.

Zenocrate, lovelier than the love of Jove,
Brighter than is the silver Rhodope,
Fairer than whitest snow on Scythian hills,
Thy person is more worth to Tamburlaine
Than the possession of the Persian crown,
Which gracious stars have promised at my birth.
A hundred Tartars shall attend on thee,
Mounted on steeds swifter than Pegasus;
Thy garments shall be made of Median silk,
Enchas'd with precious jewels of mine own,
More rich and valurous than Zenocrate's;
With milk-white harts upon an ivory sled

Thou shalt be drawn amidst the frozen pools,
And scale the icy mountains' lofty tops,
Which with thy beauty will be soon resolv'd:
My martial prizes, with five hundred men,
Won on the fifty-headed Volga's waves,
Shall we all offer to Zenocrate,
And then myself to fair Zenocrate.

Compare in quality this full-blooded verse with the effusions of the other claimants to the authorship, such as the Earl of Oxford. Compare it, too, if you can bear to, with the 'lousie Lucy' poem quoted above, which may well be an example of the work of William Shakespeare of Stratford-upon-Avon.

Then there is the speech of Faustus to Helen:

Was this the face that launched a thousand ships,
And burnt the topless towers of Ilium?
Sweet Helen, make me immortal with a kiss.
Her lips suck forth my soul: see, where it flies!
Come, Helen, come, give me my soul again.
Here will I dwell, for heaven is in these lips,
And all is dross that is not Helena.
I will be Paris, and for love of thee,
Instead of Troy, shall Wertenberg be sack'd;
And I will combat with weak Menelaus,
And wear thy colours on my plumed crest;
Yes, I will wound Achilles in the heel,
And then return to Helen for a kiss.
O, thou art fairer than the evening air
Clad in the beauty of a thousand stars;
Brighter art thou than flaming Jupiter
When he appeared to hapless Semele;
More lovely than the monarch of the sky
In wanton Arethusa's azur'd arms;
And none but thou shalt be my paramour!

Whether or not the boy playing Helen in the original production will in fact have been kissed, as the text demands, by an embarrassed Edward Alleyn, I do not know. This could be an instance of Marlowe's pressing home, in the months preceding the arrest, his sexual unorthodoxy. I shall discuss the 1592 composition date of *Doctor Faustus* in a later volume.

After the murder the dramatist had perforce to look

round for another patron. Thomas Walsingham could no longer fill the position. The risk of further overt association would have been too great for them both. The deception was therefore sealed with the posthumous dedication to Walsingham of the unfinished *Hero and Leander* in Marlowe's name, but proferred by Edward Blunt in 1598 as the self-ordained "executor to the unhappily deceased author". The poet, in other words, had been murdered, and what more natural than that he should have left behind an unfinished poem!

Now, it will be remembered that *Venus and Adonis* had been registered for publication anonymously, and about the September of the same year, published in the name of William Shakespeare. The dedication, addressed to the Right Honourable Henrie Wriothesley, Earle of Southampton, and Baron of Titchfield, was in prosaically formal terms. "I know not how I shall offend in dedicating my unpolisht lines to your Lordship, nor how the world will censure me for choosing so strong a proppe to support so weake a burthen, onely if your Honour seem but pleased, I account myself highly praised, and vowe to take advantage of all idle houres, till I have honoured you with some graver labour. But if the first heire of my invention prove deformed, etc."

The following year, on the 9th May, to be exact, *The Rape of Lucrece,* another long poem, was entered on the register of the Stationers' Company in the name of William Shakespeare, and this, too, was dedicated to the Earl of Southampton, but in words of very different emotional calibre.

"To the Right Honourable Henrie Wriothesley, Earle of Southampton, and Baron of Titchfield: The love I dedicate to your Lordship is without end: whereof this Pamphlet without beginning is but a superfluous Moity. The warrant I have of your Honourable disposition, not the worth of my untutored Lines makes it assured of acceptance. What I have done is yours, what I have to doe is yours, being part in all I have, devoted yours. Were my worth greater, my duety would shew greater, meane time, as it is, it is bound to your Lordship; To

whom I wish long life still lengthned with all happinesse."

This would seem to indicate that, during the intervening months, a certain degree of intimacy had come into
existence between the poet-dramatist and the young
nobleman.

Let us deal, in passing, with the theory advanced by
Dr. Leslie Hotson that the Sonnets attributed to Shakespeare were dedicated, not to Southampton, but to a
certain Mr. William Hatcliffe, and were composed in the
period 1587-9.

Now, I cannot believe that poems so perfect in technique could have been produced, even by Marlowe,
before the writing of much else. In supposing the years
1587-9 to have been the time of their composition, while
postulating Shakespeare as the author one frighteningly
shortens the formative period of Shakespeare, who could
have arrived in London, unlettered and unread, no
earlier than 1584-5.

Ah, but Keats, people will say, what of his tremen-
dous achievement at the age of only twenty-five. There
can be no gainsaying Keats's considerable achievement;
but he had the advantage of being able to steep himself (as he did) in the poetry of a number of great ones,
Spenser, Shakespeare, Milton and Dryden, which he
regurgitated in the form of his own sublime poetry.
The vast outpouring attributed to Shakespeare, however,
was virtually spontaneous. But there are stronger arguments against Dr. Hotson's theory, and these I shall
deal with shortly. First let us try to clear up the mystery
surrounding the person addressed in the Sonnets.

12

Since *Venus and Adonis* and *The Rape of Lucrece,*
dated 1593 and 1594 respectively, had both been dedicated to the Earl of Southampton, why, in 1597, should
there have been a change in dedicating the Sonnets? (I
shall defend the suggested 1597 later.) There is nothing
in the way of evidence to show that the young Earl
was not still the poet-dramatist's patron. Moreover, as
many scholars have noticed, Southampton's age and
appearance, and the known facts of his life, all tally
with the general scheme of the Sonnets.

There is, however, a stronger reason for believing
him to have been the dedicatee. Scholars presupposing
any other personality, a Mr. Willie Hughes or a Mr.
William Hatcliffe, for instance, cannot produce sufficient motive for the anonymity employed. The person
addressed had to be someone of importance. The elaborate concealment of his name was not devised simply
to perplex posterity. There was, on the contrary, an
awful necessity for it. People in our own day have been
sent to prison on less evidence than the open avowal
of homosexual love contained in the Sonnets; and in
the time of Marlowe and Southampton, when the
penalty for the offence was death, at least one nobleman had been sent to the block. The poems were therefore not published until many years after they had
been written.

In 1609, however, the circumstances surrounding both
the poet and the youth had changed. The affair had
waned; the poet was ill and attributed (as will be seen)
the contraction of his malady to the youth; and prose-
cutions were unlikely to be pressed. James I now occupied the thrown and was himself a practising homosexual. He was also, by fortune's dearest spite, himself
strongly attached to the youth. The Sonnets, therefore,

after having been privately circulated for many years, at last made their appearance on the bookstalls; but with an anonymous dedication and no signature, though the name SHAKESPEARE was entered on the title-page.

In attempting to elucidate the mystery of the anonymous dedicatee, I intend to make use of what I would call the anagrammatical method; and since anagrams from now on, though disreputable among scholars, are fully involved in my thesis, it will perhaps be useful first to consider the nature of these literary curiosities and, by an examination of their history through the ages, try to give them a little respectability.

The devising of anagrams is of great antiquity. According to H. B. Wheatley, writing in 1862 (*Of Anagrams*), the custom of constructing them "is not of modern or of mediaeval formation, but has come direct to us from the Greeks, the word αναγραμμα having been used among them to express the same thing".

William Camden, who by great good fortune devotes a whole chapter to anagrams in his *Remaines* (published in 1605, that is to say, during the very period that concerns us), thought it conceivable that they dated back even to the time of Moses. "For as the great Masters of the Jews testifie, Moses received of God a literal Law written with the finger of God, in the two Tables of the ten Commandments, to be imparted to all, and another Mystical to be communicated only to seventy men, which by tradition they should pass to their posterity, whereof it was called Cabala, which was divided into Mercana, conserving only the sacred names of God, and Bresith of other names consisting of alphabetory revolution, which they will have to be Anagrammatisme; by which they say Marie Resolved made Our Holy Mistress." He concludes, however, by being sceptical. "But whether this Cabala is more ancient than the Talmudic Learning hatched by the curious Jews (as some will) about 200 years after Christ, let the learned consider."

Be that as it may, it is well known that the Cabalists made frequent use of anagrams in their rituals, believing that "secret mysteries were woven in the number of letters".

The Elizabethans and Jacobeans took extraordinary delight in all forms of word play. The construction of anagrams in particular was, during those times, extremely popular. Camden seems to have been quite a devotee of the art and comments upon it rather charmingly. "Some of the sowre sort will say it is nothing but a troublous joy, and because they cannot attain to it will condemn it, lest by commending it, they should discommend themselves. Others more mild, will grant it to be a dainty service and disport of wit not without pleasure, if it be not wrested out of the name to the reproach of the person."

In giving examples, he tells us that: "To begin with his most excellent Majesty our dread Sovereign was made this, declaring his undoubted rightful claim to the Monarchy of Britain, as the successour of the valorous King Arthur:

Charles James Stuart
Claims Arthur's seat."

This obvious piece of hypocrisy on the part of Camden had had to be indulged in, if he were not to run the risk of losing his head; for the anagram had been devised in the time of Elizabeth whose side the angrammatist had been on.

Marlowe, too, understood the use of anagrams. Did he not declare that God was an anagram of dog, being simply that word spelt backwards? Did he not refer, in *Doctor Faustus,* to the magic power of "Jehovah's name, Forward and backward anagrammatis'd"? Whereas Thomas Harriott, mathematician, alchemist (one believes), Master of Raleigh's School of Night and Marlowe's friend, prepared a list, which is still in existence (according to his biographer Henry Stevens of Vermont), of twelve anagrams of his name when written in Latin.

"In the 16th and 17th centuries the making of anagrams was an exercise of many religious orders," declares *The Encyclopaedia Britannica* and continues with point: "Some of the scientists of the 17th century —for example Galileo, Christian Huygens and Robert Hooke—embodied their discoveries in anagrams with the apparent design of avoiding the risk that, while they were engaged in further verification, the credit of what had been found out might be claimed by others." Moreover, many literary personalities concealed their true identity by anagrammatizing their names. The most renowned of these was Voltaire, whose baptismal name was François Marie Arouet. His nom de plume was arrived at, it is thought, by anagrammatizing Arouet l.j. (Arouet le jeune).

Donne, Dryden, Addison and Swift all dealt with anagrams, though mainly satirically. Swift considered their use to be frivolous.

By the 19th century, however, what had been for so long an extremely popular literary device or pastime had quite fallen out of favour; so that Wheatley in the Introduction to his fascinating monograph *Of Anagrams* feels it necessary to apologize even for discussing them. "Anagrams have now for so long a period been in little esteem that they are rarely met with . . . When we consider therefore in how little regard they are now held, we shall not be surprised that there are few who are aware that these literary amusements once knew better days; that there were times, when great poets considered the making of anagrams and acrostics a pleasing and elegant relaxation; and when some individuals were so expert in their construction, that they obtained the honorable designation of 'Anagrammatists' . . . But if authors like Southey (in *The Doctor*) and Disraeli (in *Curiosities of Literature*) could amuse themselves and us by writing chapters on the subject, I think it is one that is worthy of being more fully considered."

Despite his efforts to restore them to favour, however, anagrams continued in disrepute. To-day the best that can be said for them is that they form part of the armoury of the deviser of crossword-puzzles.

So much for their history! Let us now consider the

rules governing their construction. And to whom more fitting can we turn for information than Camden, the exact contemporary of the author of the Sonnets. Let us ask, first of all, what, in the year 1605, was the definition of the word 'anagram'. Camden is ready with an answer. "The only Quintessence that hitherto the Alchymy of Wit could draw out of names is Anagrammatisme, or Metagrammatisme, which is a dissolution of a name truly written into his Letters, as his Elements, and a new connexion of it by artificial transposition, without addition, subtraction, or change of any Letter, into different words, making some perfect sence applyable to the person named." From which it will be seen that, at that time, a mystical connection was thought to exist between the character of a person and his name.

Murray, writing to-day, is perhaps clearer. According to him an anagram is "a transposition of the letters of a word, name, or phrase, whereby a new word or phrase is formed". And Webster, to his simple definition, which states that an anagram is "the change of one word or phrase into another by the transposition of its letters", adds examples. "Thus *Galenus* becomes *angelus;* and *William Noy* (the laborious attorney-general to Charles I) may be turned into *I moyl in law.*"

Bearing all this in mind, and particularly the fact that in the year 1605 the art of anagrammatizing was thought to be "a dainty service and disport of wit not without pleasure", we can now return to the Sonnets and see if anything we have learnt may be applied to the dedication.

It reads as follows:

> To the onlie begetter of these insuing Sonnets Mr. W. H. all happinesse and that eternitie promised by our ever-living poet wisheth the well-wishing adventurer in setting forth. T.T.

Let us examine this closely. The first thing one notices is that, considered as a straightforward piece of English, it does not make sense. As a whole it is curiously involuted. The verb "wisheth" has no subject, because "our ever-living poet" is governed by the preposition "by".

Now, it does not seem to have occurred to scholars that Mr. W. H. may be part of a gigantic anagram. So, instead of settling upon these two initials, as everybody in the past has been accustomed to do, and supposing them to have been those of the possible dedicatee, let us take the entire phrase "Mr. W.H. all happinesse and that eternitie promised by" and, using the anagrammatical method, see what can be wrested from it. Let us first, however, designate it by the letters MN. The dedication then reads: "To the onlie begetter of these insuing Sonnets, MN. The ever-living (though I prefer to write ever loving, since it is more sensible) poet wisheth the well-wishing adventurer in setting forth . . ." An object is now missing, for we have at the end of the dedication only the letters T.T., and these are thought to be the initials of Thomas Thorpe, the man who, in the year 1609 came to publish the poems.

But it could hardly have been Mr. Thomas Thorpe that the ever loving poet was wishing the adventurer in setting forth. It seems to me rather that the T.T. may have originally been two letters in a private code that existed between the poet and the youth (letter codes were frequently used in those days), and that these, puzzling Mr. Thorpe when he came across them and could make neither head nor tail of the dedication, caused him perhaps to substitute his own initials to the perplexity of scholars of future generations; or more simply, that the two letters just happened by coincidence to be the same as Mr. Thorpe's initials. They could, I unwarrantably and in the most arbitrary manner suggest, have stood for: "Speedy return to my arms"; for they had, by hypothesis, to be of an intimate nature, or further concealment would not have been necessary.

But their meaning is not important. What *is* important is the identity covered by MN. Let us therefore proceed to an elucidation of the anagram.

The exact dedications of *Venus and Adonis* and *The Rape of Lucrece,* it will be remembered, were identical and read: TO THE RIGHT HONOURABLE

HENRIE WRIOTHESLEY EARLE OF SOUTHAMP-
TON, AND BARON OF TITCHFIELD.

Now, in MN the word "happinesse" is already beginning to look like Southampton and "eternitie" like
Henrie (if I am not too imaginative).

Let us abstract, therefore, from MN: HENRIE
WRITHESLEY EARL SOTHAMPTEN. We are left
with the following letters:

B A P A N   T I D S P I M D

And if we alter the three recalcitrant letters, P to R—
it is a Greek R anyway; P to F and M to L, we can write
instead of the above:

B A R A N   T I D S F I L D

And Tidsfild is perfectly good Elizabethan for Titchfield. The Mr. W.H., therefore, was a "blind"; though
the initials themselves were useful as a pointer.

This does not prove anything we did not already
suspect. It does, however, make me feel fairly confident
in assuming that the Sonnets were dedicated to Henry
Wriothesley and no other; particularly when I am able
to adduce two supporting coincidences.

The first is the fact that the dedicatee undoubtedly
knew of the author's "past". The lines in Sonnet 36,

> I may not evermore acknowledge thee,
> Lest my bewailed guilt should do thee shame,
> Nor thou with public kindness honour me,
> Unless thou take that honour from thy name.

refer to a scandal which, from the details available of
Shakespeare's life, scholars have so far been unable to
pinpoint. The crime committed I have now disclosed
and that it had been confessed to Southampton seems
obvious; perhaps by Thomas Walsingham, if he knew
the youth well, in suing, on Marlowe's behalf, for patronage; perhaps by Marlowe himself, after making the
youth's acquaintance and gaining confidence in his
discretion. But it would scarcely have been confessed
to a William Hatcliffe or a Willie Hughes.

The second coincidence is even more striking and concerns the second half of the dedication: The ever-loving poet wisheth the well-wishing adventurer in setting forth T.T.

On the 11th June, 1597, John Chamberlain, Court gossip, wrote concerning the Islands Voyage: "The Erle of Essex is general both by land and sea; the Lord Thomas Howard Vice-Admiral, Sir Walter Raleigh rear-vice-Admirall, who is newly restored to the executing his place in Court of Captain of the Garde; the Earl of Southampton, the Lord Mountjoy and the Lord Rich go as *adventurers*."

Now, there is no uncertainty in my mind that the adventurer mentioned here is the selfsame adventurer of the dedication; though, I must admit, such a possibility has not occurred to other writers on the Sonnets and Southampton. Of the value of this coincidence, however, there can be no doubt; for it now becomes possible to put forward a suggestion as to the date of the last of the sonnets addressed to the young man. Because it is my belief that the dedication was written when the last had been completed. (Those to the Dark Lady I shall discuss later.) The Sonnets, up to No. 104, which was written in the spring, are thought, because of the context of this particular poem, to cover a three-year span. If we take the remainder (104 to 126) and consider each as perhaps a weekly compliment, we arrive approximately at the date of the "setting forth", which was somewhere about the 17th August. Whereas the first would have been written in the spring of 1594, or shortly before the registration of *The Rape of Lucrece*.

Everything fits in very nicely.

And for an interesting parallel in the use of anagrams in dedications I quote again from H.B. Wheatley's monograph.

"On the back of the printed title of *All the Works of John Taylor, the Water-Poet* (London, 1630) are the following anagrams on the names of those to whom the book is dedicated:

JAMES HAMILTON
I AMM ALL HONESTY

WILLIAM HERBERT, EARL OF PEMBROKE
LIBERALY MEEKE, FOR REPUTE
HONOURABLE

PHILIP HERBERT, EARL OF MONTGOMERY
FIRME FAITH BEGOT ALL MY PROPER
HONER."

13

Henry Wriothesley, third Earl of Southampton, was born at Cowdray on the 6th October, 1573. His father Thomas had been imprisoned in the Tower for his part, in 1572, in the treasonable plotting of the Catholic Duke of Norfolk against Queen Elizabeth. The hardships of the Tower had brought on a severe illness from which, though he was released in 1573, he was never completely to recover. The remainder of his life was affected by ill health and, on the 4th October, 1581, he died—two days before his son's eighth birthday.

The young Henry, in accordance with the custom of the times, was immediately made a ward of court and turned over for guardianship to William Cecil, Lord Burghley, who, it is interesting to note, played the same influential rôle in the lives of the Earls of Oxford, Rutland and Essex.

Henry Wriothesley was educated at St. John's College Cambridge, at which he was admitted in 1585, and Gray's Inn, London.

Upon his presentation at Court at the age of seventeen, he fell very much under the spell of the Earl of Essex, six (seven?) years his senior, with whom he was to be closely linked until the latter's death at the block in 1601.

And it was when he was seventeen that Lord Burghley, all too conscious of his elegibility, singled him out as a fitting suitor for his granddaughter, the Lady Elizabeth de Vere, daughter of the Earl of Oxford. But Southampton's mind was filled, just then, with the romantic conception of chivalry. The Earl of Essex was his hero: but the time had not yet come to select a "faire ladie". "To Southampton," writes Mrs. Carmichael Stopes*, "Essex became the ideal knight, to whom he

*Life of Henry Third Earl of Southampton.

was willing to become esquire, even page. Southampton's first love came in the shape of a man; his heart had no room as yet for love of woman. The youth had no active disinclination to the Lady Elizabeth, but he had a very strong disinclination to be fettered by any ties that did not leave him free to follow his own career." He therefore adopted an irritating delaying policy, avowing his affection for the Lady Elizabeth, but never coming to the point of marriage. This indecisiveness proved very embarrassing to the Lords Burghley and Oxford.

Now this singularly fortunate youth was renowned for his extraordinary good looks and his learning: so much so that, when, a fortnight before his nineteenth birthday in October, 1592, he made one of the retinue of Queen Elizabeth during a visit to the University of Oxford, one of the University officials said of him: "No youth there present was more beautiful or more brilliant in the learned arts than this young Prince of Hampshire, although his face was yet scarcely adorned by a tender down."

He was a munificent patron of the arts and was so devoted to drama that, at one phase of his life, he visited the theatres almost daily. Small wonder that, upon their reopening after the abatement of the plague in the autumn of 1593, the dramatist Marlowe, now known as William Shakespeare (and still brooding over his guilt) should have sought him as a patron.

On the 2nd May, 1594, his long widowed mother (Mary, daughter of Viscount Montague) married Sir Thomas Heneage, and this event could have been coterminous with the commencement of the Sonnets; for Marlowe, seeing the Countess about that time, compared her with her son:

Thou art thy mother's glass and she in thee
Calls back the lovely April of her prime.

(Sonnet 3)

It is of course a coincidence that April was the month in which these lines would appear to have been written;

but it is an interesting one. It is coincidental, too, that *The Rape of Lucrece,* with its dedication professing love without end, should have been entered in the Stationers' register a week after the wedding.

Henry Wriothesley came of age on the 6th October of the same year, and his bluff with regard to marriage with Elizabeth de Vere was at last called. "The young Earl of Southampton," writes a gossip of the period, "refusing the Lady Vere payeth £5,000 of present payment." And Mrs. Carmichael Stopes, who claims discovery of the snippet, comments pungently: "This is the hitherto unsuspected cause of Southampton's poverty. Just at the most critical time of his finances, when he was trying to plan a harmonious life of travel and economy, he was called upon to pay this heavy sum, *at once* —the first recorded 'breach of promise' case."

Bearing all this in mind, let us now examine the first Sonnets.

Numbers 1 to 19 are a superb efflux of poetry, slyly hypocritical, I think, in intent: in addressing the youth, the poet aligns himself with the great ones of the Court, all of whom are commenting upon the reluctance of the young Earl to marry, while at the same time feeling his way towards the desired intimacy. Marry, he urges (though not meaning it), and perpetuate, not only your family name, but also your own consummate beauty. Note the splendour of the verse.

Lo in the Orient when the gracious light,
Lifts up his burning head, each under eye
Doth homage to his new appearing sight,
Serving with looks his sacred majesty,
And having climb'd the steep up heavenly hill,
Resembling strong youth in his middle age,
Yet mortal looks adore his beauty still,
Attending on his golden pilgrimage:
But when from high-most pitch with weary car,
Like feeble age he reeleth from the day,
The eyes ('fore duteous) now converted are
From his low tract and look another way:
    So thou, thyself out-going in thy noon,
    Unlook'd on diest unless thou get a son.

                                                   (Sonnet 7)

E

It is interesting to compare this with Romeo's more lyrical acclamation of Juliet, written at about the same time.

But, soft! what light through yonder window breaks?
It is the east, and Juliet is the sun!
Arise, fair sun, and kill the envious moon,
Who is already sick and pale with grief,
That thou her maid are far more fair than she.

Also present in the poems is an obsession with the fading of youth.

When forty winters shall besiege thy brow,
And dig deep trenches in thy beauty's field,
Thy youth's proud livery so gaz'd on now,
Will be a totter'd weed of small worth held.

(Sonnet 2)

This haunting dread of life's prime absurdity is given equally clear expression by Wilde in *The Picture of Dorian Gray*. A major motif of the Sonnets, it is reiterated again and again, later with the consoling suggestion that, though the youth's beauty must inevitably fade, it will be given permanence in the poems. This is made first tentatively, then insistently, eventually superseding the idea of children.

But I forbid thee one most heinous crime,
O carve not with thy hours my love's fair brow,
Nor draw no lines there with thine antique pen,
Him in thy course untainted do allow,
For beauty's pattern to succeeding men.
    Yet do thy worst old Time, despite thy wrong,
    My love shall in my verse ever live young.

(Sonnet 19)

The poet's admiration for the youth is now unbounded.

Shall I compare thee to a Summer's day?
Thou art more lovely and more temperate:
Rough winds do shake the darling buds of May,
And Summer's lease hath all too short a date:
Sometime too hot the eye of heaven shines,
And often is his gold complexion dimm'd,

And every fair from fair sometime declines,
By chance, or nature's changing course untrimm'd:
But thy eternal Summer shall not fade,
Nor lose possession of that fair thou ow'st,
Nor shall Death brag thou wander'st in his shade,
When in eternal lines to time thou grow'st:
  So long as men can breathe or eyes can see,
  So long lives this, and this gives life to thee.

                         (Sonnet 18)

With number 20, the most controversial, the mood has become daring. The net has been cast: the seduction is imminent.

A woman's face with Nature's own hand painted,
Hast thou the Master Mistress of my passion,
A woman's gentle heart but not acquainted
With shifting change as is false women's fashion,
An eye more bright than theirs, less false in rolling,
Gilding the object whereupon it gazeth,
A man in hue all hues in his controlling,
Which steals men's eyes and women's souls amazeth.

The poet's love intensifies. He cannot sleep for thinking of the youth.

Weary with toil, I haste me to my bed,
The dear repose for limbs with travel tired,
But then begins a journey in my head
To work my mind, when body's work's expired.
For then my thoughts (from far where I abide)
Intend a zealous pilgrimage to thee,
And keep my drooping eyelids open wide,
Looking on darkness which the blind do see.
Save that my soul's imaginary sight
Presents thy shadow to my sightless view,
Which like a jewel (hung in ghastly night)
Makes black night beauteous, and her old face new.
  Lo thus by day my limbs, by night my mind,
  For thee, and for myself, no quiet find.

                         (Sonnet 27)

Then comes the first hint of a sense of unworthiness, insufficiency and guilt, which is to be rung in ever more urgently as the Sonnets progress.

When in disgrace with Fortune and men's eyes,
I all alone beweep my outcast state . . .
Haply I think on thee, and then my state
(Like to the lark at break of day arising),
From sullen earth sings hymns at Heaven's gate,
  For thy sweet love remember'd such wealth brings,
  That then I scorn to change my state with Kings.

                                          (Sonnet 29)

The image of the sun returns, this time, significantly, without reference to the pun-word "son". And there is a trace of underlying unhappiness in this truly marvellous poem.

Full many a glorious morning have I seen,
Flatter the mountain-tops with sovereign eye,
Kissing with golden face the meadows green,
Gilding pale streams with heavenly alchemy:
Anon permit the basest clouds to ride,
With ugly rack on his celestial face,
And from the forlorn world his visage hide
Stealing unseen to west with this disgrace:
Even so my Sun one early morn did shine,
With all triumphant splendour on my brow,
But out alack, he was but one hour mine,
The region cloud hath mask'd him from me now.
  Yet him for this, my love no whit disdaineth,
  Suns of the world may stain, when heaven's sun staineth.

                                          (Sonnet 33)

After which comes the guilt-racked Sonnet 36, which has already been quoted.

14

Towards the middle of 1595 the Earl of Essex had managed to introduce Elizabeth Vernon, daughter of his sister and Sir John Vernon of Hodnet (who had died several years earlier), into the service of the Queen; and it is not surprising that Southampton, on account of his devotion to Essex, should have been drawn to seek also the society of the niece who was now so much at Court.

On the 23rd September Rowland Whyte wrote to Sir Robert Sidney: "My Lord of Southampton doth with too much familiarity courte the faire Mrs. Vernon." Though Mrs. Carmichael Stopes disposes of the gossip thus: "The real fact seems to have been that, as Adonis had been able to repel the pleadings of Venus because of his heart being occupied with the pleasures of the chase, so the Earl of Southampton found as yet no room in his heart for visions of matrimony, since it was already filled with visions of glory to be won in war, somewhen or somehow, under his adored leader."

The association, however, was to become closer. For in September, 1595, the young Earl of Rutland, to whom Southampton was very much attached, went off to travel in Italy, and Southampton, instead of going with him, as he had planned to do, stayed behind; so that he would probably have turned all the more insistently for companionship to Elizabeth Vernon.

He was shortly, however, to retire from the court for some time. In 1596 an opportunity at last arose for him to give expression to his craving for adventure; but, for a reason not known, he does not appear to have taken advantage of it. A large fleet, consisting of English and Dutch ships, was sent by Elizabeth to make a raid on the Spanish port of Cadiz. The English contingent was commanded by the Lord Admiral and the Earl of

Essex. It set sail early in June; but according to Mrs. Stopes, there is no evidence to show that Southampton took part in the expedition; nor is there any of his being at Court during the course of that year. "So that we must believe that he stayed in the country, mortified and fretting."

And that Elizabeth Vernon was not the only woman in his life just then seems to be borne out by Sonnet 40, in which the poet chides the youth for stealing his mistress from him.

Take all my loves, my love, yea take them all,
What hast thou then more than thou hadst before?
No love, my love, that thou mayst true love call,
All mine was thine, before thou hadst this more:
Then if for my love, thou my love receivest,
I cannot blame thee, for my love thou usest,
But yet be blam'd, if thou thyself deceivest
By wilful taste of what thyself refusest.
I do forgive thy robb'ry gentle thief
Although thou steal thee all my poverty:
And yet love knows it is a greater grief
To bear love's wrong, than hate's known injury.
   Lascivious grace in whom all ill well shows,
   Kill me with spites yet we must not be foes.

Whereas in Sonnet 42 he affirms that the loss of the youth is of greater concern to him than the loss of the mistress.

That thou hast her it is not all my grief,
And yet it may be said I loved her dearly,
That she hath thee is of my wailing chief,
A loss in love that touches me more nearly.

Though that these sonnets are admissible of a different interpretation I shall show later; and that the affair between himself and the youth was soon to reach maximum intensity would seem to be indicated by Sonnet 56, written, there can be little doubt, from a state of repletion.

Sweet love renew thy force, be it not said
Thy edge should blunter be than appetite,
Which but today by feeding is allayed,
Tomorrow sharpened in his former might.
So love be thou, although today thou fill
Thy hungry eyes, even till they wink with fulness,
Tomorrow see again, and do not kill
The spirit of Love, with a perpetual dulness:
Let this sad interim like the Ocean be
Which parts the shore, where two contracted new,
Come daily to the banks, that when they see
Return of love, more blest may be the view.
   Or call it Winter, which being full of care,
   Makes Summer's welcome, thrice more wish'd, more rare.

An avowal of complete subjugation follows :

Being your slave what should I do but tend
Upon the hours, and times of your desire?
I have no precious time at all to spend;
Nor services to do till you require.

But the happy period is over; for the poet now enters
upon an agony of self-doubt and jealousy. We have not
far to look for a parallel to this situation; though the
youth would seem to have treated the poet less unkindly
than Lord Alfred Douglas did Wilde. There is a con-
sciousness of his advancing age and lack of physical
appeal :

. . . my glass shows me myself indeed,
Beated and chopp'd with tann'd antiquity.

(Sonnet 62)

And there is jealousy of another poet :

Whilst I alone did call upon thy aid,
My verse alone had all thy gentle grace,
But now my gracious numbers are decay'd,
And my sick Muse doth give another place.
I grant (sweet love) thy lovely argument
Deserves the travail of a worthier pen,
Yet what of thee thy Poet doth invent,
He robs thee of, and pays it thee again.

(Sonnet 79)

This theme is developed over a number of sonnets, until finally the poet cries in despair :

Farewell thou are too dear for my possessing,
And like enough thou know'st thy estimate,
The charter of thy worth gives thee releasing:
My bonds in thee are all determinate.
For how do I hold thee but by thy granting,
And for that riches where is my deserving?
The cause of this fair gift in me is wanting,
And so my patent back again is swerving.
Thyself thou gav'st, thy own worth then not knowing,
Or me to whom thou gav'st it, else mistaking,
So thy great gift upon misprision growing,
Comes home again, on better judgment making.
   Thus have I had thee as a dream doth flatter,
   In sleep a King, but waking no such matter.

(Sonnet 87)

Now the identity of the rival poet has been much discussed. Whether he was Chapman or Marlowe, Drayton or Samuel Daniel, or one of a number of others, has prompted the exercise of a great deal of speculative ingenuity among scholars. And, since my own theory as to his identity (the conventional one) has considerable bearing on the identity of the author of the plays, I shall set it down here in a short digression.

The rival poet can only have been Chapman. To begin with, the claims of Marlowe, Chapman's most formidable competitor for this rôle, must inevitably lapse as soon as it is admitted that he was the author of the Sonnets. Drayton, Samuel Daniel and a few lesser Elizabethan poets are left; but the pretensions of these, I cannot help feeling, hinging as they do mainly upon the quality of individual verse (that which is written with a "golden quill" or that which can be likened to "full proud sail") are too slim to merit analysis.

Chapman's case rests largely upon his conviction that he composed under supernatural guidance. He was a devoted, even fanatical, adherent of the Platonic doctrine, expounded in the *Ion,* that poetry is divinely inspired. This he had given an Orphic interpretation in his *Hymn to Night* :

Come consecrate with me to sacred Night
Your whole endeavours, and detest the light.
Sweet Peace's richest crown is made of stars,
Most certain guides of honoured mariners,
No pen can anything eternal write
That is not steeped in humour of the Night.

Compare this with Sonnet 86, which I quote in full:

Was it the full proud sail of his great verse,
Bound for the prize of (all too precious) you,
That did my ripe thoughts in my brain inhearse,
Making their tomb the womb wherein they grew?
Was it his spirit, by spirits taught to write,
Above a mortal pitch, that struck me dead?
No, neither he, nor his compeers by night
Giving him aid, my verse astonished.
He nor that affable familiar ghost
Which nightly gulls him with intelligence,
As victors of my silence cannot boast,
I was not sick of any fear from thence.
    But when your countenance fill'd up his line,
    Then lack'd I matter, that enfeebled mine.

The author of the sonnet, it seems to me, is through-out it obviously referring to a "mystical" technique employed in the writing of poetry and can be alluding only to the author of *Hymn to Night*.

But there is a further consideration, as I see it, which is bound up with how Chapman was able to finish *Hero and Leander*. Where was the manuscript, since the two existing sestiads had not been published, and how did he gain access to it? Even more arresting is his reason for undertaking the completion of the poem. This he gives in the dedication of the four final sestiads to Thomas Walsingham's wife Audrey. "Being drawn by strange instigation to employ some of my serious time in so trifling a subject," are the apologetic words he uses, implying that the subject was of a frivolous nature. But it is the term 'strange instigation' that has caused comment. This has been interpreted as a mystical experi-ence resembling the famous one the poet records (in 1609) in *The Teares of Peace* where he claims that the Greek Homer appeared to him when he was meditating upon a hill and directed him to translate his works:

```
. . . Sodainely, a comfortable light
Brake through the shade; and, after it, the sight
Of a most grave and goodly person shinde,
With eys turned upwards, and was outward, blind;
But inward, past and future things he sawe;
And was to both, and present times, their lawe.
His sacred bosome was so full of fire
That 'twas transparent; and made him expire
His breath in flames, that did instruct (me thought)
And (as my soule were then at full) they wrought.
```

Examine the term "strange instigation" closely, however. Does it necessarily mean the appearance of a spirit
or familiar? Might it not be possible that the "ghost"
implied, who apparently directed Chapman to complete
the unfinished poem, was Marlowe himself: which
would presuppose a singular situation: namely, that
Chapman knew the true identity of "Shakespeare".

Now this would not be surprising. In hypothesizing
an imposture, one is faced with the difficulty of how
Marlowe was able, for a protracted time, successfully
to deceive his still living friends. Greene and Kyd were
dead; so was Thomas Watson. Peele may not have
known him intimately. Nashe long before the murder
had quarrelled with him. The haughty Raleigh, viewing him from the height of his exalted social position, may not have been conscious of any deception.
Harriott may have been too preoccupied to make visits
to the theatre, where Marlowe would now be spending
most of his time, sometimes writing, sometimes acting
and sometimes indulging in little bits of business. But
with Chapman, who had also been a member of the
School of Night, it was different. His interests exactly
coincided with those of Marlowe, and he must have
known, it seems to me, of the imposture and con-
nived at it because of his belief in the divinity of the
poetic gift. This, then would be the situation of the rival
poet. Walsingham had arranged the murder. His wife
Audrey, it is almost sure, knew of it too. In 1598 Edward
Blunt "posthumously" dedicated the first two sestiads
of *Hero and Leander* to Walsingham himself; and Chapman dedicated his final four to Audrey. There seems to

me to be a cohesion between these separate literary acts and the facts of the murder.

Now, in completing the poem, Chapman can hardly have laid claim to supernatural inspiration. Homer was to draw him to the lofty task of translating *The Iliad* and *The Odyssey* from Greek into English : the work for which he is now most famous: the work which drew a cry of rapture from Keats. The question I ask is : Can he have felt himself drawn by supernatural influence, that is to say, by the intervention of Marlowe's ghost, to deal with what he considered to be "so trifling a subject". Supernatural inspiration and trifling subjects are in opposition. I cannot help feeling, therefore, that it was a Marlowe of flesh and blood, now living as Shakespeare, who was the "strange instigation" alluded to by Chapman in his dedication of his work to Audrey Walsingham, and that this veiled allusion would have been easily understood by both her and her husband; but not at all by the general audience of readers. The circumstances of the affair would perhaps have been these. The unfinished work would probably have been nagging at Marlowe, who in the end would have been led to suggest to Chapman that he should complete it. The imposture, too, from the evidence of the Sonnets, was still worrying him. And would not this completion of a work left unfinished by a "deceased" author have further stressed that author's death? Marlowe would have had constant access to Chapman's work as it progressed and might even have advised him on how to proceed. Moreover, he would have been impressed by the rival poet's handling of the undertaking; hence his use in Sonnet 86, of the phrase "the full proud sail of his great verse", which would have been under way (if my dating of the Sonnets is correct) in the middle of the year 1596, approximately two years before publication : an estimate which is conceivable. This labour, furthermore, would have brought Chapman into frequent contact with Marlowe, and with his youthful friend; and Chapman, writing under immense inspirational pressure, and gaining confidence, would have been tempted

to sue for the young Earl's patronage, thus arousing
Marlowe's jealousy. "Ah!" the scholars will now say.
"But Chapman did not praise the young man as the
Sonnets undoubtedly assert he did. You have not taken
into consideration such lines as:

> ... a better spirit doth use your name,
> And in the praise thereof spends all his might,
> To make me tongue-tied speaking of your fame."

To which I make answer that I most certainly have.
Dr. Rowse tells us that Leander, in Marlowe's first two
sestiads, was a portrait of the beautiful young Earl of
Southampton; and in his continuation of the poem
Chapman describes him just as rapturously as Marlowe
at the beginning had done—though perhaps less sensu-
ously; so that the author of the Sonnets was referring to
the praise of Southampton expressed in the continuation of *Hero and Leander*. It all fits in, and none of the
contortions is necessary that scholars are forced to
indulge in in giving Shakespeare separate existence. But
to return to our consideration of the Sonnets as a whole.

The next three poems project the same despairing
mood, which must have been indeed black, one senses;
though the emotion expressed is always muted. The
youth's exalted rank at all times prevents the poet from
inveighing against him openly.

> When thou shalt be dispos'd to set me light,
> And place my merit in the eye of scorn,
> Upon thy side, against myself I'll fight,
> And prove thee virtuous, though thou art forsworn:
> With mine own weakness being best acquainted,
> Upon thy part I can set down a story
> Of faults conceal'd, wherein I am attainted:
> That thou in losing me, shalt win much glory:
> And I by this will be a gainer too,
> For bending all my loving thoughts on thee,
> The injuries that to myself I do,
> Doing thee vantage, double vantage me.
>   Such is my love, to thee I so belong,
>   That for thy right, myself will bear all wrong.
>   (Sonnet 88)

Say that thou didst forsake me for some fault,
And I will comment upon that offence,
Speak of my lameness, and I straight will halt:
Against thy reasons making no defence.
Thou canst not (love) disgrace me half so ill,
To set a form upon desired change,
As I'll myself disgrace, knowing thy will,
I will acquaintance strangle and look strange:
Be absent from thy walks and in my tongue,
Thy sweet-beloved name no more shall dwell,
Lest I (too much profane) should do it wrong:
And haply of our old acquaintance tell.
   For thee, against myself I'll vow debate,
   For I must ne'er love him whom thou dost hate.
                              (Sonnet 89)

Then hate me when thou wilt, if ever, now,
Now while the world is bent my deeds to cross,
Join with the spite of fortune, make me bow,
And do not drop in for an after-loss:
Ah do not, when my heart hath scap'd this sorrow,
Come in the rearward of a conquer'd woe,
Give not a windy night a rainy morrow,
To linger out a purpos'd overthrow.
If thou wilt leave me, do not leave me last,
When other petty griefs have done their spite,
But in the onset come, so shall I taste
At first the very worst of fortune's might.
   And other strains of woe, which now seem woe,
   Compar'd with loss of thee, will not seem so.
                              (Sonnet 90)

But despite the misery the youth is causing the poet,
he is consummately beautiful and kind in expression:

... heaven in thy creation did decree,
That in thy face sweet love should ever dwell,
Whate'er thy thoughts, or thy heart's workings be,
Thy looks should nothing thence, but sweetness tell.
                              (Sonnet 93)

15

The following chain of reasoning should be followed carefully, since much depends on it.

Several journeys are mentioned in the Sonnets. The ones in Sonnets 27, 50 (already quoted) and 51 I am not attempting to account for. They may have been any sort of journey made on horseback. The one referred to in Sonnets 97 and 98, however, intimately concerns me.

Sonnet 104, as I have already pointed out, seems, from Southampton's departure later in the year, to have been written in the spring (April?) of 1597; and Sonnet 97, from its context, a little after the full summer of 1596:

How like a Winter hath my absence been
From thee, the pleasure of the fleeting year!
What freezings have I felt, what dark days seen!
What old December's bareness everywhere!
And yet this time remov'd was summer's time,
The teeming Autumn big with rich increase,
Bearing the wanton burthen of the prime,
Like widowed wombs after their Lords' decease:
Yet this abundant issue seem'd to me,
But hope of orphans, and unfathered fruit,
For Summer and his pleasures wait on thee,
And thou away, the very birds are mute.
  Or if they sing, 'tis with so dull a cheer,
  That leaves look pale, dreading the Winter's near.

The failure of the poet to write more than six sonnets during the intervening period is accounted for in the context of some of those six.

Where art thou Muse that thou forgett'st so long,
To speak of that which gives thee all thy might?
(Sonnet 100)

Oh truant Muse, what shall be thy amends,
For thy neglect of truth in beauty dy'd?

(Sonnet 101)

Therefore like her, I sometime hold my tongue:
Because I would not dull you with my song.

(Sonnet 102)

I am now going to make what may appear to be my most daring assumption.

In the August of 1596, that is to say in the full summer described in Sonnet 97, Hamnet, son of William Shakespeare, died in Stratford and was buried, we know from the chronology, on the 11th of that month.

And it must be accounted the most extraordinary coincidence that the journey described, and this death of Hamnet, should both have occurred at the same time. One is therefore forced to link them. Why else should the journey have been undertaken but to attend the funeral? For there can be no doubt that Marlowe, if his actions are to be brought into harmony with the Shakespeare chronology, made contact with the Shakespeare family. Is it too much, then, to infer that messages will have been sent to the absent Shakespeare concerning his son's illness and will have fallen quite naturally into Marlowe's hands; and that Marlowe, still conscience wrung, will have discussed the situation with the ever sweet Southampton who will have suggested the visit? Moreover, he had to go, if he was not to appear abnormally heartless. The continuing imposture demanded it. To have held back might have aroused suspicion.

Could the traveller not have been Shakespeare himself, is the searching question that must be answered. No, because there is no note of grief in the relevant sonnet. The predominant theme, as always when a journey is described, is the agony of separation from the beloved youth.

What of the risk?

I am convinced that the Amphitryon-like situation into which he was entering, despite the fact that it was frought with danger, need not worry us. His mind could have worked in this manner. The imposture in London had been successful. Why should this not be too? Moreover, was he not now an actor? And was not this type of deception all the rage on the London stage? Had he himself not portrayed such impostures in some of his plays? Then again, there was the unusualness of the situation offered. No dramatist avid for ideas would have avoided it; and the impetuous Marlowe, one cannot help feeling (though he was now considerably subdued) would have sought it eagerly, meeting his acquired relations with interest; sympathizing with them certainly for his conscience sake, but also acting out the new part. There would have been gifts of money to the indigent Shakespeares and the eventual application, at the Heralds' College, on John Shakespeare's behalf for a coat of arms to flatter the old man (granted on the 20th October, 1596). All this is the naive interpretation. And how peculiar that both parts of *King Henry IV* almost certainly date from the following year! One cannot help feeling that John Shakespeare may have inspired Sir John Falstaff. The Garter King of Arms assigned him "for his crest or cognizance, a falcon, his wings displayed argent, standing on a wreath of his colours". And his name was Shakespeare. The first syllable of the word 'falcon' and the last of Shakespeare, euphoniously modified, come together most aptly to make Falstaff.

I mean of course, I hasten to add, from the viewpoint of character. The stage character, or original puppet, of the source play, *The Famous Victories of Henry the Fifth*, may well have represented the historical Sir John Oldcastle, a Lollard of the early fifteenth century. The round character (I do not mean physically) the creation of whom is perhaps the playwright's most glorious achievement, and who was eventually named Falstaff (because, it is said, Queen Elizabeth at the request of one of Oldcastle's descendants commanded a change of name) was modelled on the John Shakespeare whom Marlowe met for the first time in Stratford in 1596. For it becomes more and more apparent as one studies the

plays in the light of a revised biography that many of
them, which were the original work of inferior authors,
or work of his own with which he had become dissatis-
fied, were taken up again and again by "Shakespeare"
and refurbished. His position as chief dramatist of
James Burbage's company, and later of the company in
which he himself owned a tenth part, enabled him to
do this. And in the process of transformation, even
where his own earlier work was concerned, a hitherto
non-existent magic entered into them. In *Death in
Venice* Thomas Mann outlines the slow course of this
sort of invention in describing the method of his imaginary author Gustave Aschenbach. "Outsiders might be
pardoned for believing that (his literary works) were a
manifestation of great power working under high pressure, that they came forth, as it were, all in one breath
. . . the truth was that they were heaped up to greatness
in layer after layer, in long days of work, out of hundreds and hundreds of single inspirations; they owed
their excellence, both of mass and detail (to the fact)
that their creator could hold out for years under the
strain of the same piece of work . . . devoting to actual
composition none but his best and freshest hours."
(Penguin Books: translation H. T. Lowe-Porter.) It was
a magic of language and living character that became
manifest: speeches were reclothed in magnificent language: prose was sometimes converted into verse:
characters were built up from a minute observation of
living people about him. So that in many instances it
is impossible to-day for the bewildered scholar to know
where "Shakespeare" took up his pen, where he laid it
down or what part he played in the creation of the whole
confection—apart from perceiving that much that had
been pedestrian had in some inexplicable manner become imbued with genius. It is possible that "Shakespeare" was the English theatre's first producer; that
he created his plays on the players rather than wrote
them, much as a modern *haut couturier* builds up an
elaborate "creation" on a model; that he invented long
verbal cloths of great richness to form scenes which he

adapted experimentally to the needs of the players and revised with tireless industry.

The plays, in order to ensure continuity of thought, seem to have been first sketched fully in prose (even to the imagery) which was then converted into verse. The parts which the author found most interesting, those which arrived spontaneously under the pressure of inspiration, were subjected to poetical treatment before those the conversion of which required drudgery. Order did not matter. The process can be seen at work in the unfinished *Timon of Athens* which abounds in prose much of which, on account of its imagery, seems to have been destined to become verse. And it was during this conversion that the obscurities crept in. Words proved intractable, and the exigencies of metre frequently made necessary a sacrifice of sense.

To revert, however, to my contention that John Shakespeare was the inspirer of Sir John Falstaff. When Queen Elizabeth objected to the use of the name Old-castle in the *Henry IV* plays, Marlowe had perforce to look round for another and settled on Falstaff, deriving it, I believe, in the manner I have described above. Let me see if I can substantiate the theory still further: let us glance, to begin with, at the known history of John Shakespeare and compare the points of character that emerge with those of Falstaff. I have drawn the following details from E. K. Chambers' *William Shakespeare*.

A glover or whittawer by trade, John Shakespeare also dealt in barley and timber. He "makes his first appearance in Stratford at a leet of 29 April 1552, when he was fined one shilling for having an unauthorized dunghill in Henley Street." I estimate (from the fact that his father Richard is traceable in Snitterfield only from 1528-9) that at that time he would have been no more than twenty-two, an important factor in the theory.

In 1557 or thereabouts he married Mary Arden whose father, under his Will of 1556, had left her some land called Asbies in Wilmcote and had probably "settled other property there upon her. She was also entitled to a share in a reversionary interest of his Snitterfield estate." She was therefore, in a small way, a sort of heiress, and this could have accounted for John's interest in her.

Over a period of twenty-two years the Shakespeares were to have eight children (William being the third) of which only four were surviving at the time of Marlowe's visit in 1596.

For a dozen or so years John Shakespeare prospered in business and became prominent in municipal life. "Between 1557 and 1561 he appears as juror, constable, and 'affeeror' or assessor of fines at the court leet"; but over and against this there is the inevitable contradiction: "he was himself again fined for leaving his gutter dirty and for not making presentments as ale-taster before the court of record". The upward trend, however, continues. "In 1561 and 1562 he was chosen as one of the chamberlains, and it is perhaps evidence of his financial capacity"—does Sir Edmund mean shrewdness?—"that he acted, quite exceptionally, as deputy to the chamberlains of the next two years."

"Probably he was already a capital burgess by 1561, although his name first appears in a list of 1564." And it is not unnoteworthy that "his subscriptions to the relief of the poor during that year of plague-time were liberal. In 1565 he was chosen an alderman, and in 1568 reached the top of civic ambition as bailiff." He would then have been about thirty-eight.

Now comes the journey downhill. "In 1571 John proceeded against Richard Quiney, the son of an old colleague Adrian Quiney, for £50", then worth about £500. "In 1573 he had himself to meet the claim of Henry Higford, a former steward of Stratford, for £30. He failed to appear, and a warrant for his arrest, and if not found, outlawry, was issued. He was still in a position to spend £40 on house property in 1575. But at the beginning of 1577 he suddenly discontinued attendance at the 'halls' of Corporation, and never again appeared, except on one or two special occasions. In the following year he was excused from a levy for the relief of the poor, and rated at an unusually low amount for the expenses of the musters, which still remained unpaid in 1579. His wife's inheritance was disposed of. The small reversion in Snitterfield was sold for £4. Asbies was let at a nominal rent, probably in consideration of a sum down. The other Wilmcote holding was mortgaged to Mary's brother-in-law Edmund Lambert for £40, to be repaid at Michaelmas 1580. It was not repaid."

In 1580 "John Shakespeare and one John Audley, a hat-maker of Nottingham, were bound over in the Court of Queen's Bench to give security against a breach of the peace. They failed to answer to their recogniz-ances and incurred substantial fines. That of Shake-speare amounted to £20 for his own default and £20 more as surety for Audley. In 1587 an entanglement with the affairs of his brother Henry seems to have added to his embarrassment. And in the same year the patience of the Corporation was exhausted, and a new alderman was appointed in his place, 'for that Mr. Shaxspere dothe not come to the halles when they be warned nor hathe not done of longe tyme'." Yet "further court of record suits suggest that he was still engaged in business. On 25 September 1592," that is to say, eight months before the Deptford murder and four years before Marlowe's first visit, "he was included in a list of persons at Stratford 'heartofore presented for not comminge monethlie to the churche accordinge to hir Majesties lawes'; and to his name and those of eight others is appended the note, 'It is sayd that these laste nine coom not to churche for feare of process for debtte'. As arrest for debt could be made on Sundays in the sixteenth century, the explanation seems, in the light of John Shakespeare's (ill-starred) career since 1577, extremely probable."

It would appear, therefore, that characterwise John Shakespeare and John Falstaff had several things in common. Primarily, however, I wish to stress Shake-speare's unscrupulousness as regards money matters, which in Falstaff is of course ballooned until it becomes purse-cutting and highway robbery. But Marlowe, it is evident, when he found himself in the dilemma I am

about to describe, used Falstaff as a whipping boy (much
as he was later to place his rage against Southampton
in the mouth of Thersites), vitriolically satirizing the
idleness, gluttony, drunkenness, lechery, and perhaps
treachery and cowardice, that he saw in John Shakespeare; treating them certainly with compassion and
exquisite humour; creating finally the most superbly
comic character of the English stage; but turning on
him savagely in the end. For in his relations with the
rustic Shakespeares, the highly cultivated Marlowe
would doubtless have modelled his conduct on that of
his elegant patron; and from Southampton to the youthful Prince Hal is not such a far cry; and only in the
light of some extraordinary antipathy can Prince Hal's
ruthless repudiation of Falstaff, with whom he had been
so friendly, at the end of 2 *Henry IV,* be adequately
explained.

> I know thee not, old man. Fall to thy prayers.
> How ill white hairs becomes a fool and jester!
> I have long dreamt of such a kind of man,
> So surfeit-swelled, so old, and so profane,
> But, being awaked, I do despise my dream.
> ... I banish thee, on pain of death,
> As I have done the rest of my misleaders,
> Not to come near our person by ten mile.

Yet another factor can be brought forward to substantiate the theory. John Shakespeare, at the time of
Marlowe's first visit, would have been about sixty-four
years old. Falstaff, it will be remembered, in 1 *Henry IV*
describes himself thus: "A goodly portly man, i' faith,
and a corpulent; of a cheerful look, a pleasing eye, and
a most noble carriage; and, as I think, his age some
fifty, or by'r lady, inclining to three score ..." Marlowe,
it seems likely, never knew John Shakespeare's real age,
any more than we do, and is allowing him here to be
coy about it; for Prince Hal soon exclaims: "That
villainous abominable misleader of youth, Falstaff, that
old white-bearded Satan."

The Sir John Oldcastle of the source play, on the
other hand, had been only thirty-nine years old at death,

and A. R. Humphreys, Editor of the Arden edition of
1 *Henry IV*, comments: "Since the historical Oldcastle
was certainly neither old nor unmilitary and (being a
warrior) probably not fat, these attributes of Falstaff
must arise otherwise than from history . . . The 'goodly
portly' figure" and the advanced age are "in neither
history nor *The Famous Victories* and attempts have
been made to explain" them.

We come now to the all-important question: Was
the deception successful? And I could argue with some
justification that Marlowe was indeed able to sustain
it. Mary and John were both at least sixty, a good age
in those times, and could have been suffering from
any of a number of diseases: their faculties might have
been impaired. Then, Shakespeare had left Stratford
many years earlier, and "memory grows dim". Ann
Hathaway, the acquired wife, would have been the
most difficult to fool; but even she, after the passage
of so much time, could perhaps have been successfully
deluded; for, as I shall show in a moment, he would have
refused her all marital contact.

But no! After harbouring this idea for some time,
I at last decided that it was impossible. In 1596 John
still had five years of life ahead of him, and Mary twelve.
We must therefore examine the alternative possibility,
which is that the imposture was penetrated, and estimate,
if we can, the individual reactions of the Shakespeares
to it. They were all living at the time in the so-called
birthplace in Henley Street. Let us take them one by
one.

It will doubtless have been the wiley John who made
the initial discovery, and the scene in which it dawned
upon his unscrupulous mind that this elegant, and apparently well-to-do, stranger masquerading as his son was
not what he claimed to be must have been of awe-inspiring intensity. The course of action he was going to
embark upon would have been immediately clear.

Next, Mary Arden, the mother. Married in approximately 1557, that is to say, about forty years earlier,
she would then have been probably sixty. She had had

eight children, three of whom had died in infancy, had seen her inheritance squandered and for the best part of twenty years had been trying to bring up her family (and for ten possibly William's) on the small sum of money that her husband (idler? bankrupt? tosspot? glutton? lecher? braggart? pretender?) allowed her after his own appetites had been satisfied. As William Shakespeare's mother, she could hardly have been deceived by Marlowe's imposture and would probably have discerned it with bewilderment.

Then Ann Hathaway (or Whateley, the name does not matter), the acquired wife. Eight years older than Marlowe, having been eight years older than Shakespeare, she was now forty and, after her long period of neglect, doubtless a shrew. Her relationships with John, upon whom she would appear to have been dependent, must have been delicate in the extreme; and, on first meeting her, Marlowe must have looked at her in horror; and that his relations with her from then on were at least difficult can be inferred from the fact that he left her, in his Will, only his second best bed—the one to which, in all probability, he immediately banished her. For that he abstained from her is certain and, in leaving her this strange piece of property, he perpetrated the world's supreme act of irony in relation to shrewish wives; although scholars, bent on establishing the blameless record of their dramatist, have refused to see it for what it was. Ann Hathaway, on perceiving the unusual conduct of her "husband", would have been first mystified, then furious at her further frustration.

The Will, indeed, goes a long way towards uncovering Marlowe's feelings towards the Shakespeares. For next comes Susanna. She was thirteen years old when Marlowe first met her and it is unlikely that she would have had to be let into this dangerous secret. Marlowe would therefore have been greeted with spontaneous affection. Had she not dreamed, in the manner of all little girls whose fathers are away, of the return of this adored one whom she had hardly seen; who was the vaguest memory from her earliest infancy.

Marlowe, accordingly, could have found himself the object of a ready-made ardent worship which would have moved him immensely. When he died in 1616, he left her and her husband John Hall the bulk of his estate.

Judith, now eleven, would not have remembered him at all. She, too, would therefore have been left in ignorance of the imposture. She seems, nevertheless, to have welcomed him with less show of affection. Can she have ascribed the death of her twin to the absence of her father? She received under the Will a total of only £300 (in those days certainly worth £3,000 of to-day's money, but still only a fraction of the estate) and, of his plate, only his silver-gilt bowl.

There were then the children of John himself. First Gilbert and Richard. Two and ten years younger than Marlowe respectively, they would have been approximately nineteen and eleven at the time of their brother's departure. They seem to have been, in contrast to their "distinguished" father, complete nonentities; for, whereas he is always turning up in the archives, they, apart from the notices of their christenings and deaths, and the single appearance of Gilbert's name on a document, figure nowhere in the records. They do not seem even to have married; and, having predeceased Marlowe, nothing can be learnt about them from the Will. It is not inconceivable that they were simple dull-witted men of the Warwickshire soil who gained a modest living by labouring in the fields. But both, one imagines, would have noticed some difference in the man they remembered as their brother and the one who had come to replace him.

So, too, with the sister Joan. She was now twenty-seven, and it is important to note that she had probably passed her period of elegibility. And that Marlowe's relations with her remained at least cordial can be judged from the fact that under the terms of his Will she received £20, the tenancy for life of the old Shakespeare home (she was eventually to marry) and all his wearing apparel. Her three sons received £5 each; but from the fact that he had forgotten the Christian name of one of them, for there is a blank in the Will, it would appear that, towards the end of his life he did not visit her very often.

Finally, there was Edmund. Born in the May of 1580, he was barely sixteen in the mid-summer of 1596 and was therefore the "baby" of the family. He would have been only five when his brother went away and could hardly have been conscious of any imposture. There were no photographs in those days, it should be remembered, to keep the image alive. He, too, would probably have been allowed to remain in ignorance of the secret, and a close association seems to have sprung up between him and Marlowe.

All these people, it should be noted, were, in contradistinction to the highly educated author of the plays, more or less illiterate. John "was accustomed to authenticate documents by a mark, which was sometimes a cross and sometimes a pair of glover's dividers"; although this was no proof, comments Sir Edmund Chambers, of his inability to write. Judith, too, signed with a mark. Of the others it is known only that Susanna wrote a "painfully formal" signature, and that Gilbert could write his own name, as becomes evident from his single appearance in the Shakespeare papers, where he has appended a signature to a document authorizing the transfer of property to his famous "brother". This near illiteracy of the Shakespeares, coupled with the lack of any vestige of evidence in support of William's education, has proved a considerable embarrassment to Stratfordians.

It is fairly clear from the above analysis that John was the dominant member of the household. The two commonplace brothers and the spinster daughter were hardly likely to oppose him; nor was the fruitful wife who had watched him squander her fortune in unsuccessful business ventures and perhaps roistering and profligacy. The three youngest ones would have been unaware of the deception unless he told them of it. Only Ann Hathaway, the neglected daughter-in-law, would have raised a murmur against him; and she, being dependent on him, could always have been easily brought into line. So that in all probability the decision as to whether to accept or denounce this open-handed stranger, who had come swaggering in the door, with a cock-and-bull story as to his identity on his lips and soft words for the dead Hamnet, would have been John's and John's alone.

In conjunction with the question of his dominance must be taken that of his impoverished situation. This cannot have got better since the 25th September, 1592, when the last entry concerning him appears in the records. Indeed it must have got progressively worse; for the country just then was being afflicted by a series of wet summers (1594, 1595 and 1596) which were causing havoc to the crops. There was a pitiful dearth of corn and, as a result, much hardship and discontent. The Shakespeares at the time of Marlowe's arrival could have been very poor indeed.

On the other side of the balance must be set the value the old man would have placed upon the life of this son of his who, some ten years earlier, had cleared out and left him to contend alone, not only with his own considerable (but perhaps largely ignored) responsibilities, but also with the additional one of providing for three infant grandchildren and their mother. Though in opposition to this factor can be disposed several others: first, the brutality of the times, seen in the hideous public executions which were the order of the day: hangings, drawings and quarterings, and beheadings; seen, too, in the frequency of murders and duels and sudden deaths, all of which evils would have had a carnalizing, coarsening effect upon the public mind; secondly, the fact that life was held so much more cheaply than it is to-day, because its expectation was so short; and, thirdly, the patent unscrupulousness of John Shakespeare himself.

So that, when faced with the choice of accepting or denouncing this stranger, he would have reacted, I am convinced, in only one way. He would not have unduly worried himself over the disappearance of a son, who had been virtually dead for ten years, when, by simple resort to blackmail, so much was to be gained. Here, he would immediately have seen, was the solution of his problem. This naive and naturally generous stranger, he would instantly have realized, could be "bled white". For he knew who he was. He was the brilliant London dramatist whose ever-growing fame had been filtering through to Stratford on the flow of merchant traffic: the dramatist who, contrary to all reason (for William as a boy had never shown any aptitude for such things), he had proudly believed to be his son: the dramatist of whose achievements he had even begun boasting. Here was humiliation indeed! (Further reason for accepting him.) He could now see why his urgent requests for money had met with no response.

Having arrived at his decision, he would have put his singular viewpoint to the family (none of whom, if we can judge from the strange lawsuits that some of them were later to become involved in, was terribly scrupulous either) and, in the whispered conferences that followed, the complaints of Mary Arden would have been over-ruled; the lamentations of Ann Hathaway (she had the most to lose, poor thing!) ignored; the questionings of the spinster daughter politely listened to and dismissed; and the objections of the two dull brothers (if there were any) quelled with a twitch of a scornful white eyebrow. Edmund, Susanna and Judith, one fancies, would have been held in ignorance.

When the family had arrived at agreement, John would again have approached Marlowe. There would have been a few crocodile tears (if he was anything like Falstaff), some spurious blurted protests and a demand for compensation. Where was his son, he would have asked. How had he disappeared? Marlowe's inventive genius would then have awakened. Concealing his own part in the murder, he would simply have explained why it had seemed necessary for him to take the Shake-speare name. From then on, it could have been continual blackmail, blandly and jovially applied: friendly Falstaffian blackmail: and, for all we know, the imposture might never again have been referred to, or the bona fides questioned; for a situation of some cosiness seems to have developed in the Shakespeare ménage in Stratford-upon-Avon. Thereafter Christopher Marlowe became William Shakespeare indeed. For he had now been accepted even by the Shakespeares themselves.

Why did he respond?

He could hardly have done otherwise.

But why did he respond so willingly? For it soon becomes evident that there was really no need for blackmail at all: simply the acceptance, on the part of a destitute family, of generosity that was naturally forthcoming. Here the answer is, of course, that he felt himself to be expiating his "bewailed guilt" and, in order to do so adequately, he was perfectly prepared to take upon his shoulders the support of the entire Shakespeare family.

And what of the people who had known William Shakespeare in Stratford as a boy? Will they not have become aware of the deception and denounced Marlowe? If we place the departure of William Shakespeare in the year 1585, that is to say, shortly after the birth of the twins, all of eleven years would have elapsed before his "return"; and this period can be reduced by several years without materially affecting the argument. So that the people of the town, small though it was, would hardly have been able to compare the newcomer with the boy they knew; for, whereas Shakespeare had left Stratford at the age of twenty-one, -two or -three, that is to say, in the heyday of his lusty youth, he was returning to it lame, "beated and chopp'd with tann'd antiquity" and perhaps already bald. These characteristics of age would have helped the imposture enormously. Again, the new Shakespeare was a relatively prosperous man, and simple folk are less likely to question the bona fides of the well-to-do than the poor. There is also the possibility that they may have seen him only in the distance. Marlowe, at the beginning, may have reduced the length of his visits to Stratford to a minimum and, for safety's sake, avoided all contact with the townsfolk. And the Shakespeares, because of the affluence he was bringing them, may have aided him in this, gathering round him and protecting him from the gaze of the outside world, just as the Burbages were doing in London so that the flow of new plays might not be interrupted.

At any rate, it is clear that he gained confidence in the end and emerged from his seclusion. He bought property in Stratford and settled there; for, not surprisingly, he had fallen in love with the place. It had paved streets, E. K. Chambers tells us, and much garden ground about its houses: it was embosomed in elms, and all around was fair and open land with parks and dingles and a shining river. Later he was to incorporate much that he found in it, in both situation and scene, in his plays, and in the wretchedness that was to afflict him in the following years, was to turn to it, and those he found in it, for comfort and solace.

16

We come now to the use the Shakespeares made of Marlowe.

The first to benefit was young Edmund. He was immediately whisked off to London to become a player, and it has been suggested that it was he who, a year or so afterwards, created the role of Rosalind in *As You Like It,* and that the description of her, when dressed as the youth Ganymede, was written with the boy in mind. The play, with some argument, can be dated as early as 1597, when Edmund would have been seventeen and Rosalind's remark, "I am more than common tall", perhaps necessary. At all events, one cannot help wondering whether Edmund might not have been one of the "worse essays" of Sonnet 110 (written only a few months later), who were to prove Southampton the poet's best of love. He died at the early age of twenty-seven. Two notices in the records of the London churches of the period concern him. The first in the register of St. Gile's, Cripplegate, reads:

> 12 Aug. 1607. Buried. Edward sonne of Edward Shackspeere, Player: base-borne.

The second in the register of St. Saviour's, Southwark, has:

> 31 Dec. 1607. Buried. Edmond Shakespeare (note the Marlovian spelling), a player: in the Church.

After the burial there was "a forenoone knell of the great bell", for which someone who loved Edmund paid twenty shillings.

The next to profit was John himself, and at this point a strange twist comes into the plot; for we find that Marlowe is actually taking pleasure in his newly acquired relations. His own family, from whom, on account of the contrived murder, he was now irrevocably cut off, had for four generations been only tradesmen. The Shakespeares, on the other hand, had the slightest pretensions to gentility. Marlowe, at this stage, (nonsensically) seems to be taking pride in his newly acquired ancestry; for only two months after his arrival in Stratford, that is to say, on the 20th October, 1596, there follows the issue of a grant of arms (obviously expedited by the Earl of Southampton's influence) to John Shakespeare, which in effect upgraded him (and Marlowe) from yeoman to gentleman. The citation was grossly far-fetched:

To all and singuler Noble and Gentilmen . . . William Dethick Garter principall king of Arms sendethe greetinges. Knowe yee that . . . as manie gentillmen by theyr auncyent names of families, kyndredes, & descentes have & enjoye certeyne enseignes & cottes of arms, So it is verie expedient in all Ages that some men for theyr valeant factes, magnanimite, vertu, dignites & desertes maye vse and beare suche tokens of honour and worthinesse, Whereby theyr name & good fame may be the better knowen & divulged and theyr children & posterite (in all vertue to the service of theyr prynce & contrie) encouraged. Wherefore being solicited and by credible report informed, That John Shakespeare of Stratford vppon Avon, in the counte of Warwike, whose parentes & late grandfather for his faithfull & valeant service was advanced & rewarded by the most prudent prince King Henry the seventh of famous memorie, sithence which tyme they have continewed in those partes being of good reputacon & credit, and that the said John hath maryed the daughter & one of the heyres of Robert Arden of Wilmcote in the said Counte esquire, and for the encouragement of his posterite to whom these achivmentes by the auncyent custome of the Lawes of Arms maye descend, I the said Garter king of Arms have assigned, graunted, and by these presentes confirmed: This shield or cote of Arms, etc.

As a prelude to the application for this grant, one

can imagine John Shakespeare pouring the story of his family's prowess into the ear of a Marlowe more than a little impressed; and Marlowe repeating it to Southampton later in London. The key to the situation would seem to be supplied by Sonnet 111, in which the poet refers disparagingly to what he regards as his lowly occupation:

O for my sake do you with Fortune chide,
The guilty goddess of my harmful deeds,
That did not better for my life provide,
Than public means (entertainment) which public manners
    breeds,
Thence comes it that my name receives a brand . . .

On the 4th May, 1597, there occurred a corroboratory event: the acquisition of property in Stratford. New Place in the centre of the town was purchased, together with an acre of land, for £60.

The house was large: far larger than anything the dramatist could have required for his own purposes; for, for a further ten years, he was still to reside mainly in London. It had a frontage of approximately sixty feet and a depth of about seventy, and the property as a whole included "one messuage, two barns, and two gardens with the appurtenances". It was bought presumably to shelter the Shakespeare family, which was large too, and also perhaps as a status symbol; for, from then on, William Shakespeare was known as a gentleman and householder of the town.

The next item in the chronology throws considerable light on the situation in Stratford.

On account of the dearth of corn resultant upon the three wet summers, traders had been using excessive quantities of barley for malt and hoarding supplies of corn in bulk to sell on an Elizabethan black market. The offenders were described as "wycked people in condicions more lyke to wolves or cormerants than to naturall men", and the practice, even as early as the 26th October, 1595, was declared illegal. On the 4th February, 1598, William Shakespeare was listed as being in possession of ten quarters of corn and malt. This circumstance indicates three facts. First, that a certain measure of prosperity had indeed returned to the Shakespeares, in that they were able to hoard; secondly, that it was John who was trading, and not William (who would have been playwriting in London); for this type of shady activity was in character with John, not William, and John, it will be remembered, had "dealt also in barley and timber"; and thirdly, that William, despite John's probable blackmail, was succeeding in keeping his capital in his own name.

Stratfordians will of course have been claiming for some time that the entire situation I have been outlining is only natural: that is to say, that the Shakespeares were now being generously assisted by their dutiful son, because of the improvement in his fortunes. And it is true that these were indeed flourishing. We know from Francis Meres' *Palladis Tamia* (published in 1598) that, at the time Meres was writing (late in 1597 or early in 1598), at least twelve plays (twelve are listed) by "honey-tongued Shakespeare" were already in existence and being shown to appreciative London audiences; and from the beginning of 1594 there had been the Earl of Southampton, who, Nicholas Rowe (writing in 1709) tells us, though with doubtful accuracy, had once given the dramatist as much as one thousand pounds (worth more than ten of to-day's money) "to go through with a purchase he heard he had a mind to". (If there is any truth in the story, the figure is more likely to have been a hundred given towards the end of 1597 for the purchase of New Place.) So that if there had indeed been assistance and the son *was dutiful,* one would expect it to have come sooner: in the year 1595, that is to say, when the Shakespeares' situation, on account of the dearth of corn, was already worse than it had been in 1592 and William was already prosperous. It is therefore of the utmost pertinence to observe that, although a list of people unlawfully hoarding grain had been compiled on the 7th December, 1595, and Abraham Sturley and Richard Quiney were noted, among other townsmen, as being "great corn buyers", the name Shakespeare does not appear. William Shakespeare was not yet a householder, explains Sir Edmund Chambers. But it was John, not William, who was the merchant in Stratford. We can here dispose once and for all with the Oxfordian myth that "Shakespeare was a common fellow who dealt in malt". What, then, had become of the wily John's shrewdness if his already successful son was supplying him with money and he was not investing? The truth is, of course, that the new prosperity of the Shakespeare family dated only from the death of Hamnet.

Perhaps it was Hamnet's death, the Stratfordians may counter, that brought a William Shakespeare, who was callously ignoring his family's situation, to his senses. That is possible; but it hardly improves the Shakespeare image, calling, as it does, for a degree of heartlessness in the "gentle Shakespeare", as Ben Jonson called him, which one would have thought to be quite out of character.

The next entry in the records is a pointer to the fact that the Burbages (and the Shakespeares) were indeed holding Marlowe, as it were, incommunicado.

On the 25th October, 1598, Richard Quiney happened to be in London and, knowing of the apparent wealth of the new Stratford householder, wrote him a letter craving the loan of £30:

Loveinge Contreyman, I am bolde of yowe as of a ffrende, craveinge yowre helpe with xxx^{li} vppon Mr. Bushells & my securytee or Mr. Myttons with me . . . Yowe shall ffrende me muche in helpeinge me out of all the debettes I owe in London, I thancke god . . . My tyme biddes me hasten to an ende & soe I commit thys to yowre care & hope of yowre helpe. I feare I shall not be backe thys night ffrom the Cowrte. Haste. The Lorde be with yowe & with vs all Amen. ffrom the Bell in Carter Lane the 25th October 1598. Yowres in all kyndenes Ryc. Quyney.

The letter was addressed: Haste To my Lovinge

good ffrend & contreymann Mr. Wm. Shackespere deliver thees.

Quiney seems to have been absolutely confident of being lent this money; because on the very day that he wrote to "Shakespeare", he wrote also to Abraham Sturley in Stratford telling him that he was sure of receiving it, for Sturley replied:

Yr letter of the 25 October came to mj handes the laste of the same att night per Grenwaj, which imported . . . that our countriman Mr. Wm. Shak. would procure vs monej, which I will like of as I shall heare when, and wheare, and howe; and I praj let not go that occasion if it may sort to any indifferent condicions . . .

And on the 24th November Daniel Baker wrote to Richard Quiney informing him that:

My aunt Quyny telleth me that you are to receive £20 or £30 in London, and that you will pay some money for me if need be; and in that respect I have lent her some money already to serve her occasions.

So that a part of the money was actually spent in expectation of its being received.

It is therefore strange to have to relate that Quiney's letter to "Shakespeare" does not appear to have been delivered. It was discovered in a bundle of his own correspondence which came to light in the Stratford archives in 1793. Had it reached its destination, it would have been found, not among the sender's papers, but the recipient's.

There are two points in the Quiney correspondence, as it is called, that merit attention. First, Quiney, after addressing William Shakespeare as his "loving country-man" goes on to declare: "I am *bold of you as of a friend.*" Why is he so hesitant about calling Shakespeare a friend when he had known his family even in 1571, the year in which, it will be remembered, John (in the cut and thrust of Stratford affairs) had proceeded against him for a debt of £50? A similar reticence is noticeable in Sturley's letter in which the person they are approaching is referred to in the most formal terms: "Our countryman Mr. William Shakespeare." It is as if they were dealing with some great lord, and I would hazard that neither had actually *conversed* with the person in question.

Next, Quiney, despite his emphasis on haste, which word appears twice in the body of the letter and once in the address, and the fact that the money would have to be collected, *writes* to Shakespeare rather than goes to see him. Yet from his lodgings in Carter Lane in the City to the "Curtain" (or Marlowe's residence) on the outskirts of the City, as anyone familiar with modern London will know, can have been no more than a twenty minute walk: from which we must conclude that "Shakespeare" could not find the time to receive this person from Stratford who addressed him in his letter as his "loving countryman".

What can be the explanation of this curious behaviour, which amounts to a snub, on the part of "Shakespeare"? For he could at least have seen Quiney even if he did not wish to lend him money. There can be only one: the Burbages were still protectively surrounding their valuable playwright in case he came to harm. The sequence of events would have been as follows. Quiney first tried to see "Shakespeare" at the "Curtain" and failed. He was therefore forced to write. Then, mindful of his rebuff and anxious to be sure that his vitally important letter would indeed reach the addressee, he instructed his messenger to deliver the letter to "Shakespeare" and "Shakespeare" only. The wording of the address admits of no other interpretation: "Haste To my Lovinge good ffrend & contreymann Mr. Wm. Shackespere deliver thees." The messenger was not received either and brought the letter back.

The situation is hardly complicated by the fact that Judith Shakespeare, eighteen years later, was to marry Thomas Quiney, Richard's son; although continuing bad blood between "Shakespeare" and the Quineys could have been an additional reason for Judith's doing so badly under the terms of the Will.

Joan Shakespeare was the next to benefit from the new prosperity. Somewhere about this time (1599?)

she married William Hart, a hatter, who, says Sir Edmund Chambers, was probably a good deal older than she. There is no entry in the parish register to record the event, but a son was baptised on the 28th August, 1600. Joan had therefore, despite her thirty years of age, again become eligible on account of the family's improved situation, and, since the old Shakespeare residence in Henley Street appears to have been now vacant, she will probably have been given the use of it. When the dramatist died, he left her the tenancy of it for life, it will be remembered, in his Will.

It is Ann Hathaway who figures next in the chronology—and characteristically. On the 25th March, 1601, her name appeared in the Will of Thomas Whittington of Shottery, husbandman: "Item I geve and bequeth unto the poore people of Stratford 40s. that is in the hand of Anne Shaxspere, wyf unto Mr. Wyllyam Shaxspere, and is due debt unto me, beyng payd to myne Executor by the sayd Wyllyam Shaxspere or his assigns, accordyng to the true meanyng of this my wyll . . ."

What lay behind this strange incident in the life of Ann Hathaway one cannot even guess: one can only comment that, despite the affluence in which the Shakespeares were now apparently living, she still found it necessary to incur a debt which she could not find the money to repay. This perhaps is a further indication of the relationship that existed between "Shakespeare" and his "wife". (Can *The Taming of the Shrew* have been revised about this time in the light of bitter personal experience?) It is relevant to note that Ann Hathaway never seems to have been with her "husband" in London.

On the 8th September, 1601, John Shakespeare, the records tell us, was buried in Stratford. Strangely enough, Marlowe, who, from the extraordinary intensity of his observation of the man (if he were indeed Falstaff) would appear to have developed a perverted affection for him, of the sort felt by a saint for his hair shirt, had prepared for this event by the insertion of an In Memoriam notice in the recently completed and published

Henry V, to the chronology of which the death belonged. In short he had killed the old fellow off in anticipation.

The problem now, apparently, was what was to be done with the two bumpkin brothers, Gilbert and Richard, who would have been incapable, there is no doubt, of carrying on the business with which John had been amusing himself during the last five years of his life. It is amazing how willingly Marlowe bends his back to the burden of the Shakespeares' welfare. On the 1st May, 1602, he purchased for £320, from William and John Coombe, 107 acres of arable land and 20 acres of pasture in the country surrounding Stratford, and it was Gilbert who, in the words of Sir Edmund Chambers, took delivery of this conveyance. The two bachelor brothers were then, presumably, at enormous expense, put out to grass. And on the 28th September of the same year he purchased a cottage, with a quarter of an acre of land, which was possibly for them to live in. Marlowe was expiating his "bewailed guilt" with a vengeance.

Let us now return to the early part of 1597:

In London the affair with Southampton was definitely going awry. Three years had passed since its inception.

> To me fair friend you never can be old,
> For as you were when first your eye I eyed,
> Such seems your beauty still: three Winters' cold,
> Have from the forests shook three Summers' pride,
> Three beauteous springs to yellow Autumn turn'd,
> In process of the seasons have I seen,
> Three April perfumes in three hot Junes burn'd,
> Since first I saw you fresh which yet are green.
>
> (Sonnet 104)

The poet's love is as strong as ever.

> When in the Chronicle of wasted time,
> I see descriptions of the fairest wights,
> And beauty making beautiful old rhyme,
> In praise of Ladies dead, and lovely Knights,
> Then in the blazon of sweet beauty's best,
> Of hand, of foot, of lip, of eye, of brow,
> I see their antique pen would have express'd,

Even such a beauty as you master now.
So all their praises are but prophecies
Of this our time, all you prefiguring,
And for they look'd but with divining eyes,
They had not skill enough your worth to sing:
    For we which now behold these present days,
    Have eyes to wonder, but lack tongues to praise.
                                                (Sonnet 106)

But all is not well. In Sonnet 110 he confesses having
turned to other loves in a despairing attempt to quench
this one, but all to no purpose. He swears that there
will now be eternal fidelity.

Alas 't is true, I have gone here and there,
And made myself a motley to the view,
Gor'd mine own thoughts, sold cheap what is most dear,
Made old offences of affections new.
Most true it is, that I have look'd on truth
Askance and strangely: but by all above,
These blenches gave my heart another youth,
And worse essays prov'd thee my best of love.
Now all is done, have what shall have no end,
Mine appetite I never more will grind
On newer proof, to try an older friend,
A God in love, to whom I am confin'd.
    Then give me welcome, next my heaven the best,
    Even to thy pure and most, most loving breast.

You are my All the world, and I must strive
To know my shames and praises from your tongue.
                                                (Sonnet 112)

In Sonnet 119 the poet's contrition is developed.

How have mine eyes out of their spheres been fitted
In the distraction of this madding fever!
O benefit of ill, now I find true
That better is, by evil still made better.
And ruin'd love when it is built anew
Grows fairer than at first, more strong, far greater.
    So I return rebuk'd to my content,
    And gain by ills thrice more than I have spent.

And in Sonnet 120 what had been a major quarrel
seems now to be over.

That you were once unkind befriends me now,
And for that sorrow, which I then did feel,
Needs must I under my transgression bow,
Unless my nerves were brass or hammered steel.
For if you were by my unkindness shaken,
As I by yours, y' have pass'd a hell of Time,
And I a tyrant have no leisure taken
To weigh how once I suffered in your crime.
O that our night of woe might have remember'd
My deepest sense, how hard true sorrow hits,
And soon to you, as you to me then tender'd
The humble salve, which wounded bosoms fits!
　　But that your trespass now becomes a fee,
　　Mine ransoms yours, and yours must ransom me.

Perhaps, during this period, Southampton had been restless and irritable. For adventure was again in the air. On the 2nd March, 1597, Rowland Whyte wrote to Sir Robert Sidney: "Lord Southampton hath leave to travel for a year;" and on the 9th April: "My Lord Thomas Howard, by the end of the week, goes to sea, and Sir Walter Raleigh with him. My Lord Southampton by 200 meanes hath gotten leave to goe with them, and is appointed to go in the Garland."

There was, however, to be a delay of several months before the departure. It was not until the 11th June that John Chamberlain wrote the letter from which I have already quoted: "The Erle of Essex is general both by sea and land; the Lord Thomas Howard Vice Admiral, Sir Walter Raleigh rear-vice Admirall, who is newly restored to the executing his place in Court of Captain of the Garde; the Earl of Southampton the Lord Mountjoy and the Lord Rich, go as adventerers . . . It is said that the Earl of Essex takes his leave at Court on Sunday next the 12th of this present, and hopes to be gone in ten days after."

So that it is perhaps by Sonnet 122 that news has come of the final departure. There is a swearing never to forget of such urgency that it might have sprung from a presentiment that the affair was over; as it indeed was.

Thy gift, thy tables, are within my brain
Full character'd with lasting memory,
Which shall above that idle rank remain
Beyond all date even to eternity.
Or at the least, so long as brain and heart
Have faculty by nature to subsist,
Till each to ras'd oblivion yield his part
Of thee, thy record never can be miss'd:
That poor retention could not so much hold,
Nor need I tallies thy dear love to score,
Therefore to give them from me was I bold,
To trust those tables that receive thee more.
    To keep an adjunct to remember thee,
    Were to import forgetfulness in me.

After Sonnet 126 the dedication was written, and
the adventurer set forth.

17

What happened is recorded in all the history books. Early in the year it had become known that the Spaniards were assembling a new Armada in the ports of Corunna and Ferrol; and to destroy this before it could put to sea Elizabeth had determined to send a fleet of ships under the command of the Earl of Essex, Lord Thomas Howard and Sir Walter Raleigh. But the expedition was destined to be ill-starred from the beginning. The fleet set sail from Plymouth in the middle of August and almost immediately ran into a heavy gale with which it battled for ten days. Many of the ships foundered, and the remainder were finally forced back into harbour.

Some weeks later, with the remnants of his once powerful fleet Essex set forth again; but, being now too weak to attack the Spanish ports, directed his course to the Azores with the intention of intercepting the Spanish plate fleet on its return from the Indies. He landed at Villa Franca, sacked the town and reboarded his ship with rich plunder. Seven galleons, laden with treasure, now came over the horizon; but, getting wind of the English, changed course and fled, heading for Terceira. Three strayed from the line and were taken, one by the Earl of Southampton in the Garland. The remainder, to the frustration of the pursuers, reached Terceira unharmed and took refuge in the harbour there. The Earl of Southampton now evolved a daring scheme. With Sir Francis Vere he attempted, in a small boat, to enter the harbour and cut the cables of the nearest ships so that they might be blown out to sea again. He was not successful, but for his deed of valour Essex knighted him.

On the return of the fleet at the end of October, the Queen openly showed her displeasure at the failure of the mission. Her manner towards Essex was frosty, and she did not compliment Southampton on his act of bravery. He turned for consolation to Elizabeth Vernon, and entered into a secret alliance with her.

He was now, however, more restless than ever; and early in 1598 Rowland Whyte was telling Sir Robert Sidney: "I hear my Lord of Southampton goes with Mr. Secretary to France and so onwards on his travels, which course of his doth exceedingly grieve his Mistress that passes her tyme in weeping and lamenting." And on the 2nd February was adding: "Yt is secretly said that my Lord of Southampton shall be married to his faire Mistress, but has asked for a little respite." From which it would appear that the young earl was pursuing the same delaying policy with Elizabeth Vernon that he had already pursued with Elizabeth de Vere.

On the 6th February it was officially recorded that Southampton "had final permission and Licence to travel beyond the seas, and remain two years, with ten servants, six horses and £200 in money." And on the 12th Rowland Whyte rather heartrendingly concludes the tale: "My Lord of Southampton is gone and hath left behind him a very disconsolate gentlewoman that hath almost wept out her fairest eyes." As indeed she had reason to do, for it was only a short time afterwards that she was forced to write to the traveller and tell him that she was expecting his baby. Shame-faced, he had accordingly to return and marry her as soon as possible; so that the state of matrimony he had avoided for so long he was at last forced into by fate.

The Queen raged, for he had married without her consent and in secret. Autocratic to the point of insanity, she believed that she exercised a sort of *droit de seigneur* over the affections of the nobles of her Court and flew into jealous rages if she saw them complimenting any of her women. Southampton was flung into the Fleet Prison to reflect, for a few weeks, upon the indiscretion of his act of sacrilege.

In 1599 he accompanied Essex to Ireland; and then, for his part in the ill-fated attempt to kidnap the Queen, for which Essex was executed, was committed to the Tower where he was to languish for the remainder of the reign.

When he emerged in 1603, upon the accession of James I, he was to become more and more deeply involved in the life and affairs of the new Sovereign.

18

Having examined the plays and Sonnets and found evidence of homosexuality in their author, I turn now to the author's patron to see whether a similar characteristic can be argued for him; and it seems to me that it unquestionably can. Even Dr. Rowse, who staunchly upholds the normality of the attachment goes so far as to admit that the young man himself was at least "ambidextrous". "When Southampton was General of the Horse," he tells us, "Piers Edmonds was made his Corporal General: 'He ate and drank at his table and lay in his tent. The Earl of Southampton would cull and hug him in his arms and play wantonly with him'." (Salisbury MSS.) This had been in Ireland. "Evidently," remarks Dr. Rowse astringently, "there were consolations for service in the bogs."

He was feminine in appearance and wore his hair, even for those days, unusually long. It fell, if one can judge from the portrait of him "in a suit of white", inches below his nipples.

And his behaviour proclaims it. To begin with, there was his passion for the theatre. "My Lord Southampton and Lord Rutland come not to court . . . they pass the time in London merely in going to plays every day." They were, in short, "fans". And people often become insatiable devotees of the theatre, ballet, etc., because of some sexual urge: normal men dance attendance upon actresses, homosexuals upon their own kind. Now, in the theatre of that time women's roles were played by boys, one of whom is singled out for attention in *Hamlet*:

> What, my young lady and mistress! By'r lady, your ladyship is nearer to heaven than when I saw you last, by the altitude of a chopine. Pray God, your voice, like a piece of uncurrent gold, be not cracked within the ring.

173

It is pertinent, therefore, to speculate upon whether Southampton's interest may not also have originated there, and whether the stolen mistress of Sonnets 40-42 may not have been one of these player boys, or even a player. Philip Stubbes's opinion of the morals of these player boys, expressed in his *Anatomy of Abuses* (1583), is well known. "Then, these goodly pageants being done every mate sorts to his mate, every one brings another homeward of their way verye freendly, and in their secret conclaves (covertly) they play the *Sodomits,* or worse." Well known, too, is the even more acrimonious opinion of the Puritan William Prynne, who, in his *Histrio-mastix, The Players Scourge or Actors Tragedie* written some fifty years later, takes up this passage of Stubbes and embroiders it: "Yea witnes . . . M. Stubs, his *Anatomy of Abuses* p.205 where he affirmes, that Players and Play-haunters in their secret conclaves play the Sodomites: together with some moderne examples of such, who have been desperately enamoured with Players Boyes thus clad in woman's apparell, so farre as to solicite them by words, by Letters, even actually to abuse them. This I have heard credibly reported of a Scholler of Bayliol Colledge and I doubt not but it may be verified of divers others." All of which, though probably exaggerated, leads me to speculate further. It is common knowledge that homosexuals of a certain type constantly refer to one another as "she" and "her" and have perhaps done so since they first began to form communities; and this may have been the case when the poet wrote such lines as:

And yet it may be said I loved her dearly.

One can cite next the fact that he was always fobbing off marriage and, in the end, submitted to its tyranny only because he was forced to do so by circumstance. The young woman he married was the niece of his idol Essex, and on occasions he treated her very unkindly indeed, leaving her unpredictably because some other interest was claiming his attention.

Then there is the wayward, mercurial quality, so characteristic of homosexuals, that he shows in all his dealings. He is masculine one moment, feminine the next and, despite the sweetness claimed for him by the author of the Sonnets (though it soon becomes evident that this is only a façade), often at odds with himself and exasperatingly petulant and quarrelsome. Consider, for example, the amusing incident with Ambrose Willoughby in which he had his hair pulled, and the Queen's reaction to it. Rowland Whyte is writing: "The quarrel of my Lord Southampton to Ambrose Willoughby was this. That he, with Sir Walter Rawley and Mr. Parker, being at Primero in the Presence Chamber, the Queen was gone to bed, and he being there as squire of the body required them to give over. Soone after he spake to them againe, that if they would not leave, he would call on the guard to put down the bord, which Sir Walter Rawley seeing, put up his money and went his wayes. But my Lord of Southampton took exceptions at him, and told him he would remember it, and soe, fynding him between the Tennis Court Wall and the garden, struck him, and Willoughby pulled off some of his locks. The Queen gave Willoughby thanks for what he did in the presence and told him, he had done better if he had sent him to the porter's lodge to see who durst have fetched him out."

Moreover, his acts of valour seem often to have been tinged with a sort of bravado. First there is the long pursued quarrel with Lord Grey de Wilton which Mrs. Stopes tells us about. In Ireland the Earl of Southampton, as General of the Horse, had been Grey's military superior. "At an action in the south Grey had charged on his own initiative; and, though he had been successful, the Earl of Southampton, as a lesson in discipline to an undisciplined army, had sent Grey to the care of the Marshal for one night: and Lord Grey never forgave what he thought an unjustifiable indignity, reproached Southampton openly, complained of him privately, and finally sent him a challenge." This led to the Queen's "thunderous" demand that Essex should "discharge his chief officer at once". And to separate the adversaries Grey seems to have been sent back to

England where he was "named to be captain of a company of horse." A year passed, and the quarrel persisted, but the two young men were always prevented from fighting their duel by distance. Eventually the Earl of Southampton left Ireland and went to Flanders where Grey was. The Privy Council now "directed special letters to both the adversaries (ordering them) to stop the combat." But the receipt of this did not prevent Southampton, who was at Middlesburgh in the Island of Walcheren, from writing to Grey, who was in Brabant, as follows: "I will tomorrow in the morning ride an English mile out of the ports, accompanied by none but this bearer, and a lacquey to hold my horses who shall bear no weapons. I will wear this sword which I now send you, and a dagger, which you shall see before my going, when you shall know the way I intend to go, where I will attend you 2 hours. If in the meantime I meet you, you may do your pleasure, for I will give no ground, but defend myself with the arms I carry against whatsoever you shall offer."

What came of this is not known. Mrs. Stopes suggests: "It is probable that he (Lord Grey) did meet and attack his opponent, and that he was worsted in the first encounter." It is also probable, since nobody appears to have been hurt, that Southampton's nerve failed him, and he withdrew.

Then there is the peculiar nature of the exploit at Terceira, which reminds one, in its showiness, of something done by a modern mini-submariner; but, though it was only a question of cutting the ships' cables, he was unsuccessful. One cannot help wondering, perhaps uncharitably, whether his nerve may not have failed him here too. Elizabeth, at any rate, seems to have been suspicious; for his extravagantly quick knighting by Essex caused her extreme displeasure and, on his return, she refused to acknowledge his bravery. Or was it that she was jealous of Southampton so far as Essex was concerned? For next came the excursion to Ireland, where the young man, again extravagantly quickly, was made Lord General of the Horse—this time to Elizabeth's fury. And then when Essex, after complete failure, came back so impulsively and rashly to put his case before his Sovereign, she received him first delightedly, then turned her back on him for ever, giving as one of her reasons his appointment of Southampton as Lord General of the Horse. It must surely have been apparent to her that the young man was deeply in love with his idol. He was always under his influence and was to follow him blindly into the last tragic phase of the drama, which was the foolhardy attempt to kidnap Elizabeth.

After the death of Essex, his history becomes undistinguished. Despite his association with James, who loaded him with honours and property, heroically he fades away; though this is not surprising. The hardship and illnesses of his two years of captivity in the Tower had told on him; and he had experienced the horror of his god's near-by execution, which, from his window, he may even have witnessed. He would, at any rate, have heard the hideous thud of the axe as it fell three times, we are told, before the beloved head was lopped off.

So that one is forced to ask whether this man was likely to have resisted the persuasive advances of the poet and denied him the realization of his desires.

Why did so great a personage as Southampton respond to this playwright? He was of lowly estate. But then, so was Piers Edmonds. He was much older than Southampton, being, at the outset of the affair, thirty and, at its apex, thirty-four; but so, too, was Piers Edmonds who, when in Ireland, had spent twenty years in the Queen's service; and so, too, was Essex. Southampton apparently preferred older men and, far from resisting the playwright, might even have sought him. He was bald, beated and chopp'd with tann'd antiquity, and probably lame. He was in looks, therefore, far from the heroic Essex; though perhaps not so far from Piers Edmonds whose old hurts, in the year 1600, when he wrote of them, were "bursting out afresh". It does not matter. Several reasons can be brought forward to

explain why Southampton would have been attracted
to this homely man. What young homosexual, who loved
the arts, could have failed to respond to the persistent
importunity indicated in the Sonnets? Would have been
unmoved by the poet's conversation which must have
been more marvellous even than Wilde's? He had travelled, of that we can be certain, and if, in their "walks"
together, he described the places he had visited in the
language he has left behind for us, and recounted his
adventures, then the young Earl, who was himself desir-
ous of adventure and travel, must have been as enthral-
led by it as the boy Raleigh was by the seafaring tales
he heard at Hayes Barton. No wonder Southampton was
taking Italian lessons with his friend Rutland and longing to visit Italy!

Then there was the flood of poetry with which the
poet was dazzling him. Dr. Rowse places the writing
of *A Midsummer Night's Dream* in 1593-4. It is generally agreed, he says, that it was written for a wedding
ceremony, and concludes that the wedding in question
was the one already mentioned of the Countess of
Southampton to Sir Thomas Heneage on the 2nd May,
1594. "We have no reason to doubt that *A Midsummer
Night's Dream* was produced to grace the occasion." I
am in full agreement. *A Midsummer Night's Dream*
would have been the very thing with which to impress
the young man with whom its author was falling so
terribly in love. And was there not a secret message
contained in it? A little speech of fourteen lines, in
other words, sonnet-length, spoken by Puck and destined
specially for the heart of the boy who would be watch-
ing in the audience? Whom else should Oberon and
Titania be quarrelling over!

> The king doth keep his revels here to-night:
> Take heed the queen come not within his sight;
> For Oberon is passing fell and wrath,
> Because that she as her attendant hath
> A lovely boy, stolen from an Indian king;
> She never had so sweet a changeling:
> And jealous Oberon would have the child

Knight of his train, to trace the forests wild;
But she perforce withholds the loved boy,
Crowns him with flowers, and makes him all her joy:
And now they never meet in grove or green,
By fountain clear, or spangled starlight sheen,
But they do square, that all their elves for fear
Creep into acorn cups and hide them there.

From then on, for a number of years, the plays were to incorporate Southampton, almost without exception. The author, as I shall show in a later book, was to become quite obsessed by this brilliant youth, portraying him in guise after guise monotonously.

People in love are capable of many foolish things. It is the distraught Venus who cries:

How love makes young men thrall, and old men dote;
How love is wise in folly, foolish-witty!

These words were written when the Earl of Southampton's fascination was just beginning to bite in.

19

Now it is fitting to believe that, after the departure of the beautiful youth, melancholy of a severe nature had fallen upon the poet. A black night of the soul had set in, which was to endure for some time; and the twenty-eight Sonnets usually referred to as those to the Dark Lady, or, as the poet himself calls her, the Black Woman (though some of them are addressed to the youth) I believe to be an expression of this. They have been named the "Back Slums" of the Sonnets and likened to a disordered appendix. Mr. Walter Thomson, whom we have seen to be a sensitive critic, says of them: "The 'Dark Woman' Sonnets drag their unwholesome length along like some wounded and weary reptile, leaving an impression of misery and defeat. Whatever nastiness there is in the Sonnets is concentrated in them. They are often the ravings of a thwarted soul tortured by jealousy."

Myself I believe them to be an addition, penned after the dedication to the first one hundred and twenty-six poems had been devised; but still addressed to the "onlie begetter"—as a reaction when it had become clear to the poet that his days of requited love were over.

The clue to their meaning, I think, is to be found in *Hamlet*.

QUEEN: Good Hamlet, cast thy nighted colour off,
    And let thine eye look like a friend on Denmark.
    Do not for ever with thy veiled lids
    Seek for thy noble father in the dust:
    Thou know'st 'tis common; all that lives must die,
    Passing through nature to eternity.

HAMLET: Ay, madam, it is common.

QUEEN: If it be,
    Why seems it so particular with thee?

HAMLET: Seems, madam! nay, it is; I know not 'seems'.
'Tis not alone my inky cloak, good mother,
Nor customary suits of solemn black,
Nor windy suspiration of forced breath,
No, nor the fruitful river in the eye,
Nor the dejected haviour of the visage,
Together with all forms, moods, shapes of grief,
That can denote me truly: these indeed seem,
For they are actions that a man might play:
But I have that within which passeth show;
These but the trappings and the suits of woe.

Compare this with the first of the Black Lady Sonnets.

In the old age black was not counted fair,
Or if it were it bore not beauty's name:
But now is black Beauty's successive heir,
And Beauty slander'd with a bastard shame,
For since each hand hath put on Nature's power,
Fairing the foul with Art's false borrow'd face,
Sweet Beauty hath no name, no holy bower,
But is profan'd, if not lives in disgrace.
Therefore my Mistress' eyes are raven black,
Her eyes so suited, and they mourners seem,
At such who not born fair no beauty lack,
Sland'ring Creation with a false esteem,
    Yet so they mourn becoming of their woe,
    That every tongue says Beauty should look so.

The poet, then, is mourning the death of his love and has selected the Black Woman (negress) to be the symbol of that mourning; swinging, in his mood of black despair, from life to death; seeking consolation in the opposite of everything he has so far known; swinging from male to female, white to black, fair to dark, beauty to ugliness, attractiveness to repellent horror.

My Mistress' eyes are nothing like the Sun,
Coral is far more red, than her lips' red,
If snow be white, why then her breasts are dun:
If hairs be wires, black wires grow on her head:
I have seen roses damask'd, red and white,
But no such roses see I in her cheeks,
And in some perfumes is there more delight,
Than in the breath that from my Mistress reeks.

I love to hear her speak, yet well I know,
That Music hath a far more pleasing sound:
I grant I never saw a goddess go,
My Mistress when she walks treads on the ground.
  And yet by heaven I think my love as rare,
  As any she beli'd with false compare.

(Sonnet 130)

From the first onslaught of this mood of terrible despair Marlowe eventually emerged to write *Hamlet*, the greatest of his tragedies, in which Southampton's hopeless indecision is portrayed and his own guilt for which he perhaps superstitiously believed his unhappiness was a punishment.

Consider the King's speech :

O, my offence is rank, it smells to heaven;
It hath the primeval curse upon't,
A brother's murder. Pray can I not,
Though inclination be as sharp as will:
My stronger guilt defeats my strong intent . . .
My fault is past. But O, what form of prayer
Can serve my turn? 'Forgive me my foul murder?'
That cannot be, since I am still possessed
Of those effects for which I did the murder . . .
May one be pardoned and retain the offence? . . .
O wretched state! O bosom black as death!
O limed soul, that struggling to be free
Art more engaged! Help, angels! Make assay!
Bow, stubborn knees, and, heart with strings of steel,
Be soft as sinews of the new born babe!
All may be well.

But the king cannot pray :

My words fly up, my thoughts remain below:
Words without thoughts never to heaven go.

There is another point of similarity already mentioned. The assassins while waiting for Shakespeare to die had walked in the garden of Eleanor Bull's house at Deptford; and it was in an orchard that King Hamlet was lying asleep when the poisonous juice was poured into his ears.

And in writing this play which was perhaps undertaken to expiate his crime, Marlowe at the same time perpetrated a peculiar act of vengeance upon Kyd who had betrayed him and made the murder necessary. He took Kyd's unpublished play, written about the year 1587 and to-day known as the ur-Hamlet, which he must have read when staying with Kyd (in 1591) and seen often performed on the stage, and converted it to his own purposes. So that there was achieved a blend of the two playwright's talents. "For Kyd was much stronger dramatically than Marlowe," writes Dr. Boas in his introduction to *The Works of Thomas Kyd*. "And that Marlowe had improved during his stay with Kyd is evident from *Faustus*. But he was vastly superior poetically, and in creating character; so that now what had been merely a well-wrought stage play and nothing more" and perhaps even "a flamboyant presentment of the Prince of Denmark's irresolution" was transformed by the master dramatist "into the subtle study of diseased emotion and palsied will with which the world is familiar". The ur-Hamlet then disappeared, and it is only by means of the most advanced form of scholarship that it has been possible to restore to Kyd the credit of having been the first to put Hamlet on the stage.

We are now in a position to attempt an elucidation of some of the problems posed by *Love's Labour's Lost*, several of which disappear when one accepts Marlowe's authorship of the plays.

According to Frances M. Yates, *Love's Labour's Lost* was an attack on Raleigh's School of Night: "a move in a controversy which was then afoot between two rival groups and which turned, in part, upon the question of what is the best way of qualifying as a poet, of achieving full development as a man and—to take it at its highest level—of seeking the Light of Truth. One side maintained that all these things were best and most quickly learned in the school of life and of experience of the world. The other side believed that they could only be achieved at the cost of the most rigid intellectual discipline and study, necessitating a certain degree of retirement from the world." (*A Study of Love's Labour's Lost.*)

Miss Bradbrook suggests that the teachings of the School of Night were Hermetic. They were also Orphic. The goddess Night held a powerful place in the Orphic Mysteries. "Oceanus is the father of all the gods; Zeus is referred to as younger and more potent; Night even Zeus fears to offend." (Damascius.) And a key to an understanding of the significance of the School, it has been thought, may lie in Chapman's poem *The Shadow of Night,* from which the following extract has already been quoted:

> Come consecrate with me to sacred Night
> Your whole endeavours, and detest the light.
> Sweet Peace's richest crown is made of stars,
> Most certain guides of honoured mariners,
> No pen can anything eternal write
> That is not steeped in humour of the Night.

Ganymede figures in this poem as the symbol of the beauty of the soul.

Both Raleigh and Chapman, it seems obvious, were mystics. Raleigh was grappling with the problem of the nature of the soul, upon which he discoursed learnedly. Chapman, less talented than Marlowe, sought inspiration (it is clear from the above) in the School's activities for his writing. Harriott's interest was experimental. But all, I think it can be safely concluded, no matter how high the mental plane upon which they individually approached the School, were dabbling in alchemy and the occult. Marlowe, for one, shortly before the Deptford murder, wanted nothing better than physical wealth: wealth that could be obtained by transmutation. The Hermetic word 'gold', or its adjective, occurs in the first two sestiads of *Hero and Leander* no fewer than fifteen times (indicating surely an obsession) base bullion once, silver and diamonds (both Hermetic words) each four times, pearls five times; and the fact that the whole poem was Hermetic in conception is perhaps indicated by the frequent use of words to do with flame and fire, which also occur fifteen times. But then, if Dr. Rowse's theory is valid, and Leander is indeed a portrait of the young Earl of Southampton, whom Marlowe had just seen and by whom he had become inspired, it would certainly be wealth that, in his existing state of development, he wanted—and love —and life in which to enjoy them. Hence the decision, in the midst of his unbounded fear, to contrive his salvation by means of murder.

Love's Labour Lost, therefore, did not form part of a controversy. Marlowe had been a member of the School of Night; so that the play, viewed as his work, is first a reminiscence, then a satirical comedy. I believe the King of the play to have been Raleigh for the following reasons. Henry of Navarre had, in July 1593, re-renounced Protestantism and embraced the Catholic religion so that he might the more easily succeed as King of France. English troops supporting him were withdrawn in the November of that year. Navarre is the ostensible King; Raleigh, in whose conduct the author discerned a parallel, the target. He had betrayed the School of Night in 1592 by disregarding his vows of abstinence so that he might court, and finally marry, one of the Queen's Maids of Honour, Elizabeth Throgmorton. This courtship and marriage had led to his downfall and to the consequent removal of his protection from the other members of his possibly atheistic School; which removal of protection had led, in its turn, to Marlowe's downfall: sufficient reason surely for the writing of a satirical play after the volte-face of Henry of Navarre had become known in the latter part of 1593.

I believe the play to have been revised in the spirit of disillusionment, shortly after the Southampton affair had come to its unfortunate climax in 1597-8, when the attributes of the Dark Lady, symbol of mourning and the author's betrayal, were superimposed upon the existing, but perhaps renamed, Rosaline.

KING: By heaven, thy love is black as ebony.

BEROWNE: Is ebony like her? O wood divine!
A wife of such wood were felicity.
O, who can give an oath? Where is a book?
That I may swear beauty doth beauty lack,
If that she learn not of her eye to look:
No face is fair that is not full so black.

KING: O paradox! Black is the badge of hell,
The hue of dungeons and the school of night;
And beauty's crest becomes the heavens well.

BEROWNE: Devils soonest tempt, resembling spirits of light.
O, if in black my lady's brows be decked,
It mourns that painting and usurping hair
Should ravish doters with a false aspect;
And therefore is she born to make black fair.
Her favour turns the fashion of the days,
For native blood is counted painting now;
And therefore red, that would avoid dispraise,
Paints itself black, to imitate her brow.

DUMAIN: To look like her are chimney-sweepers black.

LONGAVILLE: And since her time are colliers counted bright.

KING: And Ethiopes of their sweet complexion crack.

DUMAIN: Dark needs no candles now, for dark is light.

Here the peculiar reversal that the dramatist's aesthetic sense underwent on the youth's departure is again underlined.

20

As the years passed, Marlowe found himself drawn more and more, perhaps on account of his affection for Susanna, who was not to marry until the 5th June, 1607, to Stratford; so that it is not surprising to learn that, in 1612 or thereabouts, when he retired "big with honours" and, as I shall show in a moment, stricken with disease, he did not go to his native Canterbury, where they did not care for him, because "whenever he visited the place he was drunk", and from which, in any case, he had been inexorably cut off since the first days of his imposture, but to the town of his adoption where he had built his home. There he was to write no more until a few days before his death on the 23rd April, 1616. Then he took up his pen and devised his epitaph. One can imagine his resentment of the fact that the fame deriving from his immense achievement (though that fame was not nearly so great then as it was to become) should all have accrued to the provincial Shakespeare about whom Henry James was to write so disparagingly: "I am haunted by the conviction that the divine William is the biggest and most successful fraud ever practised on a patient world." How then, to reveal his identity while concealing the crime of Thomas Walsingham, committed on his behalf, and the connivance of Southampton, both of whom were still living?

It is now time to consider the decipherment of the epitaph.

21

I understood from the beginning that the solution could not be too involved. The error that cryptologists have always made in dealing with suspected Shakespearean ciphers has been in supposing that the author's purpose was to conceal his identity rather than to reveal it. They have therefore treated the underlying message as if it were one sent out by a ship in wartime in a code which, for the sake of national security, must above all not be cracked. His purpose, however, was to reveal to later generations an identity which, at the time of writing, he could not openly proclaim; because persons who had been concerned with him in a criminal deception, or who knew about it and had remained silent, were still living and he owed them a debt of loyalty and gratitude. The message had to be concealed for a time and then, when he and his friends had passed beyond reach of the law, revealed; or at any rate written in such a manner that any hint of incrimination could be denied. Attempts at decipherment have therefore been, I saw in a book which covered them, of an extreme, and even laughable, complexity; and have achieved nothing. Having understood the nature of this mistake, I set out to look for a cipher that was simple. There had to be, I felt sure, certain clue words on the surface, which would stimulate curiosity and provide a thread, as it were, that could be pulled; and there were indeed so many of them—four in all—and the solution was so easy that I was amazed no one had arrived at it before me. The cipher employed was purely anagrammatical. Any crossword-puzzle addict could have mastered it, had he applied himself to the task with sufficient concentration; and since anagrams are again involved, let us go back for a moment to Camden for further light on the technique of anagrammatizing. His remarks, dating as

they do from the year 1605, are of the utmost importance to my decipherment; for if the *Remaines* was published in 1605 by so important a writer as Camden, then
it is extremely likely that the author of the Shakespeare
plays will have read it. "The precise in this practice
strictly observing all the parts of the definition, are only
bold with H either in omitting or retaining it, for that it
cannot challenge the right of a letter. But the Licentiats
somewhat licentiously, lest they should prejudice poetical liberty, will pardon themselves for doubling or
rejecting a letter, if the sence fall aptly, and think it no
injury to use E for AE; V for W; S for Z, and C for K,
and contrariwise." To which I would add that, in the
case of the deviser of the epitaph, it seems that P could
also be substituted for its fellow labial B.

Remembering these rules (or should I rather call them
licences?), let us now turn to the verse and examine it
carefully. On the tomb it looks like this:

GOOD FREND FOR IESVS SAKE FORBEARE

TO DIGG ÞE DVST ENCLOASED HEARE

BLESE BE Ý MAN Ý SPARES ÞES STONES

AND CVRST BE HE Ý MOVES MY BONES

The first thing one notices is that there are several
ligatured, or fused, letters in the script: TH in the THE
of the second line and HE in HEARE; TE in BLESTE
in the third line and TH in THES. The only point I
wish to make concerning them is that in the underlying message each letter of the fused pair, in each case,
is to be taken separately: each in the decipherment is
to play its separate part.

Then, in the third and fourth lines, there are a series
of Y's all of which have a minute E or T superimposed.
These, in the rhyme, represent the double consonant TH,
which, with the superimposed E or T, becomes respectively THE or THAT. But since the TH of THE in the
second line and of THES in the third line is ligatured,

that is to say, not represented by the old-style Y, I feel that I am justified in considering the Y, used as TH in the ciphered version, to be in all cases in the underlying message the letter Y itself. The minute superimposed letters will therefore, in the decipherment, be discarded. It may be objected that I am already adding to the complexity of the puzzle; but in an anagram of such length certain letters were bound to prove intractable. For the rhyme is in reality an immense anagram, not, as would have been more usual, of a name with a play on that name; but of an entire message, the words of which were changed only when the sense demanded it.

Let us now turn to a consideration of the verse line by line; for the decipherment, it soon becomes clear, has to be undertaken in a series of stages, most of which involve separate anagrams within the line itself. It is only at the end, when we have to carry out a sort of mopping up operation, that there is an interchange of letters between lines.

The first thing one observes is the key-word SAKE, one of the threads to be pulled. Remove the FOR of FORBEARE, the word next to it, and place it in front of SAKE, and you have FOR SAKEBEARE: enough, surely, to make even the simplest of us wonder whether this similarity to the great name could be wholly fortuitous! Then, since the rhyme is the anagram, and, in the underlying message from which the author was working, he was allowed to be "bold with H either in omitting or retaining it", because it could not challenge the right of a letter, replace the H he has dropped after S. Change B (more arbitrarily) into its fellow labial P, and the result is FOR SHAKEPEARE. The name is still defective, for an S is missing. Let us therefore insert a dot where the letter should be so that when we come to the final mopping up we shall not forget that a vacant place remains to be filled. We now have FOR SHAKE. PEARE. And it is here of importance to remember that, in the first edition of the Sonnets (1609) the printing of which is said to have been supervised by the author himself, the name on the title page is similarly spelt: SHAKESPEARES SONNETS NEUER BEFORE IMPRINTED. IESVS also responds to treatment. With a slight rearrangement of the letters it becomes VISES. But according to the rules V is interchangeable with W, and H, if dropped, may be replaced. VISES therefore becomes WISHES; so that the first line and a half can now be made to read: GOOD FREND FOR WISHES FOR SHAKE.PEARE TO DIGG THE DVST.

Now the word "friend", in Elizabethan times, was often spelt FFREND; indeed the letter F, when used as an initial, was frequently doubled. Marlowe's contemporary and fellow poet, Michael Drayton, in inscribing for Sir Henry Willoughby of Risley a presentation copy of *The Battaile of Agincourt* writes: "To the noble knyghte and my most honord ffrend." And the Rawlinson Bright copy of *The Muses Elizium* shows a similar quaintness of spelling: "To the Noble Knight and my heighly esteemed ffrend Sir Richard Brawne all health and happiness ffrom his servante and ffrend Michell Drayton." And the fact that this latter example is said not to be in the author's hand only goes to show that the doubling of the F in "ffrend" was not just a personal trick of Drayton's. I quote further instances, also drawn from *Michael Drayton and His Circle* by B. H. Newdigate. The endorsement of a bond dated 1607, on which Thomas Woodforde sued for a debt of £120, contains the phrase: ". . . if the within bounden lordinge Barrye William Treveele Edwarde Sybthorpe & Michaell Drayton . . . doe well and truelie pay . . . the somme of three score poundes of lawfull money of England on the ffyve and Twentieth day of November now next cominge att or on the ffirst stone in the Temple Churche neere fleetstreet london . . . then this present obligacion to be voyde . . ." In the same book one also finds: fforfieture, ffebruary, ffor his person was very comely, etc.

On the other hand, the dying Sidney, in his last Will, claimed Sir Henry Goodere for "my good cousin and Friend"; and Ben Jonson wrote to Drayton:

It hath beene question'd, Michael, if I bee
A Friend at all: or, if at all, to thee.

Moreover, the author of the epitaph, who used the word frequently in the Sonnets, always spelt it "friend" thus:

To me faire friend you neuer can be old.

Nevertheless I believe it quite likely that, in working from the underlying message, he would not have hesitated to employ the less familiar (and perhaps more vulgar) spelling in order to obtain an additional F if he needed one. Furthermore the dropped I adds substance to this argument: the word was spelt either FRIEND or FFREND; rarely FREND, as it is on the epitaph. And since my own need to dispose of this conjured letter is as urgent as the author's was to obtain it, I now take the F of FOR (the third word in the first line) and give it back to its neighbour FREND to which I believe it belongs. The first line and a half now reads: GOOD FFREND OR WISHES FOR SHAKE.PEARE TO DIGG THE DVST. And for the moment let us be content with that, imperfect though it be, and set it aside. We shall return to it later.

We come now to the peculiar spelling of ENCLOAS-ED. In Elizabethan and Jacobean times it seems always to have been spelt ENCLOSED, as it is to-day, or INCLOSED. I quote from the Folio of 1623:

If therefore you dare trust my honestie,
That lyes enclosed in this trunke. (Winter's Tale.)

Titinius is enclosed about with horsemen. (Julius Caesar.)

And would under-peepe her lids to see th'inclosed lights.
(Cymbeline.)

The dead with charitie enclos'd in clay. (Henry V.)

Whereas in the first edition of the Sonnets one finds:

Oh in what sweets doest thou thy sinnes inclose.

And it was spelt ENCLOSED much earlier than that:

The paradies terrestre . . . is enclosed with fyre brennynge.
(Caxton, 1481.)

In the orisoun of the Paternoster hath oure Lord
Jhesu Christ enclosed most things. (Chaucer, 1386.)

It would seem, therefore, that in the cipher an unnecessary A has been forced into ENCLOASED—because it was the only place that could be found for it. This can be taken out and given back to the following word, to which it appears to belong, to produce, when the letters have been slightly rearranged: ENCLOSED HEAE AR. There is an imperfect letter in the word that is obviously meant to be HERE, and the E of ARE is missing; but for the moment let us not worry about these defects.

The next line, being in its entirety an anagram of its fellow in the underlying message, needs considerable manipulation. Reading at present: BLESTE BE Y MAN Y SPARES THES STONES, it can be re-rendered thus: PLAYES BY THE MAN BERSES (T)HES SONNETS. This I derive as follows. The ligatured TE of BLESTE adds a dropped H and becomes THE. The B of BE sheds its E and picks up the adjacent Y to become BY. MAN remains as it is. The shed E of BE joins the remaining BLES of BLESTE (the second key-word) and Y SPARES to form PLAYES and BERSES; while STONES (the third key-word) becomes SONNETS. The second N of SONNETS has in the anagram been rejected; but then, "the Licentiats somewhat licentiously . . . will pardon themselves for doubling or rejecting a letter, if the sence fall aptly".

AND . . . And what? The appealing voice comes ringing down the years packed (for Stratfordians) with awe-inspiring significance.

Remember that B can apparently be used for P, and that V is interchangeable with W. CVRST BE HE Y MOVES MY BONES can therefore become, with the addition of a dropped H, the arrangement of several letters and the arbitrary interpolation of three dots and an apostrophe: CHRYSTEPHEV M . . . OWE'S (MY) BONES. (CVRST is the fourth key-word, the one indeed that gave me the clue as to where the solution might lie.) But before discussing this, let us hark back to the meaningless OR of the first line for the purpose of reversing another piece of sleight of hand (similar to the doubling of the F in FREND) made necessary by the difficulty of finding appropriate letters in this lengthy anagram. Interchange the R of OR with the V of CHRYSTEPHEV, which now becomes CHRYSTEPHER, add a dropped H, and OR emerges as OWH, an anagram of WHO. The first line and a half is now intelligible: GOOD FFREND WHO WISHES FOR SHAKE.PEARE TO DIGG THE DVST; and the jingling rhyme, which has for so long perplexed scholars (because they were too learned to believe that the great dramatist could have descended to the construction of anagrams) now reads:

GOOD FFREND WHO WISHES FOR SHAKE.PEARE
TO DIGG THE DVST: ENCLOSED HEAE AR
PLAYES BY THE MAN, BERSES (T)HES SONNETS
AND CHRYSTEPHER M . . . OWE'S (MY) BONES.

Of this the first line and a half is an apostrophe which can be recast thus:

O thou who art wishful of digging the dust for
Shakespeare:

and the remaining two and a half lines list the contents of the tomb:

Enclosed here
Are playes by the man, verses his sonnets
And Christopher Marlowe's bones.

The meaning is already perfectly clear. But there are still many imperfections, the most vital of them being the three missing letters in the name Marlowe. Christopher is explicit; Marlowe is not. In Elizabethan times and later, it is true, when relatively few people were writing, abbreviations of names were common, even on the title pages of published literary works. Compare the title page of *Doctor Faustus* (1604) on which the name of the author is shortened to Chri. Marl., of the 1628 edition where it becomes Ch. Marloe, and of *Edward II*, where it is given as Chr. Marlow. Whereas on those of *The Massacre at Paris* (?), *Hero and Leander* (1598) and *The Jew of Malta* (1633) the spelling in every case varies, the name becoming Christopher Marlow, Christopher Marloe and Christopher Marlo respectively. But, in this modern age of exaggerated scepticism, if the three missing letters cannot be produced, scholars will remain unconvinced. Let us therefore return to the rhyme and see if we can clear the imperfections up.

It will be remembered that I have converted the words ENCLOASED HEARE into ENCLOSED HEAE AR; and this phrase, it soon becomes evident, is the focal point of the anagram, a sort of clearing house which the author used for his final polishing. The most significant thing about it is that it contains all the letters missing from the words SHAKESPEARE and MARLOWE: those which we have represented by dots. Let us therefore abstract the S, the AR and the L from the phrase and place them where they seem to belong. In the clearing house we are left with ENCOED HEAE, and SHAKESPEARE and MARLOWE are now written in full.

Let us next begin an interchange of those letters which are obviously wrong in our decipherment as it now stands: first the B of BERSES which we move up to the clearing house, replacing it with—what?

There has here been another piece of prestidigitation. The C does not have to be taken as a C at all. The author, desperate for a C and having only a V at his disposal, has been forced to resort to trickery. If the page is turned, the C will be seen to be a U lying on its side. But how does this U become the V of verses? The answer is simple. In the first edition of the Sonnets the

letter 'u' when internal did service for both 'u' and 'v'.
I give examples.

Then these old nine which rimers inuocate.   38.10.
So oft haue I inuok'd thee for my Muse.   78.1.
Nor taste, nor smell, desire to be inuited.   141.7.

Whereas the letter 'v' did service for both 'u' and
'v' when either appeared at the beginning of a word.

Vnthrifty louelinesse why dost thou spend,
Vpon thy selfe thy beauties legacy?   4.1,2.
Thy vnus'd beauty must be tomb'd with thee.   4.13.
For euery vulgar paper to rehearse.   38.4.
Vnlesse you would deuise some vertuous lye.   72.5.
That you were once vnkind be-friends mee now.   120.1.

This lack of distinction between the two letters (and
between 'i' and 'j') is summed up by L. C. Hector in
The Handwriting of English Documents. "The convention which treats the forms *i* and *u* as vowels and
the forms *j* and *v* as consonants did not gain general
acceptance in England until the beginning of the 18th
century. For earlier writers *i* and *j* on the one hand
and *u* and *v* on the other were variant forms of one
letter; and *Judas* was a perfectly permissible anagram
of *Davis.*"

It therefore follows that if a 'u' appearing intern-
ally as the C does in ENCLOASED, be moved to the
initial position, it automatically becomes a 'v'; or,
more simply, would be written as a 'v'. Compare:

For nothing this wide Vniuerse I call,
Saue thou my Rose . . .   109.13,14.

So that the C of ENCLOASED first turns to become
a U, then changes places with the initial B of BERSES
and becomes a V; and the clearing house now looks
like this: ENBOED HEAE.

Now for the bracketed MY in the last line. It is
obvious that this has to be moved, since it makes a

syllable too many in AND CHRYSTEPHER MAR-
LOWE'S BONES, besides interfering with the sense.
The M goes straight to the clearing house; the Y replaces
the E of (T)HES in the line above it, which loses the
initial T to the clearing house and becomes HYS. The
clearing house now reads ENBMTOED HEAE. And
ENBMTOED is a perfect anagram of ENTOMBED.
Notice, moreover, in passing the different shades of
meaning of ENCLOSED and ENTOMBED. The dust
was enclosed; the documents and bones are entombed:
which is as it should be. Compare the use of the word
in *Timon of Athens*:

Timon is dead; Entomb'd upon the very hem
o' the sea.

And more tellingly in the Sonnets:

Thy vnus'd beauty must be tomb'd with thee,
Which vsed liues th'executor to be.   4.13.
When you intombed in mens eyes shall lye.   81.8.

But what happens to the displaced E of (T)HES?
Before proceeding to a solution, let us place it tempor-
arily in the clearing house and restate the underlying
message thus:

GOOD FFREND WHO WISHES FOR SHAKESPEARE
TO DIGG THE DVST: ENTOMBED HEAE E
PLAYES BY THE MAN, VERSES HYS SONNETS
AND CHRYSTEPHER MARLOWE'S BONES.

The letter E, it is obvious, has to be appended to
DIGG. The word 'dig', in those days, was usually written
DIGGE, and occasionally DIG; but never (so far as I
have been able to ascertain) DIGG. Among the
examples of this word's usage given in Bartlett's *Con-
cordance to Shakespeare's Works,* I found, on referring back to the Folio Edition, that all but two (both
in *Titus Andronicus*) were spelt DIGGE. The two exceptions were written as we write the word to-day. The
following are extracts from the Folio:

Wilt thou go digge a grave to find out warre?   (2 Henry VI)

I with my long nayles will digge thee pig-nuts.   (The Tempest)

I'le hide my master from the flies, as deepe
As these poore pickaxes can digge.   (Cymbeline)

The Scripture says Adam dig'd; could hee digge without
    armes.   (Hamlet)

More conclusive, however, is the single use of the word in the Sonnets, which is similarly spelt in the first edition.

When fortie Winters shall beseige thy brow
And digge deep trenches in thy beauties field.   2.1,2.

The decipherment is now almost perfect and reads as follows:

GOOD FFREND WHO WISHES FOR SHAKESPEARE
TO DIGGE THE DVST: ENTOMBED HEAE:
PLAYES BY THE MAN, VERSES HYS SONNETS
AND CHRYSTEPHER MARLOWE'S BONES.

Only two blemishes remain. The A in HEAE, which in a way resembles an R, and the E in the middle of CHRYSTEPHER. The Y's in CHRYSTEPHER and HYS I do not apologize for. Y was frequently used for short I in the literature and letter writing of the period. The following examples are taken at random from *Drayton and His Circle.*

Adorned wyth wytte, and skyll to rule the same.

Synce Fortune frownde.

Whych in thy brest dyd boyle.

Yf yt please good that he and I lyve.

At any rate I can do no more. The verse as written above allows of no further modification.

It remains to consider words that have so far not called for comment.

HERE is spelt HEERE almost throughout the First Folio. It is spelt HERE, however, wherever it occurs in the first edition of the Sonnets. (13.2; 39.14; 42.13; 49.9; 110.1).

GOOD in the Sonnets is always spelt GOOD.

And yet methinks I haue Astronomy,
But not to tell of good or euil luck.   14.2,3.
Which in their wils count bad what I think good.   121.8.

DVST is written DUST and BONES BONES.

When that churle death my bones with dust shall cover.   32.2.
Waighes not the dust and iniury of age.   108.10.

The U in DVST has been written as a V in the epitaph to bring it into accord with the U's in CVRST and IESVS.

WISHES (rather than the WISHETH of the dedication to the Sonnets) occurs frequently in the plays:

I shall think my brother happy in having what he wishes for.
                    (As You Like It. V.2.52.)

Love make your fortunes twenty times above
Her that so wishes and her humble love!
                  (All's Well that Ends well. II.3.89.)

If never, yet that Time himself doth say
He wishes earnestly you never may.   (Winter's Tale, IV.1.32.)

WHO referring to a person occurs frequently.

For certain friends that are both his and mine,
Whose loves I may not drop, but wail his fall
Who I myself struck down.   (Macbeth, III.1.123.)

Of thee my dear one, thee my daughter, who
Art ignorant of what thou art.   (Tempest, I.2.17.)

Not only with what my revenue yielded
But what my power might else exact, like one
Who having into truth.   (Tempest, I.2.100.)

My son is lost; and, in my rate, she too,
Who is so far from Italy removed
I ne'er again shall see her.   (Tempest, II.1.115.)

Finally the word SONNETS is similarly spelt on the title page of the first edition of the Sonnets.

22

Now, in assessing the value of this discovery, it will be helpful to elicit the aid of "the doctrine of chance, or, as it is technically termed, the Calculus of Probabilities", as Auguste Dupin did in Poe's *The Mystery of Marie Rogêt*. Certain Paris newspapers, it will be remembered, had, in this story, by stressing the coincidences of the known facts, set out to prove that the corpse found floating in the Seine was not Marie Rogêt's, but that of another woman. Dupin was convinced that they were wrong. I quote his comments, replacing, for brevity's sake, the coincidences he mentions with algebraical symbols.

"Had M. Beauvais, in his search for the body of Marie, discovered (a) (a corpse corresponding in general size and appearance to the missing girl), he would have been warranted in forming an opinion that his search had been successful. If in addition he had found (b), his opinion might have been justly strengthened, and the increase of positiveness might well have been in the ratio of the peculiarity or unusualness of (b). If there was also (c), the increase of probability (of his having arrived at truth) would not have been an increase in a ratio merely arithmetical, but in one highly geometrical, or accumulative. Add to all this (d) and you so far augment the probability as to verge upon the certain. What of itself would be no evidence of truth, becomes, through its corroborative position, proof most sure. Give us then (e)", which has subsections, each successive one of which "is multiple evidence—proof not added to proof, but multiplied by hundreds of thousands, and we seek no further. Let us now discover (f) and it is almost folly to proceed". But (f) is found to be characterized by (g). "It is now madness or hypocrisy to doubt."

Using this method of reasoning, then, let us proceed to an examination of what we have found in the epitaph.

The Baconians would claim that the poor quality of the verse was further evidence of the fact that their champion Francis Bacon had written the plays. Also to be taken into account, however, is the possibility that the jingle conceals an underlying message. It has now been treated anagrammatically, and something intelligible has emerged. This is coincidence (a).

Then SONETS, at the end of the third line, is the only anagram that can be wrung from the word STONES (except perhaps TEN SONS, which is hardly applicable). Can this be by chance? To discover its presence in the casual "effusion" of a layman would certainly be accidental; but to find it prominently placed, in anagrammatical guise, in the already suspect epitaph of a poet and playwright, whose sonnets form an important part of his collected works, is much less so. This is coincidence (b). And when the word PLAYES (with Elizabethan spelling) falls at the beginning of the same line (c) and VERSES in the centre of it (d); and the entire line is an almost perfect anagram of its fellow in the ciphered version (e), the probability of accident is considerably reduced. Add to all this the facts that the three literary words, and indeed all four lines, are bound together by the cohesive force of meaning (f); that no ciphered word, and no letter, have been excluded in returning to the underlying message (g); and that the last half of the resultant verse has an unmistakable Shakespearean ring (h) — varied definite rhythm, strongly marked caesura between MAN and VERSES, and a characteristic ultimate line of three feet; and the degree of likelihood that all the features so far mentioned have been fortuitously assembled becomes very small indeed. Add, next, the presence in the first and last lines of the names SHAKESPEARE and CHRYSTEPHER MARLOWE (i); the important fact that CHRYSTEPHER MARLOWE provides the rhythm necessary to the last line (whereas the name of no other claimant does) (j); and the strange circumstance that all the derived words, even DIGGE, are spelt as they would have been by the early 17th century cipherer (k); and the case for suspension of disbelief becomes very strong indeed. There is then, in the last line, the dramatic employment of allusion, so natural in a poet, rather than direct statement (1). The message is not baldly expressed in sentences like "Bacon wrote Shakespeare", "Oxford wrote the plays", "Shak'stspur never writ a word of them", or something else equally naive; but allusively. The whole complex situation with all its dramatic overtones is gathered up with overwhelming succinctness in the one simple assertion: ENTOMBED HERE . . . CHRISTOPHER MARLOWE'S BONES. How could this be by accident? And I must at this point emphasize the fact that I did not contrive the verse; I discovered it. So that, if its validity is not accepted, I must be given the credit of having been shrewdly inventive as regards, not only the general assembling of the words, but also the devising of the implied situation, which would have had to come first. And the task of thinking up a plot so complex, and expressing it allusively in four lines, would have required a mind much more gifted than mine. Indeed, even the creative genius of the author of the plays might not have dealt with it successfully—had he not lived through the experience.

Finally, there is the coincidence (m) that Camden's rules for the construction of anagrams, as set down in the 1605 edition of his *Remaines,* are obeyed in the conversion of epitaph into message, and vice versa. They in fact make it possible; and here I can only assert, with the hope of being believed, that I became acquainted with the *Remaines* after I had made my initial discovery. It was Camden's treatment acting as a key that enabled outstanding difficulties to be cleared up. If I had contrived the verse, I should have had to be acquainted with the rules first. How did it come about that this extraneous piece of the jigsaw of evidence should fit so accurately into place?

Next to be considered is the likelihood of the author's using this type of cipher, and one can quote two instances in the canon where letters are seriously played with (n). The first occurs in the opening scene of *King Richard III*.

> And if King Edward be as true and just
> As I am subtle, false and treacherous,
> This day should Clarence closely be mew'd up,
> About a prophecy, which says that G
> Of Edward's heirs the murderer shall be.

Which leads to:

> He hearkens after prophecies and dreams;
> And from the cross-row plucks the letter G,
> And says a wizard told him that by G
> His issue disinherited should be;
> And, for my name of George begins with G,
> It follows in his thought that I am he.

Here an entire identity is supposedly concealed in the letter G.

The second instance is to be found in *Twelfth Night*. Malvolio in the Letter Scene, having read that "M.O.A.I. doth sway my life", remarks. "M.—Why that begins my name . . . But then there is no consistency in the sequal . . . A should follow, but O does . . . And then I comes behind . . . M,O,A,I. This simulation (i.e., hidden significance) is not as the former; and yet to crush (force) this a little, it would bow to me, for every one of these letters are in my name."

That which convinces me most, however, is the falling together in the last line of CVRST and CHRYST, the first syllable of Christopher meaning Christ-bearing (o). From the tragic story that has now been told, it would seem obvious that the cipherer felt himself to be cursed: and that this idea must often have occurred to him; so that when the time came to devise an anagram of Christopher, "cursed" immediately suggested itself; whereas "blessed", its antonym, suggested plays.

The argument can be taken a good deal further; for the strange passage between Christ and cursed, and the obsession with being cursed, are (not surprisingly) features of *Doctor Faustus*.

Ay, go, accursed spirit, to ugly hell!
'Tis thou has damn'd distressed Faustus' soul.

which is followed a few lines later by:

Ah, Christ, my Saviour,
Seek to save distressed Faustus' soul.

To which Lucifer replies:

Christ cannot save thy soul, for he is just:
There's none but I have interest in the same . . .
Thou talk'st of Christ, contrary to thy promise.

Then, in the scene with the Pope and the Cardinal
of Lorrain, Mephistophilis says:

. . . we shall be cursed with bell, book and candle.

And Faustus rejoins:

How! bell, book and candle,—candle, book and bell,
Forward and backward, to curse Faustus to hell!

And this, oddly enough, is followed word for word
by the formula of the epitaph, repeated, in all, five times
in a dirge sung by a group of friars.

Cursed be he that stole away his Holiness' meat from the table!
    maledicat Dominus!
Cursed be he that struck his Holiness a blow on the face!
    maledicat Dominus!
Cursed be he that took Friar Sandelo a blow on the pate!
    maledicat Dominus!
Cursed be he that disturbeth our holy dirge!
    maledicat Dominus!
Cursed be he that took away his Holiness' wine!
    maledicat Dominus!

This extract comes, it is true, from a comic scene
thought by some critics to fall below the general level
of the play's writing and therefore judged by them to
be suspect as genuine Marlowe. The fact, however, that
it hammers home the formula of the curse is rather

proof (if one allows oneself for a moment to beg the question) of the scene's authenticity.

The next instances of the recurrence of the Christ-cursed theme are to be found in the scene in which the old man seeks to reform Faustus.

> Break heart, drop blood, and mingle it with tears,
> Tears falling from repentant heaviness
> Of thy most vile and loathsome filthiness,
> The stench whereof corrupts the inward soul
> With such flagitious crimes of heinous sin
> As no commiseration may expel,
> But mercy, Faustus, of thy Saviour sweet,
> Whose blood alone must wash away thy guilt.

After the old man's exit Faustus comments:

> Accursed Faustus, where is mercy now?
> I do repent; and yet I do despair:
> Hell strives with grace for conquest in my breast:
> What shall I do to shun the snares of death?

The most telling examples, however, come in the play's great concluding passage.

> See, see, where Christ's blood streams in the firmament!
> One drop would save my soul, half a drop: ah, my Christ!
> Ah, rend not my heart for naming of my Christ!
> Yet will I call on him: O, spare me, Lucifer!

which is followed a moment later by:

> O God,
> If thou wilt not have mercy on my soul,
> Yet for Christ's sake, whose blood hath ransom'd me,
> Impose some end to my incessant pain;
> Let Faustus live in hell a thousand years,
> A hundred thousand and at last be sav'd!

Then the formula of the epitaph appears again.

> Curs'd be the parents that engender'd me!
> No, Faustus, curse thyself, curse Lucifer
> That hath deprived thee of the joys of heaven.

Now Marlowe wrote *Doctor Faustus* (it has come to be believed) in 1592, much of it (one concludes) from experiences gained at meetings of the School of Night which will have disbanded no later than the

June of that year when Raleigh fell from favour. And from the agonized soul-searching of Faustus, so convincingly represented, it would seem that the author was exploring his own soul. Atheist he was called, and atheist he may have been; but only externally, in discussion; and then probably only from bravado. Within, his mind was constantly questioning the meaning of life and the universe, just as Raleigh's was. After his long religious training, his belief was too deeply ingrained ever to be completely renounced. His doubt was of the mind, rational: his belief of the unconscious, intuitional. Hence his appalling Christ-cursed conflict.

The man from Stratford, on the other hand, whose life is inferred in all its immaculateness by the scholars, never had reason to feel himself anything but blessed. Respectable parentage, particularly on the side of the mother; quiet youth spent peacefully at the local grammar school; early marriage to a young woman eight years older than he was, who was able doubtless to mother him, and who presented him with three children before he was twenty-one; journey to London eventually to become famous as an actor and playwright; nervous breakdown in middle age, his only misfortune apparently (we are coming to this); death from unknown causes after four years of bucolic retirement. It is all insisted upon by the scholars. Reason for profound soul-searching? It would seem none! But then, if William Shakespeare was the contriver of the epitaph, there was no anagram, and the Christ-cursed conflict (since Christ, in this instance, is the first syllable of Chrystepher) does not apply.

In our list of coincidences we have now gone much further than the point where Auguste Dupin declared that it would be "almost folly to proceed"; though whether or not it would yet be "madness or hypocrisy to doubt" I shall not ask the discriminating reader to decide until I have fully expounded, and summarized, my thesis. Before continuing with the argument, however, it will be of value to discuss an example of what would seem to be the only serious criticism that can be levelled at my anagrammatical decipherment of the epitaph. It is given expression by a friendly critic (whose books I admire) in a letter addressed to an associate of mine, who had asked him to look at the manuscript. The first paragraph states quite simply that anagrams prove nothing; the letter continues:

"Take the opening sentence of (the) book. Take the concession that W (Double U) can be split into UU (as in fact it often is in early printed books). Now look: (And U is, of course, V.)

OPENING SENTENCE
IT IS THE MOST TRAGIC IRONY, IN THE LIGHT OF WHAT I AM ABOUT TO DISCLOSE,

ANAGRAM
VILLIAM HONEY UTTERS A TRACT NO IDIOTIC BOSH, SO HAT MIGHT FIT, I VOTE G

If you cross off the letters one by one you will find they tally to a coma. Now comes the enigma (No fun in anagrams without enigmas). What does 'I VOTE G' mean? Well, 'G' is the commonest mark on a school essay for GOOD: and it might mean that. In fact, that is what I believe (the author) meant to tell us in that cryptic opening sentence of his: but it could be the initial of some other name (compare the opening speech of Richard III which plays with the letter G) *either* perhaps some nickname of (the author's), or possibly of some friend of his who habitually called him Villiam (for fun) rather than William. So is the book really by (this author) at all?

Now I dashed this anagram off on receipt of your letter at breakfast and no doubt if I spent longer at it I could work out a dozen more equally convincing and contradictory. But I will spare myself, and you!"

In other words, the devising of *all* anagrams is as easy as the drinking of coffee and eating of hot buttered toast.

Now the proposition "All anagrams prove nothing"

is not necessarily valid. Fallacious reasoning of this nature is termed argument by defective induction, which means simply that, if in a scientific investigation too few instances are sought to sustain a conjectured universal, then that universal may turn out to be false; just as the proposition "All swans are white" did when the English discovered Australia and found to their surprise that "Some swans are black". The author of the Shakespeare plays saw the possibility of disproving apparent universals when he wrote: "All that glistens is not gold."

The only truth demonstrable, therefore, is that "Some anagrams prove nothing." Equally true is its fellow "Some anagrams prove something", as I hope I shall have shown by the time I get to the end of this book.

Again, there is a difference of treatment in my anagram and that of my critic. In his the letters are moved individually, a mathematical procedure which is infinitely simpler, in that no restrictions have to be observed. He has selected 56 letters and 2 commas from my opening sentence, and the possible permutations of these would number 58 x 57 x 56 . . . 3 x 2 x 1, or 58!, clearly a very large figure indeed, one that would reach a magnitude of millions of millions of millions.

Yet, despite this abundance of opportunity, his anagram amounts only to a piece of telegraphese: amusing perhaps; but not very witty, and certainly not sensible. For that reason it proves nothing: not even that my own proves nothing.

In mine, on the other hand, very few letters are moved: in some words none is moved at all. Let us go back to the first stage and see what happened.

In the first line, out of a total of 29 letters, 5 were moved, and 2 syllables, containing in all 7 letters, were inverted. In the second line the A of ENCLOASED was transferred merely for the sake of clarity, so that no letters had to be moved at all. In the third line 10 were moved; and in the fourth 4, two of which were simply transposed.

Then, in the second stage, 10 were involved in the polishing process, making a grand total of 36: fewer than a third of the 110 the verse contains, and an average of only 9 per line.

So that to conform with the rules that I myself have been able to observe, my critic should have moved only 20 letters of the 58 he selected, and still achieved an intelligible result. The task, it will be seen, is already much less easy; because the randomness of choice has been considerably narrowed. If, instead of 58 letters, he had selected 110 (so that we might both have started with equal handicaps) the comparison could be mathematically expressed thus: $110 \times 109 \times 108 \ldots \times 3 \times 2 \times 1$ (his opportunity), as against $110 \times 109 \times 108 \ldots \times 77 \times 76 \times 75$ (mine): which represents a good deal of difference, though the latter figure is still very large indeed.

There are further rules to be observed, however; and I wonder how my critic (or anyone else) would fare if, in attempting to wrest an alternative from the jingle (surely a more practical exercise than anagrammatizing my opening sentence) he were to abide by them, while limiting himself to moving an average of only 9 letters per line!

First, the result should be rhythmic; and that this condition enormously restricts selection can be judged from the fact that if, in all English literature, the highly prized section called verse were set against the immense mass of unrhythmic material called prose, the one would amount to the merest fraction of the other; partly, of course, because the inclination to compose verse comes to only few people; but mainly because the difficulty of inventing it is so much greater. Even when a dictionary of words is available to choose from, it is difficult to produce a four-line poem of any merit. How much more difficult, then, is it to conjure one from the handful of words that make up the epitaph particularly when the changing of only an average of 9 letters per line is permitted. The ratio of verse to prose could possibly yield a factor: if it were a fraction of 1 per cent, the probability of producing verse, rather than prose, from any given selection of letters, might also be, approximately, the same fraction of 1 per cent. I shall

H

not labour the point beyond stating that ease of performance is what is implied in the proposition
"Anagrams prove nothing", and the condition of having
to produce verse rather than prose introduces an
element of considerable difficulty. My critic has been
able to produce only telegraphese.

Secondly, there should be rhyme. But the rhyme is
the same in my verse as it is in the jingle, it may be
argued. True! But if it should be altered, the EARE,
HERE endings would have to be abandoned and others
found, a procedure that would be very extravagant in
the use of the 36 letters available. Moreover, if the first
two lines of the original are examined, the possibility
of an alternative rhyme seems remote, as does that
(incidentally) of alternative anagrams. Besides WISHES,
IESVS yields ISSUE; but what can be got from GOOD
FREND or TO DIGG THE DVST? Would such
phrases as END OF DOG R (9 letters moved) or
EIGHT DUGGS DOTT (12 moved) or SIGHT TV
DODGE T (12) make much sense in the context? And
what do the enigmas R and T (which will not fit in)
mean? (But then, no fun in anagrams without enigmas.)

Thirdly, the result should be a Shakespearean pastiche.
The typical caesura in PLAYES BY THE MAN,
VERSES HYS SONNETS should, if possible, be reproduced somewhere else, and the spelling throughout
should agree with that of the Sonnets.

Fourthly, all lines should be linked by allusive meaning; and, fifthly, the name of a rival claimant should be
put forward, no matter how ridiculous. Bacon? Oxford?
Derby? Queen Elizabeth? Queen Victoria?

All this I have been able to accomplish; for, in the
opinion of my critic, I am the one who composed the
verse.

But, working from the same material, I could not
produce another! Because with each added restriction
the difficulty of the task increases to the point of virtual
impossibility, as the Calculus of Probabilities shows. The
anagram I am demanding, if my own is to be proved
invalid, could not be dashed off at breakfast. It could

not be dashed off at all. I did not dash mine off. I discovered it.

The only satisfactory answer, of course, from the viewpoint of the Stratfordians, would be:

GOOD FREND WHO WISHES FOR MARLOWE
TO DIGGE THE DVST: ENTOMBED HERE:
PLAYES BY THE MAN, VERSES HIS SONNETS
AND WILLIAM SHAKESPEARE'S BONES

But in this instance, unfortunately, the 9-letter rule has been ignored; most of the words are mine (and it is an alternative we are seeking); the rhyme has disappeared; the scansion in the first line staggers and in the fourth halts; and CVRST BE HE Y cannot possibly be converted into William.

The truth is that no alternative exists; and the cipherer, I am convinced, knew it. In his message to posterity, how could he have been so incautious as to leave behind an ambiguity? That, however, is to beg the question.

Lastly, there is the problem of style, and here I am anticipating criticism to come. Poetic perception depends upon a well or badly developed ear, and numerous critics (with tin ears) are bound to assert that the underlying message is not Shakespearean in character. In defence I refer them to the several instances in the canon where the words DVST, TOMB and BONES are variously combined.

Where dust and damn'd oblivion is the tomb
Of honour'd bones indeed.

(All's Well That Ends Well)

Hang her epitaph upon her tomb
And sing it to her bones.

(Much Ado About Nothing)

When that churl death my bones with dust shall cover.

(Sonnet 32)

Or lay these bones in an unworthy urn,
Tombless.

(Henry V)

And by the honourable tomb he swears
That stands upon your royal grandsire's bones.

(Richard III)

. . . that his bones,
When he has run his course and sleeps in blessings,
May have a tomb of orphans' tears wept on 'em!

(Henry VIII)

This reiteration of the motif TOMB—BONES which, in one instance, becomes DVST—BONES and in another DVST—TOMB—BONES, together with the fact that the word BONES with connotation 'corpse' is used over thirty times in the plays, would seem to indicate a pattern of unconscious thought found again in the underlying message. The author of the epitaph, it will be remembered, did not write ENTOMBED but ENCLOASED.

But the author of the message, if he were not Marlowe, is a hypothetical person, to be identified, in the opinion of my critics, either with me myself (as supposed pseudo-cipherer) or chance. As for the first of these possibilities, I have shown (successfully, I believe) that the contrivance of such a verse, when undertaken within the restricted limits laid down, is virtually impossible. Whereas the second would seem to be absurd, involving, not a single, but a double, highly improbable coincidence: the emergence, from something Shakespearean in origin, of a second something, both intelligible and reminiscent of Shakespearean form. It is here that the absurdity arises. For to claim that a Shakespearean verse, emerging from another Shakespearean verse, should be an accidental pastiche, is tantamount to saying that chance has taken lessons in the writing of Shakespeare.

We come to the vital question. Can the pattern of thought discernable in the plays, and apparently repeated in the underlying verse, be accepted as proof of the fact that the verse was written by the play's author?

If it can, then the implication as to authorship must also be accepted.

It was not William Shakespeare, the actor from Stratford-upon-Avon, who wrote the plays, but the poet-dramatist Christopher Marlowe.

23

It will now be clear that the argument of this entire book, complex though it has become, stems from the single clue so succinctly and unambiguously expressed in the message underlying the epitaph: ENTOMBED HERE . . . CHRISTOPHER MARLOWE'S BONES. It was this which indicated an imposture and led me to seek corroboration elsewhere: corroboration in the hunt for which coincidence added itself to coincidence until I had eventually built up a structure of evidence so comprehensive that it was capable not only of supporting the truth of the message, but also of standing by itself and, in a strangely compelling vicious circle, reinforcing the authenticity of the decipherment: if there had indeed been an imposture, as it now seemed certain there had, then the decipherment was of necessity correct. The original argument can be reduced to three major hypotheses.

1. If the decipherment is valid, then it was the body of Christopher Marlowe, and not William Shakespeare, that, on the 25th April, 1616, was entombed in Holy Trinity Church, Stratford-upon-Avon. Copies in manuscript of the Shakespeare plays were also put into the grave, and they were the work of the man whose bones they were accompanying.

2. If Marlowe's body is buried in Stratford, then Shakespeare and Marlowe must have changed places at some point in their individual careers, and that can have been only where one of them disappeared, that it to say, at Deptford.

3. If Shakespeare died at Deptford, and Marlowe replaced him, then the only person who can have made contact with the Shakespeare family three years later, and acquired property at Stratford, was Marlowe.

It is as simple as all that.

As for the details of the imposture: the slipping into the "Theatre" in order to avoid detection, and the virtual bribery of the Shakespeares to ensure their silence: it will be understood that concealment is implicit in the very nature of such a deception and to have to arrive at truth from the few signs unwittingly left behind is no easy task. Nevertheless, though the clear stream of evidence here frequently vanishes underground, there is still much to indicate its direction.

We come now to the cause of death.

In 1608 there seems to have been a hiatus in "Shakespeare's" work, which Dr. Rowse from the elegance of All Souls and Sir Edmund Chambers from the respectability of the Education Department, suggest was due to a nervous breakdown.

"The chronology of the plays becomes difficult at this point, and it is therefore frankly a conjecture that an attempt at Timon of Athens early in 1608 was followed by a serious illness, which may have been a nervous breakdown, and on the other hand may have been merely (sic) the plague." (E. K. Chambers in *William Shakespeare.*)

It was, however, I think, due to the onset of the tertiary stage of syphilis. For in *Pericles,* the play that preceded *Timon,* there is a savage attack on the brothels. "The brothel scene (in *Pericles*)," writes Eric Partridge in *Shakespeare's Bawdy,* "is perhaps the lowest in Shakespeare." And one speech from it, I diffidently suggest, provides a slender clue to the nature of the dramatist's malady. The Frenchmen, "Monsieur Veroles brought his disease hither: here he does but repair it."

Now, Vérole is the French word for pox; and Monsieur Veroles, when abbreviated to M. Vérole, is an almost perfect anagramme of Marlowe. It is a trivial observation, I admit, but such a detail would not have escaped the eye of the dramatist himself when writing. So that one is drawn to speculate that Marlowe was the person who took his disease to the Mytilene brothel. I had much conversation with an expert* over this pos-

*Dr. G. W. Csonka of St. Mary's Hospital, Paddington.

sibility. My first question was: "If the onset of the tertiary stage of the disease, that is to say its 'repairment'
or recrudescence, had been in 1608, when would it have
been first contracted?" And the answer: "Some ten
years earlier: no more than eighteen and no fewer
than five."

I then asked: "Does death follow rapidly upon the
onset of the tertiary stage?"

"No, the onset can be sudden, but the development is
usually gradual, lasting a number of years."

My next question was: "If the disease had been contracted in the late fifteen nineties, and the tertiary stage
had manifested itself in 1608, would a deterioration
have been likely in 1612 which would have made further
writing impossible and a retirement necessary with
death following in a further four years?"

The answer was: "That would have been an accept-
able time programme; though I would like to know
more details: had there been, for instance, loss of
memory, blackouts, fits, tempers?" Most interesting,
however, was the remark: "Patients in the tertiary stage
are very happy. A state of euphoria seems to protect
them from a full knowledge of their illness." For the
dramatist had stated in his Will, redrawn up on the
25th March, 1616, that he was "in perfect health and
memory, God be praised". This phrase was often included in the Wills of the period, but in this instance
it was false, since all work had perforce been abondoned.

On my asking whether it would have been possible
for a person afflicted with the disease to have devised
the epitaph, the answer given was: "Not usually. There
is considerable impairment of the faculties and not
much insight. But one patient I had, a brilliant engineer,
turned to an invention a few days before he died and
succeeded admirably."

My next task was to find, somewhere in the works of
the dramatist, a reference to the contradiction of the
disease approximately ten years earlier than 1608; and
I looked for it in the place it was most likely to be: in
the Sonnets to the Black Woman, written in 1597-8

during that period of despair that had followed Southampton's desertion. I came quickly to Sonnet 146, which
I quote in full.

> Poor soul the centre of my sinful earth,
> (Which feeds) these rebel powers that thee array,
> Why dost thou pine within and suffer dearth
> Painting thy outward walls so costly gay?
> Why so large cost having so short a lease,
> Dost thou upon thy fading mansion spend?
> Shall worms inheritors of this excess,
> Eat up thy charge? Is this thy body's end?
> Then soul live thou upon thy servant's loss,
> And let that pine to aggravate thy store;
> Buy terms divine in selling hours of dross:
> Within be fed, without be rich no more,
>   So shalt thou feed on Death, that feeds on men,
>   And Death once dead, there's no more dying then.

What else could this be but a description of the recently contracted disease that was feeding on the poet?
Syphilis was rife at the time, having been brought, according to Dr. A. H. Hudson of Wisconsin, the world
authority on its history and pathology, not from Haiti
by the crew of Christopher Columbus, as was originally
thought; but from Africa by the slavers. And when it is
realized that the rebel powers that were arraying the
guilt-ridden poet's sinful earth, painting its outward
walls so costly gay, were the marks of the disease in its
primary stage (nobody who has seen them could deny
their gaiety) or the equally bright rash that appears six
weeks later to characterize the secondary stage, the rest
of the poem falls into line.

Just as convincing is Sonnet 147 where there is a
constant uneasy passage between love as a disease and
the disease of love, both of which are persisting. Here
the wretched poet seems to be on the very brink of
lunacy, and the reproach at the poem's conclusion, addressed unquestionably to the beautiful youth who has
so cruelly betrayed him, is the bitterest he has ever dared
fling at him.

My love is as a fever longing still,
For that which longer nurseth the disease,
Feeding on that which doth preserve the ill,
Th'uncertain sickly appetite to please:
My reason the physician to my love,
Angry that his prescriptions are not kept
Hath left me, and I desperate now approve,
Desire is death, which physic did except.
Past cure I am, now reason is past care,
And frantic mad with evermore unrest,
My thoughts and my discourse as mad men's are,
At random from the truth vainly expressed.
　For I have sworn thee fair, and thought thee bright,
　Who art as black as hell, as dark as night.

Remorse, however, at his unrestrained chiding of the youth, soon follows (Sonnet 151); and here there can be no doubt as to the identity of the person addressed. Compare "gentle cheater" with "gentle thief" in Sonnet 40. The adjective could hardly have been applied to the Black Woman. And the gentle cheater was the "thee" of Sonnet 147, or there could have been no reason for the remorse.

Love is too young to know what conscience is,
Yet who knows not conscience is born of love,
Then gentle cheater urge not my amiss,
Lest guilty of my faults thy sweet self prove.
For thou betraying me, I do betray
My nobler part to my gross body's treason,
My soul doth tell my body that he may
Triumph in love, flesh stays no farther reason,
But rising at thy name doth point out thee,
As his triumphant prize, proud of this pride,
He is contented thy poor drudge to be
To stand in thy affairs, fall by thy side.
　No want of conscience hold it that I call,
　Her love, for whose dear love I rise and fall.

The entire poem is addressed to the "gentle cheater" Southampton. The last two lines are a little obscure only because the word "thou" has been omitted. They can be recast as follows: O thou for whose dear love I rise and fall, hold it no want of conscience that I call her Love. "Her" refers to the Black Woman, the negress from Africa from whom he had probably caught the disease: the prostitute Lucy Negro, perhaps, Abbess de Clerkenwell, mentioned in the *Gesta Grayorum*.

The phallic significance, acknowledged by scholars, of the sonnet's last two lines should not be overlooked. It does away once and for all with the idea that there had been no physical tie between the poet and the youth. And from it we may perhaps deduce that the bitter satire of *Troilus and Cressida* also had its origin in this affair. The play consists of two divided plots. One details the love of the constant Troilus for the false Cressida; the other relates how the Greeks, offended by the sulking of Achilles in his tent, cause Ajax to meet the Trojan Hector in friendly combat; how Hector afterwards slays Patroclus, Achilles' young friend and companion; and how he is himself slain in revenge by Achilles.

These interpenetrate without appearing to interact. They are, I hazard, two entirely separate tales both built on the character of Southampton. It has been suggested before that Achilles represents the Earl of Essex and Patroclus Southampton; and it is difficult not to identify Troilus, with his oft reiterated cry of constancy, with the playwright himself abandoned by the youth who disaffects (the exchange of Cressida is only a dramatic device) to the opposing camp of the Greeks to yield, strumpet-like, to Diomedes and become confused (in the mind of the dramatist) with Patroclus, termed scathingly by Thersites "Achilles' bitch", "Achilles' male varlet" and his "masculine whore", which latter insult is followed by a stream of venereal obscenities. For the part of Cressida had been written for a boy player, and it is a very small remove to attribute the bitter treatment of Cressida's falseness, "O Cressid! O false Cressid! False, false, false! Let all untruths stand by thy stained name, And they'll seem glorious!" to the playwright's personal reaction to his own betrayal by his master-mistress.

The scene in which Cressida's falseness is actually

witnessed by the distraught Troilus is perhaps one of the most powerful and subtly handled in all the plays. Its depth of passion cannot be attributed simply to the need of an author to conjure up a scene; any more than the stream of vituperation which Thersites directs at Patroclus can be said to be motivated by anything in this puzzling drama. Both find their origin, I am convinced, in the emotional life of the playwright.

Moreover it is an added coincidence that publication of the Sonnets, and of *Troilus and Cressida,* "never staled with the stage, never clapperclawed with the palms of the vulgar", in other words, likewise virgin in having been kept secret from the moment of its distracted creation some ten years earlier, and of *Pericles, Prince of Tyre* should in all three cases have been in the year 1609. Perhaps the giving of these three embittered works to the world was an act of vengence when the unfortunate dramatist realized that the recrudescence of his disease was his death warrant.

Further corroboration for this theory that syphilis was the cause of death can be found in the six extant authentic signatures of the playwright, all of which date from the last few years of his life. These appear under:

1. His deposition in a law-suit brought by Stephen Belott against his father-in-law Christopher Mountjoy. The document is dated the 11th May, 1612, and the signature reads: Willm Shakp.

2. The conveyance of a house in Blackfriars, London, purchased by the dramatist. This is dated the 10th March, 1613, and the signature reads: William Shakspe.

3. The mortgage deed of the same property. This is dated a day lated than the conveyance, and the signature is difficult to decipher. Sir Edmund Chambers believes it to read: Wm Shakspe.

The remaining three appear in the Will, one at the foot of each sheet. The document is dated 25th March, 1616, and the signatures read: William Shakspere, Willm Shakspere and By me William Shakspeare.

Many writers, some of them Baconians, have been appalled by the poor quality of penmanship evidenced

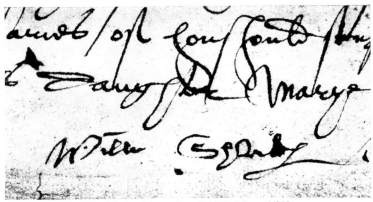

The Deposition, dated 11th May, 1612.
(Reproduced by courtesy of the Public Record Office)

The Conveyance, dated 10th March, 1613.
(Reproduced by courtesy of the British Museum)

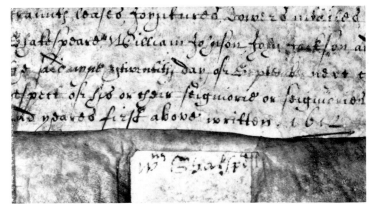

The Mortgage, dated 11th March, 1613.
(Reproduced by courtesy of the London Guildhall)

Shakespeare's Signatures

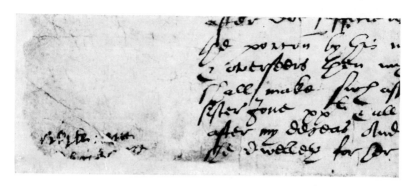

SHEET 1

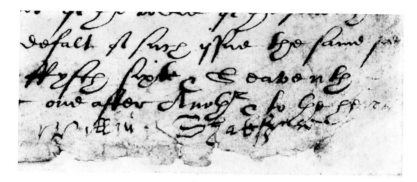

SHEET 2

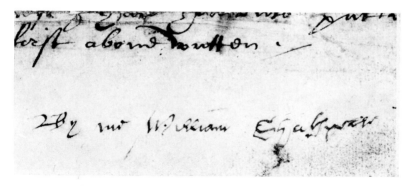

SHEET 3

Shakespeare's Signatures from the Will
Dated 25th March, 1616.
(*Reproduced by courtesy of the Public Record Office*)

by these specimens of the dramatist's handwriting. Though again, as always in Shakespearean criticism, widely divergent views are to be found. Whereas the Baconians would have it that the signatures are those of a semi-literate peasant, Dr. S. A. Tannenbaum attributes the scrawled handwriting, not to the playwright himself, but to the poor tracing and primitive methods of reproduction of early scholars. The signatures, he argues, are those of an educated man writing at speed. More significant, however, is the opinion expressed by Sir Edward Thompson and others that the dramatist, during the last two or three years of his life, suffered from "writer's cramp", of which they find in the scrawls no fewer than eighteen clear signs. It is extraordinary how the minds of scholars, when forced to account for unexpected phenomena, so often produce theories of extreme awkwardness: theories which cannot satisfy the intuition (I deliberately do not say critical faculties) of anyone with a modicum of creative ability. How many clerks, scratching away with quill pens, have spent a lifetime producing a volume of work perhaps hundreds of times that of Shakespeare's collected plays, and shown no evidence of writer's cramp at all. It is a theory of the most fanciful, and again the whitewashing tendency has come into play. For the truth is (in my opinion) that in the years 1612, 1613 and 1616 the dramatist was far advanced in the tertiary stage of syphilis, and the tremor so evident in his handwriting was the result of locomotor ataxia consistent with the malady. The six signatures, moreover, are not equally bad, but reflect rather a history of progressive degeneration, those on the Will being by far the worst.

It is interesting to compare them with the vital, confident, beautifully formed signature of Christopher Marlowe as a young man. I reproduce the unique example which is to be found on the surviving Will of Catherine Benchkin of Canterbury. This, in the November of 1585, together with his father and two others, he witnessed. (Public Record Office, Canterbury, 39/11. 3.)

Marlowe at this time was twenty-one and a half years old. The most astonishing thing, however, that emerges from such a comparison is that, if one allows for the passage of time and the state of health of the declining "Shakespeare", there is an extraordinary similarity in

the formation of some of the letters. The "C" of Christofer bears a strange resemblance to the "S" of Shakespeare. It is as though the open "S" were a memory of the round ornate "C" which had slid so naturally into the Elizabethan "h" which follows. Then the "h"s of the Deposition and Conveyance signatures and the "h" of Christopher are almost identical, allowing for the loss of vigour in their execution. Alike, too, are the Italian "l"s and the "a" of William in the Conveyance signature and the "l" and "a" of Marley; whereas the final "e" of Shakespe is of the old reversed type, just as are those in both Christofer and Marley. I am not troubled, incidentally, by the fact that the spelling of these two names here differs from that of the decipherment. Raleigh and others signed in a variety of ways.

One should not, of course, allow oneself to be misled by the old letter forms into discerning a greater similarity than actually exists. Most "h"s were written with long tails in those days. For comparison there are several by other hands above the Shakespeare signatures. It would therefore be rash to claim that any such similarity could not fail to be evidence of similar identity; one must be cautious and say simply that is not inconceivable that the signatures of both personalities were written by the same hand. Nevertheless a scholar steeped in the reading of medieval documents said, when I showed him the signatures together, that the similarity "fairly hit you in the eye".

In Sonnet 152 there is a return to the mood of 147.

And then the Sonnets formally end. Love lays by his brand and falls asleep, and the poet at last finds relief: perhaps because the maddening beauty of the youth has mercifully faded.

It would appear, then, that, but for the desertion of Southampton, the miraculous, seemingly inexhaustible fountain-head of the plays would not have been so pitilessly and tragically blocked when the dramatist was only forty-eight years old and had just arrived at his apogée of perfection. But life is such a wretched tangle of irony and circumstance that perhaps it does not do to be too precise in the apportionment of responsibility.

That, then, is the case for Marlowe.

The following is a recapitulation of the major coincidences that have been enlarged upon:

(a) The precise falling together of Marlowe's supposed death and Shakespeare's emergence as a writer, linked with the fact that Shakespeare's name is nowhere evident until after the Deptford murder.

(b) The probability that Marlowe survived the 30th May, 1593.

(c) The lameness of the author of the Sonnets, coupled with the unlikelihood that the actor Shakespeare was lame.

(d) The similarity of the situations portrayed in *The Comedy of Errors,* written about the time of the murder, to the first days of the imposture; and the guilt and blood obsessions manifest in *Richard III.*

(e) The many close parallels in *Hero and Leander* and *Venus and Adonis,* which seem to indicate that the two poems are the work of one author.

(f) The undoubted homosexuality of the author of the Sonnets, and of Marlowe, coupled with the unlikelihood that the actor Shakespeare was homosexual.

(g) The success of the anagrammatical method in deciphering the dedication to the Sonnets.

(h)   The reference to "my bewailed guilt" in Sonnet 36.

(i)   The falling together of the travel sonnet (97) and the death of the actor Shakespeare's son Hamnet, linked with the fact that there is no expression of grief in the sonnet.

(j)   The proof of the deciphered epitaph.

(k)   The strange circumstance that the French word *vérole,* when joined to the letter "M" standing for Monsieur, should be an almost exact anagram of Marlowe, and that the author of the Sonnets would appear to have suffered from syphilis.

(l)   The similarity between the signature of the young Marlowe and those of the declining "Shakespeare".

(m)   The fact, not yet mentioned in so many words, that, when the vacuum of the traditional Shakespeare is filled with the character and actions of Marlowe, the figure immediately comes to life. Many of the plays seem to spring out of the man and to be dictated by his emotional experiences.

Most important of all, however, is the inescapable truth (n) that the education and early reading of "William Shakespeare", which can only be deduced, exactly corresponds to the education and reading of the young Marlowe, which can at all points be substantiated by documentary evidence. It is indeed ironical that scholars, in seeking to establish the one, should only succeed in producing a perfect Identikit picture of the other.

That he had sinned is sure. But who could deny he had also suffered? And who could expect an author of such transcendent genius and vast range of expression to have been morally blameless? Only the most naive could demand of him the respectability of the English country gentleman that Stratfordians would have us believe he was.

Again we have progressed beyond the point where

Auguste Dupin would have said that it was "folly to proceed" and "madness or hypocrisy to doubt". If, however, there are any who do still doubt, the opening of the tomb would prove the matter conclusively; for it contains, it would seem, a treasure of priceless manuscripts — all those that have been missing over the centuries — or the residue of such manuscripts. People have suggested that, since Holy Trinity Church stands so close to the Avon, the tomb will have been inundated at least twice during the three and a half centuries that have elapsed since the dramatist's burial. If this turns out to be true, it will indeed be unfortunate; but provided something recognizable as the residue of old documents is found, its very existence will point to the accuracy of my decipherment and the true identity of Shakespeare.

And since, if my decipherment is correct, documents or their residue must be found, it is perhaps worth while to review theories concerning the contents of the tomb.

But first, why was "Shakespeare" buried in the chancel of Holy Trinity at all? The answer is that, having purchased the great tithes of the church, he had become a lay rector, and had the right to have himself and his dependents buried in its most sacred part. The custom was, however, that when there was no further room for such dignitaries in the sanctuary, the bones of an earlier rector were dug up and thrown into the adjoining charnel house. Such, in a race where there is no ancestor worship, is the inconsistency between the exaggerated homage of a man's contemporaries and the indifference of posterity. And according to tradition it was just this jettisoning of his bones that had caused the dramatist to include the curse in his epitaph. E. K. Chambers quotes from an anonymous writer of the eighteenth century (1777): "At the side of the chancel is a charnel house almost filled with human bones, skulls, etc. The guide said that Shakespeare was so much affected by the charnel house that he wrote the Epitaph (Good friend etc.) for himself, to prevent his bones being thrown into it." Whatever the truth of this story, the curse has certainly ensured "Shakespeare" and his supposed relations a peaceful sleep in their chancel tombs for more than three hundred years.

As for the contents of the tomb, a well-known Stratford personality commented in a letter to me: "How any human remains could survive after 400 years (he meant 350) in gravel subsoil on a river bank passes my comprehension."

It is true that there has been danger in inundation. "Like most other rivers in this country," I learn from the Engineer to the Severn River Board, "the Avon at Stratford has considerable potential for flooding. When a major flood occurs then there is a vast area of land adjoining the river which is inundated with flood waters and this may be to an average depth of 2 or 3 feet."

There are, however, several reasons why, in any such inundation, the tomb may not have been affected.

First, the church stands on a small rising and erosion of the surrounding graveyard is prevented by a retaining wall which rises sheer from the river bank. On a rough estimate the chancel floor is some fifteen feet above the normal level of the river and ten above the bank. So that, if the above mentioned figures are correct, there would be in any maximum flood a clearance of seven feet. Six is the normal depth that a coffin is put down. Moreover, the river's potentiality for flooding must have been known, and would probably have been allowed for, particularly if anything requiring preservation was also going to be buried in the tomb.

Secondly, the body of such an important person would probably have been enclosed in a lead casket which would have resisted the corrosive effects of any inundations, and one hopes that, if there were documents, they would have been accorded similar treatment.

Finally there are layers of clay in the region, and if the church by good fortune should stand on clay foundations, then these, too, would have prevented any seepage of water.

But there are other agencies besides flooding which

could have led to the destruction, or disappearance, of whatever the tomb contained when it was first sealed. It could have been robbed; though this I find difficult to believe, since any robber would have had to contend with the curse. Curst be he who moves my bones, the epitaph reads regardless of the underlying message; and this, in a more superstitious age than ours, has probably proved a powerful deterrent. Moreover, anything that had been "salvaged" would surely by now be in the museums, or on the market: if there are no known relics, then the tomb must surely be intact.

There are some who claim that the vault contains "nothing but dust". And this story originates in Washington Irving's *Sketch Book*. During a visit to Europe in 1815 this author visited Stratford-upon-Avon and records his sight-seeing of the church. "In the course of my rambles I met the grey-headed sexton, Edmunds . . . He had lived in Stratford, man and boy, for eighty years . . . (He) and his companion had been employed as carpenters on the preparations for the celebrated Stratford jubilee and they remembered Garrick, the prime mover of the fête . . . The inscription on the tomb has not been without its effect. It has prevented the removal of his (the dramatist's) remains from the bosom of his native place to Westminster Abbey, which was at one time contemplated. A few years since also, as some labourers were digging to make an adjoining vault, the earth caved in, so as to leave a vacant space, almost like an arch, through which one might have reached into his grave. No one, however, presumed to meddle with his remains, so awfully guarded by a malediction; and lest any of the idle or curious, or any collector of relics, should be tempted to commit depredations, the old sexton kept watch over the place for two days until the vault was finished and the aperture closed again. He told me that he had made bold to look in at the hole, but could see neither coffin nor bones; nothing but dust. It was something, I thought, to have seen the dust of Shakespeare."

Sir Edmund Chambers gives the date of what was

apparently the first opening as 1796, adding that "R. Hendrie saw a hole much about 1827 made by the sinking of the stone and was (also) told that no workman would meddle with it, because of the curse. There was an intention to put fresh slabs round."

Now if Irving's old sexton was eighty in 1815, he would have been approximately sixty in 1796. What was the state of his eyes? Would they, in the dim light of the new vault within the chancel (if there were indeed such a thing, for I have been able to find no vault coinciding with this description) have given him accurate information as he raised his lantern and looked fearfully in? Or was he, because of the curse, perhaps anxious *not* to see anything? Again, could it be possible that a swathing of cobwebs had taken on the appearance of dust under the light of his trembling lantern? But to proceed with Irving's story. "I was grieved to hear these worthy wights speak very dubiously of the eloquent dame who shows the Shakespeare house. John Ange (the companion) shook his head when I mentioned her valuable collection of relics, particularly her remains of the mulberry tree; and the old sexton even expressed a doubt as to Shakespeare having been born in her house. I soon discovered that he looked upon her mansion with an evil eye, as a rival to the poet's tomb — *the latter having comparatively few visitors.*" Which would also weigh against the theory that the tomb might have been robbed.

One final suggestion: it is possible that, on account of the danger of inundation, the coffin and casket containing the manuscripts were set down high on oak beams, the coffin first, the casket on top. This would not have been unusual. A professional gravedigger of my acquaintance, a man who has had a great deal of experience in the putting away of bodies, assures me that the coffins of many people buried either in churches or graveyards before the regulation came into force that the topmost coffin in a multiple grave should be at least six feet down, are just below the surface. Moreover, it would explain the old sexton's report that the tomb, which he had peered into only from the side, contained "nothing but dust". It would also mean that the manuscripts were probably still in a fair state of preservation.

That he had sinned is sure! What of the formidable ethical problem posed? How far was Marlowe justified in allowing Thomas Walsingham to take the less complex life of William Shakespeare so that his own mighty genius might be conserved? It is a question that cannot be answered, beyond saying that, had he been executed, the works of "Shakespeare" would never have been written; and it was Goethe, I think, who stated that, if an observer on another planet looked down on this one, the glory that he saw would be Shakespeare.

BIBLIOGRAPHY

Adams, J. Q., *Shakespearean Playhouses*, Houghton Mifflin Co. Boston, 1917.
Aldis, H. G., in *The Cambridge History of English Literature*.

Boas, F. S., *Christopher Marlowe*, Clarendon Press, 1940. *Marlowe and His Circle*, Clarendon Press, 1929. *Works of Thomas Kyd*, Clarendon Press, 1955. (Editor). (Extracts by kind permission of the Clarendon Press.)
Bradbrook, M. C., *The School of Night*, University Press Cambridge, 1936.

Camden, William, *Remaines*, 1605.
Chambers, E. K., *The Elizabethan Stage*, Clarendon Press, 1923. *William Shakespeare*, 1930. (Extracts by kind permission of the Clarendon Press.)
Chettle, Henry, *Kind-Harts Dream*, 1592.

Falconer, Lieutenant Commander A. F., *Shakespeare and the Sea*, Constable, 1964.

Gibson, H. N., *The Shakespeare Claimants*, Methuen & Co., 1962.
Gray, A. K., *Marlowe as Government Agent*, P.M.L.A., September, 1928.
Greene, Robert, *A Groates-Worth of Witte*, 1592.
Greg, W. W., *Records of the Court of the Stationers Company*, 1576-1602. Bibliographical Society, 1930.

Harrison, G. B., *Elizabethan Plays and Players*, G. Routledge & Sons, 1940. *Introducing Shakespeare*, Penguin Books, 1954.
Hector, L. C., *The Handwriting of English Documents*, Edward Arnold & Co., 1958.
Henderson, Philip, *And Morning in His Eyes*, Boriswood, 1937.
Hoffman, Calvin, *The Man Who Was Shakespeare*, Max Parrish, 1955.
Hotson, J. L., *Mr. W. H.*, Rupert Hart-Davis, 1964.
Humphreys, A. R. (Editor), *Arden Edition of Henry IV*.

Irving, Washington, *Sketch Book*, 1820.

Joseph, B. L., *Elizabethan Acting*, Clarendon Press, 1951. (Extracts by kind permission of the Clarendon Press.)

Kalb, Eugenie de, *Death of Marlowe*, in *T.L.S.*, 21 May, 1925.

231

Mann, Thomas, *Death in Venice*, Penguin Books, 1957.
McKerrow R. B., *A Dictionary of Printers and Booksellers in England, Scotland and Ireland and Foreign Printers of English Books from 1557 to 1640*, Bibliographical Society, 1910.
Murray, John Tucker, *English Dramatic Companies*, Constable, 1910.

Newdigate, B. H., *Michael Drayton and His Circle*, Basil Blackwood, 1961.
Norman, Charles, *The Muses Darling*, Falcon Press, 1947.

Oppenheim, M., *A History of the Administration of the Royal Navy*, John Lane, 1896.

Parsons, J. Denham, *R. Field and the First Shakespeare Poem*, Chiswick, 1935.
Partridge, Eric, *Shakespeare's Bawdy*, G. Routledge & Sons, 1947.
Poe, Edgar Allan, *The Mystery of Marie Rogêt*.
Prynne, William, *Histrio-mastix, The Players Scourge or Actors Tragedie*, 1633.

Reese, M. M., *Shakespeare: his world and his work*, Edward Arnold & Co., 1953.
Rowse, A. L., *Christopher Marlowe*, Macmillan & Co., 1964.
William Shakespeare, Macmillan & Co., 1963.

Simpson, Percy, in *Shakespeare's England*, 1916.
Stopes, C. C., *Life of Henry, Third Earl of Southampton*, University Press Cambridge, 1922.
Stubbes, Philip, *Anatomy of Abuses*, 1583.

Thomson, Walter, *The Sonnets of William Shakespeare and Henry Wriothesley*, 1938.

Wheatley, H. B., *Of Anagrams*, Hertford, 1862.

Yates, Frances M., *A Study of Love's Labour's Lost*, University Press Cambridge, 1936.

INDEX